EVENTS IN THE LIFE OF
PHILLIP TAPSELL

EVENTS IN THE LIFE OF
PHILLIP TAPSELL
'THE OLD DANE'

Researched and edited by
Jonathan Adams

Oratia

FRONT COVER AND FRONTISPIECE: Phillip Tapsell (Hans Hömman Falk). A retouched portrait of the famous trader, c.1870s, taken by an unidentified photographer (1/2-005486-F: Alexander Turnbull Library, National Library of New Zealand · Te Puna Mātauranga o Aotearoa, Wellington). Background image on cover and pp. 14–15: The *Cort Adeler*. Colour drawing by Christoff Wilhelm Eckersberg (1808) of an attack on the *Cort Adeler*, 20 August 1808, in Snekkersten Bay, Øresund (00028730: Museet for Søfart, Helsingør). Pages 52–53: The Tapsell manuscript (qMS-1977: Alexander Turnbull Library, National Library of New Zealand · Te Puna Mātauranga o Aotearoa, Wellington). Pages 186–87: page 154 of the Tapsell manuscript (qMS-1977: Alexander Turnbull Library, National Library of New Zealand · Te Puna Mātauranga o Aotearoa, Wellington).

Published by Oratia Books, Oratia Media Ltd, 783 West Coast Road, Oratia, Auckland 0604, New Zealand (www.oratia.co.nz).

ISBN 978-0-947506-92-6

Editor: Carolyn Lagahetau
Designer: Sarah Elworthy

First published 2021
Printed in China

Contents

Foreword

WHAT STRUCK ME ON FIRST HEARING from Jonathan Adams and reading his manuscript was how he had taken Phillip Tapsell — Te Tāpihana — into a new era. His work extends our tipuna's story beyond the version that James Cowan established in the popularised *A Trader in Cannibal Land* (1935). Cowan was a gifted writer who in the telling, romanticised Phillip Tapsell 's life and created the sense of a 'mythical Dane'. Jonathan has countered this perspective, showing our ancestor as a real person at the heart of unimaginable events. This is a remarkable life story that needs no glamourising.

    A Trader in Cannibal Land addressed an immigrant readership, portraying a past New Zealand as a land untamed. Cowan placed Tapsell among the British vanguard where, through their endeavours, Pākehā settlers were able to thrive in a new land. Cowan was one of a number of popular writers who objectified the noble savage through his regular newspaper articles. His narratives set the civilising foundation by which the brutal realities of colonisation were first historicised and justified, then later mis-remembered or even forgotten. By the early 1930s, when Cowan's book was published, New Zealand had changed dramatically from when our ancestor first stepped ashore in the Bay of Islands in 1809. But Cowan's story wasn't written for Māori. His readership was the million-plus Pākehā who were thirsty for frontier stories and their own Daniel Boone.

    Tapsell is a North-Eastern English name and his biography has an intriguing English back story of teenage appropriation, Icelandic romance, imprisonment and adventure. Yet it was from Denmark that our ancestor embarked across the oceans in the era when doing so ran a high risk to life and limb. In the story he reminisced to Edward Little, it was almost as if the man born in Copenhagen as Hans Hömman Falk downplayed the feats he undertook — perhaps because adventure was just integral to the times or at least to his character. As his descendants we also think of our Māori ancestors who crossed the ocean in great voyages of adventure.

The arrival of Phillip Tapsell in the Bay of Plenty reopened our people to international influence. We had endured 12-plus generations of isolation since Aotearoa became cut off from the rest of the Pacific around the 1400s. From the late 1700s, following the arrival of Tupaea (Tupaia) on the *Endeavour*, waves of sealers, whalers, missionaries and traders all assisted us to reconnect to our Pacific relations and the wider world. We can only imagine that moment for Māori: after hundreds of years in relative isolation, their imaginations expanded anew. Where Cowan viewed that process through Pākehā settler eyes, Jonathan sees this moment through a multicultural prism as experienced by Tapsell himself.

The name Te Tāpihana, by which Te Arawa still recognises this Danish-English settler and his progeny, reflects the mana he held within and beyond the Bay of Plenty. This, after all, was the man who provided the means by which the many hapū from Tauranga to Whakatāne, Maketū to Tongariro and Tarawera to Maungatautari were able to protect themselves from external forces that already had the musket. These were desperate times when unarmed kāinga (villages) of the central North Island were being wiped out by heavily armed northern raiders. Before Te Tāpihana's arrival the Ngāti Whakaue people of Rotorua were seriously contemplating joining Te Rauparaha in the south, taking refuge on Kapiti Island alongside his well-armed followers.

Te Tāpihana's arrival and willingness to trade firearms for muka (dressed flax fibre) was pivotal. Thoughts of migration ceased and for a period Te Arawa relocated to the Maketū-Matatā coastal regions to harvest muka. Te Tāpihana's allocation of firearms was not haphazard: he ensured no one hapū gained an unfair firearm advantage. War was inevitably bad for business, but in simple terms we needed Te Tāpihana's muskets to survive. By the time Te Waharoa's army attacked Maketū, destroying Te Tāpihana's trade station, the Bay of Plenty hapū confederations were adequately armed and successfully reasserted their ancestral borders.

Te Whānau a Tāpihana regard our Danish ancestor in the same way as any Māori ancestor. He transcended ethnicity and culture, and had a mana that saw him married to three high-ranking daughters of powerful rangatira. While the first two of Ngāpuhi descent lost their lives before bearing children, it was Te Tāpihana's third wife, Hineitūrama, who enabled commercial success. Her whakapapa through Ngatokowaru and Ngāti Huia directly connected her to powerful leaders of the day seeking arms, including Te Wherowhero, Te Rauparaha and Tupaea II. Te Tāpihana's personal mana was enhanced by the fairness of his interactions with Arawa leaders Te Pukuatua, Te Amohau, Tohiteururangi and Te Haupapa.

But Tapsell was also an outsider, who had already lived a full life of adventure before settling in the Bay of Plenty. In his youth he found himself on the wrong side of imperial history with the destruction of the Danish fleet in Copenhagen by Admiral Nelson. Against the background of Danish trading with northern England, the young Falk easily moved in British maritime circles; he learned English proficiently alongside other trade languages of northern Europe. His ability to acquire languages was a trade asset and he became fluent in te Reo Māori long before he arrived amongst our Arawa people. A lifetime of being culturally open and flexible assisted the Dane (previously at war with the English) to blend in to the British world of sailing adventure and exploration in a way that didn't antagonise the Crown.

His Te Arawa-raised sons, however, were less forgiving of British brutality as colonisation began to rip the Māori world apart. The death of their mother Hineitūrama and sister Ewa at the Battle of Orakau, at the height of New Zealand's civil wars, was a turning point for Te Whānau a Tāpihana. In the coming decades Retireti, Perepe and Ieni worked behind the scenes to prevent land loss through colonisation. Similar to their father, and to the annoyance of government officials, they played key roles in maintaining the peace, ensuring fairness, and preventing Crown granting of lands that would lead to alienation and poverty.

What emanates from *Events in the Life of Phillip Tapsell*, and the extensive research and analysis that Jonathan has put into this edition, is how much Tapsell came to belong in the Bay of Plenty. He was one of the originals, a generation older than most other Pakeha-Maori, and so one of the first Europeans to be accepted by and integrated into Maori society in a fluid way, not just for commercial motives. Before he settled at Maketū he had already accumulated more than 20 years of experience in New Zealand; had been present at the retribution by whalers for the 1809 burning of the *Boyd*; was a key figure in the capture of the brig *Wellington*; saw close engagement with Hongi Hika; acquired a navy licence to trade — not to mention many other adventures. That is why the life of Phillip Tapsell – Te Tāpihana – resonates far beyond the Bay of Plenty, throughout Aotearoa New Zealand and across the oceans to Denmark, and helps us all to understand the dynamics of European colonial history from a uniquely biographical perspective.

Paora Tapsell
Honorary Professorial Fellow
Centre of Heritage and Museum Studies, Australian National University

Introduction

IN 1790, SOME 20 YEARS AFTER CAPTAIN COOK circumnavigated and mapped New Zealand for the first time, a woman in her twenties gave birth to a baby boy in Copenhagen, Denmark. Christened Hans Falk, he was to become the ancestor of more than 3000 New Zealanders alive today, the vast majority of whom identify as Māori. His story is not well known in his country of birth, even though his memoirs, written shortly before his death, are without doubt the most important written account by a Dane of the early European settlement of New Zealand. Furthermore, they bear witness to an eventful and adventurous life that reads like a 'who's who' of the nineteenth century — Napoleon Bonaparte, Horatio Nelson, Samuel Marsden, Thomas Kendall, Hongi Hika and Te Waharoa — with descriptions of dramatic events such as the bombardment of Copenhagen, the massacre on the *Boyd* and the recapture of the *Wellington*, to name a few. We might have expected that all this would have catapulted Hans Falk into Danish history books as one of the nation's swashbuckling heroes, a modern-day Viking who took advantage of the opportunities offered by the age of exploration.

Like thousands of his compatriots nine centuries earlier, Falk spent years sailing the oceans and visiting distant lands, sometimes having to resort to combat and violence but more often than not simply engaged in peaceful fishing and commercial activities. Also like many of those earlier Danish Vikings, he settled far beyond the borders of his country of birth, in a foreign land where he successfully integrated into the local community and created new trading networks that had a huge impact on the development of the region.

Aged 14, Falk left Copenhagen for a life at sea. Although Denmark was allied with Napoleon against Britain, it was in fact London — the capital of enemy England — that became his gateway to the world. He falsified his papers, changing his name to Phillip Tapsell, and by the age of 20 had sailed vast distances aboard British whaling ships to far-flung destinations such as St Helena, Timor, New South Wales, Tasmania and New Zealand. However, he never forgot his Danish origins and during the Gunboat War (1807–14) between Britain and Denmark, Tapsell returned to Copenhagen to fight for his homeland. He subsequently travelled back to London using his false papers.

Phillip Tapsell's career started in the lucrative business of whaling in the waters around New Zealand. He made contact with the various Māori iwi (tribes) and the Pākehā (Europeans) living among them, and in 1823 married a young Māori woman, Maria Ringa. The wedding was the first Christian marriage in New Zealand, and probably one of the shortest: it lasted just a few hours. In 1830 he married a second time. The marriage was successful but his wife, Karuhi, died two years later without the couple having any children. About the same time, he purchased land from local chiefs in Maketū in the Bay of Plenty and set up business trading flax, a natural product that could be made into rope, twine and sailcloth, and that was in great demand. The flax was produced and worked by local Māori and shipped to trading houses in Sydney. Even if it did not make Tapsell rich in the long term, the business provided him with an income and he married for a third time. Hineitūrama, a Ngāti Whakaue woman of mana (prestige, authority), gave him eight children, six of whom survived to adulthood.

From their home in Maketū and later in Whakatāne, the Tapsells were witness to growing European control over New Zealand and to frequent and violent intertribal warfare. Often the trader ransomed the captured slaves, but on several occasions he too came close to becoming a victim of the bloody feuds. In large part he survived because of his peaceful and deep commitment to the Māori people and their culture, as well as his ability to supply them with muskets, powder and trading goods. He died in 1873, aged 83, of natural causes. He is the founding father of the well-known Tapsell family/Te Whānau a Tāpihana, now numbering hundreds of families and including leaders in community affairs, politics, education, research and business.

At some point before his death Tapsell told his life story to a magistrate's clerk, Edward Little. The result is a fascinating manuscript that not only details events in the life of Hans Falk/Phillip Tapsell, but also provides us with a valuable account of the social and economic history of early nineteenth-century New Zealand and the development of the colony as seen through the eyes of a non-British settler. The world that Tapsell describes is not one of governors, admirals and high-ranking officials: he sees the world from below decks and from the trading station. It is a world of two parts: a Pākehā world populated by sailors, whalers, sealers, traders and convicts, and a Māori world

11

made up of men, women, warriors, friends and family. Tapsell's encounters with captains and missionaries usually did not go well and he repeatedly was shown to be more understanding, brave and intelligent than these men of status. Indeed, despite being a common man, he was able to count chieftains among his closest friends and he even convinced the Catholic bishop Jean-Baptiste Pompallier to officiate at his wedding.

Tapsell's story is unique and he told it with incredible attention to minute detail even though he was recalling the events many years after they took place. For the first time, the manuscript, now kept in the Alexander Turnbull Library in Wellington, is discussed, edited and transcribed accurately and in full. It is my hope that this book will be of interest to the general reader and that by making Tapsell's valuable account more widely available it will also be of use to historians of colonial affairs and maritime history as well as those interested in Pākehā-Māori relations.

In Part 1, 'The Pacific Viking', the concept of Pākehā-Māori is discussed, including its changing associations and how the phenomenon shows that the binary relationship between Pākehā and Māori has been illusory from the beginning of European settlement. Part 2 is an edition of Phillip Tapsell's reminiscences as they were written down by Edward Little, now preserved at the Alexander Turnbull Library in Wellington (qMS-1977). The reproduction here retains the spellings, punctuation and division into paragraphs as they appear in Little's handwritten notes, even when they conflict with modern practice. Little published a serialised version of Tapsell's reminiscences based on these notes in the *Daily Southern Cross* (1867), but that account varies somewhat from the manuscript in the Turnbull Library. The newspaper version contains five episodes that are missing in the original manuscript pages. They have been included here and are marked with a reference to the newspaper. The newspaper included sections headings that are occasionally missing in the Tapsell manuscript. As they are useful for structuring the narrative, they have been included here but are reproduced in italics to show that they do not appear in the original manuscript. Notes have been provided at the end of the chapters to identify or explain names, places, events or phenomena mentioned in Tapsell's story that are not necessarily self-evident. Drawing a satisfactory line in determining the criteria for these explanatory comments has not been easy, but the guiding principle has been to provide a note wherever the text might not be understood by the reader who may not be from New Zealand or Denmark, or where further background information might be of interest. References to secondary sources or further reading have also been included.

In Part 3 the Phillip Tapsell story is placed within a broader context. The most significant events in the three major phases of Phillip Tapsell's life — childhood in Denmark, youth at sea, adulthood in New Zealand — are summarised using Tapsell's own reminiscences, supplemented with archival sources from Denmark and New Zealand, as well as informants.

Tapsell's story is held up to scrutiny and its facts, motives and veracity questioned. In 'The Tapsell manuscript' the physical artefact, the manuscript, is investigated: how did it come into being and what happened to it after it was written? Historian James Cowan's stewardship of the work is of particular interest. He clearly came to feel a sense of ownership over the material; he was happy to cut and change the manuscript in order to publish an amended version of the text as his book *A Trader in Cannibal Land* (1935). Publications about Tapsell in Denmark are discussed in 'The Tapsell story in Danish' showing that the Danish have followed a different path to how such nineteenth-century reminiscences are now understood in New Zealand. Finally, 'Contemporary accounts of Phillip Tapsell's life' includes newspaper articles and letters that mention Tapsell and refer to events found in his memoirs as told to Edward Little.

Jonathan Adams
2020

PART 1

THE PACIFIC VIKING

Pākehā-Māori

AS THE FIRST HUMANS TO DEVELOP THE SKILLS and technology to cross vast stretches of ocean, the Polynesians arrived in Aotearoa (Land of the Long White Cloud) some time during the thirteenth century. The descendants of these settlers, the Māori people, developed a distinct culture and a flourishing society that for centuries remained untouched and unaffected by the wider world until the arrival of explorers from Europe. Although first sighted by Abel Janszoon Tasman in 1642, it was not until well over a hundred years later in 1769-70 that Europeans — James Cook and his crew aboard HMS *Endeavour* — landed on the islands of Aotearoa for the first time. Within just a few decades, the waters around New Zealand (as Cook named it)[1] were being visited regularly by whaling ships and sealing gangs from Britain, France, USA and New South Wales. The crews aboard these ships, known to Māori as tauiwi (outsiders, people from afar), traded Europeans goods (principally muskets, ammunition, metal tools and alcohol) with Māori in exchange for food, water, wood and harakeke (flax). However, not all interaction was fleeting or based solely around trade. Thousands of sailors as well as some convicts from New South Wales, Van Diemen's Land (Tasmania) and Norfolk Island settled among coastal and interior Māori, living as members of the iwi (tribe), sometimes as mere taurekareka (captives), but more often acting as trading intermediaries.[2] Some of these new arrivals achieved positions of respect and became white rangatira (chiefs), tohunga (priests) and toa (warriors). To be accepted as a member of the iwi, Pākehā-Māori usually had to learn the language, have a Māori spouse, observe — or at least respect — Māori customs and rituals, and subordinate their own interests to those of the iwi.[3] These Pākehā-Māori came to play an important role in the social, political and economic history of New Zealand at the beginning of the nineteenth century, often acting as a bridge between the newcomers and tangata whenua (indigenous peoples) and between the government and trading networks.

For many years, opinions about Pākehā-Māori in historiography tended to be rather negative. They were portrayed as criminal degenerates and troublemakers who were overly fond of violence and alcohol and who hindered governmental progress and the development of the colony. In recent years, however, there has been a revisionist trend (not least thanks to the work of historian Trevor Bentley)[4] that has attempted to demolish this view and re-evaluate the role of Pākehā-Māori more fairly: as 'a unique class of men (and women) possessed of the knowledge, skills and courage necessary to live and prosper among a warrior society rent by intertribal gun warfare'.[5]

Many Pākehā-Māori assimilated fully and have left no trace. Most others remain largely unrecorded or merely as names in documents, but a few have left clearer historical traces. From the hundreds of known cases, it is possible to gain a clearer picture of the range of men and women who lived as Pākehā-Māori throughout New Zealand. Some stayed for just a few years among the Māori people where they could enjoy freedoms that had been denied them in their earlier lives. Australian convict and mutineer Charlotte Badger escaped imprisonment and sailed from Tasmania to New Zealand in 1806. She settled among Māori in the Bay of Islands for about ten years before running off with a New England sea captain.[6] Others became 'naturalised' Māori who identified completely with their iwi, engaged in intertribal warfare and even fought against former compatriots (who in turn treated these 'white savages' with contempt). Sealer James Caddell, who at age 16 was the sole survivor of a shipwreck in 1810, settled among Ngāi Tahu in South Otago. He became fully assimilated and it is said that he nearly forgot his English.[7] Kimball Bent, an American deserter who became a Pākehā tohunga and lived among Ngāti Ruanui in Taranaki from 1865 until his death in 1916, was interviewed many times by historian James Cowan.[8] Indeed, from earliest times, the lives of Pākehā-Māori were considered newsworthy and often were turned into tantalising tales of men and women 'going native' that circulated by word-of-mouth and through the colonial press. Many, like Phillip Tapsell, wrote or dictated accounts of their lives and activities. For example, Jacky Marmon's long life from the 1820s among Hokianga Māori was serialised in newspapers.[9] Generally, these descriptions and narratives focused on sensational events and gruesome activities such as warfare, cannibalism and 'native superstitions', which would whet the appetite of nineteenth-century Pākehā readers. In spite of their journalistic slant, these accounts provide us with insights into the challenges faced by Pākehā-Māori 'crossing over' and what they did — or had to do — to succeed in their new environment. Moreover, they describe the benefits of creating a new life among tangata whenua and the opportunities given to Pākehā-Māori that had been denied them in their former lives.

17

The Tapsell manuscript is one such source for understanding the Pākehā-Māori phenomenon and aspects of culture-crossing in early nineteenth-century New Zealand, not least by showing how the cultural and racial categories of Māori and Pākehā are unstable and permeable. Although the memoirs themselves strive in places to uphold the colonialist categories of Māori savagery and European civilisation (for example, in its descriptions of Māori warfare and superstition), the boundaries became blurred in Tapsell's life when he threw his lot in with Te Arawa, acquiring a new family and close friends, acknowledging the power of mākutu (sorcery) and, according to some sources, adopting Māori practices such as smearing himself in ochre and declaring himself tapu (sacred, set apart, under supernatural protection) at certain times.[10] His occasional irritation with and scoffing at the missionaries and their work among Māori also placed him in opposition to Pākehā/European culture and 'civilising influences'. The memoirs admittedly do tend to present Tapsell as a 'civilising force' — his grand house, his peace missions, his ransoming of captives — but the facts of his life point toward a much more nuanced and complex role. Indeed, even though they tend to focus on sensational events, Tapsell's memoirs show how the binary relationship between Pākehā and Māori, between 'positivity' and 'negativity', is entirely illusory:[11] the Dane finally gained love, respect and fulfilment living among Māori and a domestic family life he had not been able to enjoy since he was a young child in Denmark. Tapsell's memoirs present an intertwined bicultural Pākehā-Māori past based on interaction and exchange, cooperation and compromise, and equality and integration.

Hans Falk: the child

HANS FALK WAS BORN IN 1790.[12] His parents, Jens Hansen Falk and Gjertrud Johanne Homan, who had married five years previously in Roskilde,[13] lived in a rear building on Strandgade (Beach Street) in the Christianshavn district of Copenhagen. Jens worked as a carpenter and labourer, later becoming a *vandmester* (sanitation supervisor; literally 'water master') responsible for parts of the city's sanitation and water supply, while Gjertrud worked in the home and also earned extra income as a cleaner. They called their little boy Hans and on 22 August of that year had him baptised in the Church of Our Saviour in Copenhagen. The entry in the parish register of births and deaths is one of the few sources of information we have about the family: 'Jens Hansen, labourer, and Gjertrud Johanne Homan: A son, Hans Homan. Godparents: Madam Lassen; Madam Sünckenberg; Merchant Høvisk;

Phillip Tapsell
(Hans Hömman Falk).
A retouched portrait
of the famous trader,
c.1870s, taken by
an unidentified
photographer.

1/2-005486-F: Alexander Turnbull
Library, National Library of New
Zealand · Te Puna Mātauranga o
Aotearoa, Wellington

Book-keeper Lykke; Clerk Larsen. Baptism.'[14]

At some point, the Falks moved to Laksegade (Salmon Street) in the city centre, and when Hans turned four, his brother, Niels Christian, was born and the family was complete. However, just a few years later on 12 May 1798, tragedy struck and the boys' mother Gjertrud passed away: 'Building carpenter Jens Falk [...] living in rented accommodation at 311 Laksegade [...] his wife Gjertrud Johanne Homan [...] died 12 May 1798 [...] leaves behind from the marriage two sons Hans aged 10 and Niels Christian aged 4.'[15] Hans' father subsequently sent him to live with his grandparents in Jutland and the voyage there was the first of his many adventures at sea. Indeed, whether fact or fiction, the episode sets the tone for the remainder of the narrative that focuses on the dramatic and affective events of his life. According to Tapsell the vessel he was sailing in caught fire in the middle of the night and the eight-year-old had to make his escape together with the crew in a small boat. After three days drifting at sea with no provisions, they were rescued and the boy was sent on his way to Jutland once again — this time in a boat sheathed with copper that would not burn. Hans stayed there for two years attending the local school, but after the death of his grandparents he returned to Copenhagen to live with his father.

While Hans had been living in Jutland, his father Jens had married the widow Marie Dorothea Arentsen (née Esmark) in the Church of the Holy Ghost in Copenhagen: 'On 26 October [1799], the undersigned read the banns

Church of Our Saviour (Vor Frelsers kirke). The church in Copenhagen where Hans Falk was baptised. Photograph taken c.1897 by an unidentified photographer.

Photocrom Prints Collection, the Library of Congress, in the public domain

AN ICELANDIC TAPSELL FAMILY?

A certain Hans (Hansen) Falk is listed in the Icelandic parish censuses for 1806 and 1807. Aged 25, he was in Reykjavík at Petræusar Hús (Petræus' house) during the winter of 1806 when the parish census was taken. On 25 September 1806, he reported the theft of some food to the authorities in Reykjavík and in February 1807, when a new parish census was taken, he was at Sýslumannshús (Sherriff's house), aged 26. He was an employee of Lieutenant M. Smith, a Norwegian in the Danish navy, responsible for mapping the coast of Iceland for the military. The crew were caught out by early Atlantic storms and forced to winter 1806–1807 in Reykjavík. During his stay in Iceland, Hans met Margrét (1782–1842), the daughter of pastor and dean Illugi Hannesson, a respected scholar of a prominent family. Margrét and Hans had a relationship, and on 22 December 1807 their son, also named Hans, was born at the Landfógetahús (Magistrate's House) in Reykjavík. The child was brought up by his grandfather Illugi rather than being sent away to paid foster-parents as was the usual custom for illegitimate children in prominent families. When he grew older he began to prepare for higher education, but after the death of his grandfather he changed course, probably due to a lack of financial support, and trained as a weaver. He married Ólöf Jónsdóttir and had two children Hans (b. 1832) and Pétur Þórarinn (b. 1851). Pétur Þórarinn was the great-grandfather of Anna Pétursdóttir who kindly shared this story with me. Hans Falk had probably left Iceland by the time his son was born. There has been some discussion whether this Hans Falk is the same man as our protagonist – indeed, photographs of Pétur Þórarinn bear an uncanny resemblance to Hans Falk/Phillip Tapsell's offspring – but the age of the 'Iceland Falk' (25, rather than 15) and his patronymic (Hansen, rather than Jensen) suggest we are dealing with another person, although the two may possibly be closely related.

of marriage for widower Jens Falk, acting sanitation supervisor, and widow Marie Dorothea, widow after the late ship carpenter Arentsen, [...] married on 22 November.'[16] When Hans was reunited with his father and brother, the family were living in a new home on Lavendelstræde (Lavender Street) in the western part of the city and the census for 1801 records the four residents in the home: 'Lavender Street, plots 87 and 89, no. 145: Jens Hansen Falk — husband, 40, sanitation supervisor/Marie Esmark — his wife, 40/both in their second marriage/Hans Falk — at home, 10, unmarried/Niels Falk — 6, unmarried/sons of first marriage.'[17] Hans continued his schooling in Copenhagen until the age of 13 or 14 in 1803 when his father indentured him to a ship owner and his long career as a sailor began.

According to his memoirs, Hans Falk first began working on a Danish ship that was trading in the Baltic and Mediterranean seas, but soon took up a position on an American brig sailing for Boston. However, the ship did not make it across the Atlantic but instead stopped off in London where it was sold. Fortunately, Hans quickly found employment and was engaged first on the *New Zealander* and then the *Eliza* as first mate under American captain, Jonathan Clarke of Nantucket. However, to secure work the young Dane had to reinvent himself. At the beginning of the nineteenth century Britain was at war with several European nations, including Denmark, that were allied with Napoleon, and foreigners were viewed with suspicion — indeed, they were not permitted to work on British vessels. In order not to be refused employment, Hans adopted a more British-sounding name, taking it, according to James Cowan, from the word 'topsail' — and explained his unusual accent by claiming to hail from the Isle of Man. Phillip Tapsell the sailor was born.

Phillip Tapsell: the sailor

TAPSELL MERGED HIS TWO FIRST VOYAGES in his memoirs: the *New Zealander* 1808, under Captain William Elder, and the *Eliza* 1810, under Captain Jonathan Clarke. Although we know nothing about his first voyage, his time on the *Eliza* was anything but a happy experience. Contrary to first impressions, Captain Clarke was tyrannical and cruel, and while whaling off the coast of Timor his maltreatment of the crew became so brutal that seven men, including Tapsell, decided to desert ship and hide on a nearby island. They were all recaptured in a matter of hours and Tapsell had to spend the entire voyage back to England suffering many iniquities at the hands of the vengeful captain. When the ship arrived back at port the 'crew [were] mutinous

TAPSELL AND TOPSAIL

The explanation of Falk choosing 'topsail' as a name was proposed by James Cowan in *A Trader in Cannibal Land* (1935) and it has since become accepted without question as a family fable. However, Enid Tapsell was derisive of Cowan's story and said that the name was not unknown to young Hans while he was living with his grandparents in Jutland. They knew traders from across the North Sea and were familiar with the northern English accent. Furthermore, Hans deliberately took the Tapsell name, an English east county family name with its own coat of arms, as he knew it was a recognised trade name in London.

23

and suffering with the scurvy'.[18] This was the first of several run-ins Tapsell was to have with various captains and authorities during his career as a sailor, a career that spanned over 25 years.

Although the Dane Hans Falk had transformed himself into the Manxman Phillip Tapsell to gain work in London, and in spite of the state of war between Britain and Denmark, he maintained contact with family and friends in Denmark, even returning home between voyages. On one such occasion, in 1807, he claims to have witnessed the British navy's horrific bombardment of Copenhagen when nearly a thousand Danes were injured or killed, with at least as many buildings destroyed by fire, and the Danish fleet was confiscated ('Copenhagenised'). In defence of his country of birth, Tapsell

The *Cort Adeler*. Colour drawing by Christoff Wilhelm Eckersberg (1808) of an attack on the *Cort Adeler*, 20 August 1808, in Snekkersten Bay, Øresund.

00028730: Museet for Søfart, Helsingør

became a privateer and took part in attacks on enemy, that is, British-allied mercantile vessels. His prowess was recognised and he was put in command of the ship *Cort Adeler*. However, luck was not on his side for long, and Tapsell was badly wounded in the stomach and spent over a year in Swedish captivity as a prisoner of war.

After his release Tapsell went to Copenhagen and then, using falsified papers, returned to London by way of a Dutch ship. A short voyage in a brig loaded with government stores for the British troops stationed in Malta was followed by one as first mate on the whaling ship, *New Zealander*. It was on this voyage that young Tapsell saw his future homeland, New Zealand, for the first time.[19]

In the summer of 1810, aboard the *Eliza*, while whaling off the East Cape, news reached the fleet of the massacre that had taken place aboard the *Boyd* in December 1809. The *Boyd*, a 395-ton brig, had put in to Whangaroa Harbour on the northern coast of Northland to collect a load of kauri. As utu (retribution) for earlier wrongdoings committed against them by Europeans, local Māori conspired to attack the

OPPOSITE A South Seas whale fishery. 'A Representation of the Ships *Amelia Wilson* and *Castor* off the Island of Bouro, with their Boats & Crew, in the various process of Fishing, shewing the manner the Spermacetti Whales are caught, also the mode of cutting them into the Ship & Boiling the Oil upon Deck'. By Williams John Huggins (1781-1845) and engraved by T. Sutherland, London, 1825.

D-002-036: Alexander Turnbull Library, National Library of New Zealand · Te Puna Mātauranga o Aotearoa, Wellington ship. In all, 66 of the 70 people aboard were murdered. On hearing news of the event, the captains of the whaling ships agreed to immediately send seven or eight vessels to the Bay of Islands to wreak revenge. The decision had tragic consequences. The name of the chief who had orchestrated the massacre had apparently become garbled in reports of the event, and the whalers set out to punish Te Pahi, who had no part in the massacre, rather than the actual instigator, Te Puhi. On arrival at Te Pahi's pā (fort, stockade) at Rangihoua, the whalers, including Tapsell, launched a devastating attack, shooting the innocent villagers, burning their homes and destroying their crops.[20] Their vengeance wrought and the slaughter complete, the vessels returned to the fishing ground where the whales were plentiful and the hunt successful.

Although the vast majority of his sailing career was taken up with whaling, in 1813 Tapsell was engaged as first mate aboard the *Catherine*, a convict ship under Captain Robert Graham, transporting 120 women and children from Cork to the penal settlement in New South Wales.[21] The offences for which the women had been sentenced ranged from murder to relatively trivial matters: one woman claimed to have been sentenced to transportation for being out on the streets late at night after accidentally locking herself out of her dwelling. Tapsell seems to have felt great pity for some of the convicts, one of whom — 'Kitty' Lynch — would repay his kindness some years later by saving him from falling into a dangerous trap one night in Hobart Town.

Another area of business for Tapsell was transporting paying passengers. For example, late in his sailing career in 1827, he was appointed captain on

the schooner *Darling* headed to Hihifo, Tongatapu, with Wesleyan missionary William Weiss and his family as passengers.[22] When they arrived in the island kingdom they were met by several other missionaries residing there who begged to be taken back to Sydney — they were afraid of being murdered by the islanders. After receiving reassurance from the local chief that the missionaries would not be harmed, Tapsell offered them passage, but only if they accommodated themselves in the hold. This event and continual arguments with Weiss during the voyage led to Tapsell facing serious charges, of which he was cleared, upon arrival back in Sydney.[23]

Tapsell met many Māori during his years as a sailor. Māori men were hired as crewmembers on his and other ships, and he met traders and residents when in the Bay of Islands. Not all contact was peaceful, however, and there were episodes of violence and conflict — the attack on Te Pahi's pā during his first sojourn in New Zealand being the most notable. On one occasion in 1814,[24] while at anchor off Kororāreka (Russell), a canoe came alongside the *Catherine* with a number of large kete (woven baskets, kits) from which blood was streaming. Tapsell enquired of one of the men in the canoe what the kits contained and he was told in a confidential whisper 'tangata' (human [flesh]). This is the first time Tapsell mentions cannibalism, a theme he returns to several times in his reminiscences and that occupies a surprisingly large place in his depictions of life among Māori.[25] In 1822 he was the first mate under Captain William Darby Brind aboard the *Asp*. When the ship arrived in the Bay of Islands the victorious war party of the Ngāpuhi leader Hongi Hika was at the same time returning home from a campaign against Ngāti Whātua, Waikato and Rotorua (1821–25). Without hiding his disgust, Tapsell provided a detailed description of the execution, cooking and subsequent eating of some 40 prisoners of war by Ngāpuhi men as well as the drowning of a slave boy by Hongi Hika's wife, Turikatuku. The killing of the prisoners was in response to the loss of Hongi's son, Hare Hongi, during the campaigns in the Battle of Te Ika-a-Ranga-nui.[26]

On 23 June 1823, Tapsell married Ngāpuhi woman Maria Ringa at Oihi (Hohi) Mission Station, Bay of Islands (the location is now marked by Marsden Cross). This was the first Christian wedding in New Zealand and the first registered marriage between a Māori and a Pākehā.[27] The ceremony was officiated by Thomas Kendall of the Church Missionary Society, but without the consent of his brethren. Maria had first to be baptised by Kendall and some missionaries were not convinced that her conversion, the first in New Zealand, was sincere. Indeed, they may have been right: Maria disappeared into the bush just hours after the wedding took place and was never seen by her husband again. Unable to find his wife, Tapsell returned with the *Asp* to London.[28]

At the time of his marriage to Maria Ringa, Tapsell may well have already

Phillip Tapsell and Maria Ringa's wedding certificate and registry of marriage. Tapsell's marriage to Ngāpuhi woman Maria Ringa at Oihi Mission Station was the first Christian wedding in New Zealand.

Bay of Islands Missions/Waimate – Register: marriages (1823–1835), baptisms (1815–35), burials (1821–35 [MICRO2792], Archives New Zealand, The Department of Internal Affairs · Te Tari Taiwhenua, Wellington [Original: Anglican Church in Kaikohe] been entertaining the idea of settling in New Zealand among the Māori people. Relating various events of 1823, Jacky Marmon who at the time was a Pākehā tohunga in the Bay of Islands, wrote:[29]

> ABOUT THIS TIME I had another visit from Tom [Phillip] Tapsell, who gave me all the latest news from Sydney[30] [...] Tom Tapsell seemed to consider my life a perfect heaven upon earth, and was hot upon becoming a Pakeha-Maori at once, but I dissuaded him from it at present, partly because I did not want any other pakeha to share the influence I held, and partly because I wanted to be brought in contact as little as possible with men likely to suspect what my previous history had been.

One incident more than any other had consequences for Tapsell's future, namely the quelling of the most famous Norfolk Island convict mutiny: the recapture of the *Wellington*. Sixty-six convicts under the leadership of John Walton seized the *Wellington* on 21 December 1826 as it made its way from Sydney to the penal settlement on Norfolk Island. The mutineers chained the captain (John Harwood), the crew and the soldiers, and kept them aboard as prisoners. They then sailed to the Bay of Islands where the arrival of the convict ship attracted much attention, not least from the *Sisters* on which Tapsell was working under Captain Robert Duke. According to his memoirs and contemporary newspaper accounts, Tapsell played a key role in the recapture of the *Wellington* and in making sure that the mutineers were sent to Sydney for trial.[31] The praise for his actions that he received in the newspapers infuriated Duke, who according to Tapsell intended to take all the credit for the recapture himself, despite having actually been opposed to the operation. This led to a heated altercation in Sydney between the two men and Duke had Tapsell 'broken' (flogged) in front of the crew. Shortly afterwards Tapsell was also attacked and left for dead while ashore — perhaps something to do with Duke and the *Wellington* affair or maybe just a coincidence. Nonetheless, he had so many enemies in the town at this point that he felt his life was in danger and he decided to move his base of activities from Sydney to the Bay of Islands.

In 1830 Tapsell married for a second time, this time to Karuhi, sister of Tungaroa and the chiefs Wharepoaka and Waikato, who had been living for many years among the missionaries. The wedding ceremony was performed by missionary Samuel Marsden in Kerikeri.[32] At first the couple lived together under the protection of Karuhi's brother Wharepoaka at Rangihoua pā overlooking the mission station.

Tapsell was never again able to secure passage back to England. He relates

Rangihoua pā. A hand-coloured glass curio showing Rangihoua pā (left) and the Oihi (Hohi) Mission Station (right); London, c.1852–57.

Curios-021-008: Alexander Turnbull Library, National Library of New Zealand · Te Puna Mātauranga o Aotearoa, Wellington

how he tried to board the only whaler in the Bay of Islands heading for London but was refused. The reason, he was told, was that the ship's owner had given orders that she take no passengers. Nonetheless, Tapsell believed this to be a ruse arranged between his enemy Captain Duke and the other whaling captains to refuse him passage to England. The motive? So that Duke might get back first and tell his version of the story of the rescue of the *Wellington* and claim a handsome reward. The impossibility of returning to England marked the end of Tapsell's days as a seafarer. From this point on, his fate and fortune lay ashore in New Zealand among his Māori family and friends rather than at sea among European whalers, sailors and convicts. Again it was time for him to reinvent himself: Tapsell the Sailor became Te Tāpihana the Trader.

Te Tāpihana: the trader

HAVING JUST TURNED 40, Tapsell went into the flax trade with the Sydney company Jones & Walker, who had a government contract for the commodity.[33] Tapsell was contracted to act as an agent, trading muskets, powder, blankets, tobacco and other desirable goods with Māori in return for scraped flax that he would ship to Sydney. There it would be processed into rope, twine and sailcloth, or shipped on to London. At the time, a hundredweight (approx. 50 kg) of flax was equivalent to one musket, and a ton (approx. 1016 kg) was exchanged for a 5 lb (2.7 kg) cask of gunpowder.[34] In this way Tapsell became an important source of muskets, powder and ammunition for Māori across the North Island. On the advice of Karuhi's brother Wharepoaka, he settled in the Bay of Plenty, purchasing unoccupied land in Maketū near Tauranga from Hōri Tūpaea for a case of muskets, a cask of tobacco, a case of pipes, a quantity of pig lead, 36 axes and 36 tomahawks. A document of purchase was drawn up at a later date (probably by Jones & Walker in Sydney) and is dated 5 January 1831.[35]

THIS INDENTURE made the Fifth day of January in the year of our Lord, One Thousand Eight Hundred and Thirty one, Between, Tupiah and Hekarea on the first part and Phillip Tapsell Gentleman of the second part now residing at Maketu in New Zealand WHEREAS the said Tupiah and Hekarea being chiefs of the tribe of Ngai-tauhau now residing at the Tumu in the Bay of Plenty in the territory of New Zealand, and having right and authority to alienate the land hereinafter described hath contracted with the said Phillip Tapsell for the sale to him of the said land for the price and consideration as hereinafter mentioned AND the same is now intended to be [—] and conveyed to the said Phillip Tapsell in the manner hereinafter expressed.

NOW THIS INDENTURE WITNESSETH that in consideration of One Case Muskets, One Cask Tobacco, One Case Pipes, Seven 'cwt' Lead, Thirty-six Axes and Thirty-six Tomahawks in hand well and truly paid by the said Phillip Tapsell to the said Tupiah and Hekarea before the sealing and delivery hereof the receipt whereof and that the sum is in full for the absolute purchase of the Inheritance in Fee Simple in possession of the Land and hereditaments hereinafter described and intended to be hereby [—] and conveyed the said Tupiah and Hekarea doth hereby acknowledge and from the same and every part thereof doth acquit release and for ever discharge the said Phillip Tapsell his heirs and assigns and also the land THEY the said Tupiah and Hekarea HATH given, granted and [—] and by these presents DOTH give grant [—] and confirm into the said Phillip Tapsell and his Heirs ALL THAT piece or parcel of land situate lying and being Maketu from Town Point in a South-West direction to Huri Taupoki or howsoever the said land and any part thereof is bounded situate known or distinguished TOGETHER with all paths waters woods timber and other trees Minerals and all appurtenances to the said land premises belonging or in anywise appertaining AND all the right and title whatsoever of them the said Hekarea and Tupiah or any of the said Tribe of Ngaitautau in or to the same TO HAVE and TO HOLD the said land hereditaments and premises hereinafter described and hereby granted [—] and confirmed or intended so to be with their and every of their rights privileges advantages and appurtenances whatsoever unto and for the use and behoof of the said Phillip Tapsell his Heirs and Assigns for ever And the said Tupiah and Hekarea for themselves and their Heirs doth hereby convenance with the said Phillip Tapsell his heirs and Assigns that they the said Tupiah and Hekarea and their heirs do shalt and will warrant and forever defence unto and to the use of the said Phillip Tapsell his heirs and Assigns ALL the said land and premises hereby granted and [—] against them the said Tupiah and Hekarea and their heirs and against all and every person whomsoever claiming the said land and premises or any part thereof IN WITNESS whereof the said parties to these presents have hereunto set their hands and seals the day and year first written above.

SIGNED SEALED AND DELIVERED by the said
Tupiah and Hekarea the same having been first
read over and explained to which they seemed
perfectly to understand in our presence.
Albert Jno. Nicholas
James Farrow
Tupiah
Te Omanu

Local chiefs were keen to invite Tapsell to establish a flax station at Maketū as their neighbouring enemy, Ngāi Te Rangi (or Ngāiterangi), had taken a

THE VOYAGES OF PHILLIP TAPSELL

Departure	Return	Destination	Vessel	Master	Tapsell
08-11-1808	14-04-1812	NZ	New Zealander	William Elder	1st mate
19-02-1810	16-09-1812	Timor	Eliza	Jonathan Clarke	1st mate
13-12-1813	15-06-1816	NSW fishery	Catherine	Robert Graham	1st mate
13-12-1816	20-05-1819	NZ	Catherine	Robert Graham	1st mate
15-12-1818	14-08-1821	Galapagos	Asp	James/John Kenny	Master
22-07-1819	31-05-1822	Galapagos	Catherine	?	1st mate
17-07-1822	26-05-1825	NZ	Asp	William Darby Brind	1st mate
11-03-1823	18-07-1825	NSW fishery	Sisters	Robert Duke	Master

gun trader into their iwi in 1829. Although Te Arawa could obtain guns from traders stationed at Tauranga and Te Tūmū, this was largely dependent on the goodwill of Ngāi Te Rangi and was not a satisfactory arrangement.[36] In the emerging 'arms race' Tapsell could help Te Arawa rebalance the power.[37]

Within no time Maketū was transformed into a place of activity and habitation with people coming from the Rotorua and Tarawera regions and settling there: within two years from 1830 the population in and around Maketū increased from 200 to 3000 souls, transforming the previously abandoned site into a lively papa kāinga (village). Tapsell developed an inland network of traders and came to monopolise the flax trade in the central North Island and the Bay of Plenty, setting up outposts in Maungatautari (Ngāti Raukawa), Mokoia (Te Arawa), Matatā (Ngāti Tūwharetoa) and Whakatāne (Ngāti Awa). The scale of the trade was so great that it led to entire hapū (subtribes) relocating to the trading stations he established and to the flax growing areas and swamps. In Maketū he built a house and store on the beachfront from which the flax could easily be transported onto a waiting ship. A couple of years later he constructed a new house in dressed timber on top of the bluff at Pūtangaru on the site of an ancient pā of Te Arawa and overlooking the shore. Alongside the house he erected a large store for flax and surrounded the property with a battery of 12 cannons as a precautionary measure — he never fired a single shot from them.[38] About this time in Denmark Tapsell's father, Jens Falk, passed away: '26 October 1832: Sanitation supervisor Jens Hansen Falck ... died 25 October (1832) leaving behind his wife Marie Dorothea Falk, née Ismarck [...] from a previous marriage one son, Hans Homan Falck, about forty years old, sea captain in New Zealand [...] in his last marriage no children.'[39]

Karuhi proved to be of huge importance for Tapsell's initial success in Maketū. As sister of the prestigious chiefs Wharepoaka and Waikato,[40] she was a well-respected woman whose years among the missionaries had given her a good knowledge of English. She was able to act as an interpreter for her husband and assist him in avoiding the cultural and political pitfalls for a European living among and establishing trade agreements with Māori. Consequently, Tapsell was on best of terms with people of Tauranga, Waikato, Rotorua, Taupō and Tarawera. In particular, he forged a special friendship with Hōri Tūpaea who built a pā at Te Tūmū to be nearer the flax industry that was developing in and around Maketū.

In the beginning, Maketū traded in fish, sending portions of its catches to Rotorua in return for potatoes and kōura (crayfish). The first year went well: there was peace, plenty of activity and extra income from the fish. But the good times came to an end in 1831 when a taua (war party) of Ngāpuhi under the command of Te Haramiti launched an attack in the Bay. They slaughtered the majority of the inhabitants of Mayor Island (Tūhua) and Mōtītī Island before they were defeated and killed by warriors from Tauranga and Waikato.[41] Many Ngāpuhi killed on Mōtītī were relatives of Karuhi and Wharepoaka, and consequently the latter chose to leave the area and return to the Bay of Islands with the next ship taking flax there.[42]

Before long, Ngāpuhi returned and set up camp near Otūmoetai pā in Tauranga Harbour. The subsequent fighting lasted for months. About the same time, Karuhi was taken seriously ill with measles, a disease that arrived with Pākehā settlers and against which Māori had no immunity. She wished to see her brother one last time, so Tapsell took her to the site of the fighting where she could meet Wharepoaka at the Ngāpuhi camp, while he himself entered Otūmoetai pā to visit Hōri Tūpaea. During the night Tapsell was the victim of an attempted murder when a rival European flax trader tried to shoot him while he slept.[43] Fortunately Tapsell escaped unscathed and was able to return safely with Karuhi to Maketū. Shortly afterwards Ngāpuhi gave up

'A SKETCH OF MAKETU'

Maketu is situated on the East Coast, about 18 miles south of Tauranga, on the river Kaituna. It was at one time a place of great importance to the Maoris, the pa being thickly peopled and very strongly fortified. It was however stormed and taken in 1836 by Waiharoa. At the present time it has a considerable native population. Maketu must always be a place of considerable trade, being as it is one of the keys to the interior. Vessels can enter the river and discharge their cargoes, which, by means of a good road already made, can in a few days be distributed over the Rotorua. This road is not of that uninteresting character one so often meets with in New Zealand. Here the traveller at one time is riding through an avenue of willows, interspersed with peach trees, affording at the proper season both shade and refreshment. Besides the pa mentioned previously, Maketu has the remains of a large redoubt built by the Imperial and Colonial forces in 1865, who garrisoned it for a considerable time. The rebels, 700 strong, on one occasion marched on Maketu, but were met and driven back at Waihi. Maketu cannot be looked upon as a European settlement, all the lands being in native hands, who, however, cultivate a considerable quantity. At Waihi is a flax mill, worked by steam, the raw material being supplied from the neighbouring swamps. Although there are few Europeans engaged in agricultural pursuits, Maketu has a fair number of settlers. There are two very comfortable hotels, two or three large stores, church, and schoolhouse. The school, principally of native children, is spoken highly of. There is a telegraph station, and in fact all the elements of a town, not forgetting a Resident Magistrate and a Court-house. The Mission house and grounds, a little distance from the river, must not be missed. Everyone must acknowledge that we have to thank these early pioneers of civilisation for the introduction and distribution of English and other trees not indigenous to the country. It would be hardly fair to close this slight notice of Maketu without mentioning the name of Tapsell. Mr. Tapsell is most probably the oldest European resident in New Zealand – oldest in years (being over 100 years of age), and oldest in settlement. He has been identified with Maketu and the neighbourhood many years. Years ago when the country was disturbed by tribal wars, and many places now pleasant to the eye were scenes of slaughter and cannibal feasts, Tapsell was there. Even when Te Waharoa made his raid, it was in Tapsell's whare where the head chief of the defenders died.

Daily Southern Cross, 12 October 1872, p. 3

the siege of Otūmoetai and moved to Maketū to
attack the pā of Hōri Tūpaea's at Te Tūmū. There
was a massacre and the subsequent cooking
of and feasting on the victims of the attack is
described in detail in the memoirs. Tapsell's
special role as a Pākehā-Māori, providing access
to European commodities (principally weapons),
and his mana, meant that for the time being he
could live in peace with his Arawa neighbours
in Maketū, even during times of war in spite of
the fact that he had family and friends among
Ngāpuhi and Ngāi Te Rangi, who were among Te
Arawa's greatest enemies.

Karuhi died, and in order to fulfil her last
wish Tapsell sailed with her coffin to Rangihoua
so that she might be buried among her family.
Her death and the following tangihanga (rites
for the dead) caused several misunderstandings
between Tapsell and some of her relatives, who
accused him of violating tapu. Wharepoaka
intervened and came to his friend's aid by arguing

35

Hand-drawn map of
Maketū. This sketch map
of country around Waihi
Estuary and Maketū Pā
from 1870 shows the
location of Tapsell's store
and whare [house]. The
creator is unknown.

MapColl-832.16a/[187-?]/Acc.1848.
Alexander Turnbull Library, National
Library of New Zealand · Te Puna
Mātauranga o Aotearoa, Wellington

Maketū clifftop. The site of Tapsell's house at Pūtangaru above the shore as it is today.

Author's photograph, 2015

that his sister had married a Pākehā and that the laws and customs of the iwi did not apply.

The adaptations required of Pākehā-Māori in becoming part of an iwi are previously discussed; here it is pertinent to acknowledge and comprehend the compromises, dislocations and changes that Māori women (and to a much lesser extent men) who married Pākehā-Māori were required to implement. They too underwent a process of crossing cultures and blurring boundaries, with consequences for themselves and their families. Karuhi was buried at the top of the hill and the missionary John King performed the service over the grave, which Tapsell then had fenced in and covered with a monumental wooden structure.

A few months after Karuhi's death Tapsell set up home with Hineitūrama, a Ngāti Whakaue woman of mana, born about 1818 in Ōhinemutu to Te Koiki (Ngāti Whakaue) and Te Koha-a-Ngatokowaru (Ngāti Raukawa). When missionaries brought Christianity to Ngāti Raukawa around 1825, the family was christened and Hineitūrama was baptised Maria. In 1831,

'Te Haupapa'. Tapsell's last surviving cannon, now located by the shore in Maketū.

Author's photograph, 2015

her uncle, Te Amohau, presented Hineitūrama to Tapsell as a puhi-bride (woman of high rank set aside for political marriages) to ensure that he remained at Maketū. The couple lived happily together for many years, and Kataraina, the first of eight children (six lived to adulthood) was born in 1834:[44]

1. Kataraina (1834–1917; Catherine). Born in Maketū. Married George Simpkins, the first European to settle in Whakatāne, in 1853, and had one child, a daughter called Eliza. Kataraina died in Whakatāne on 21 October 1917. The obituary in the *Auckland Star* (3 November 1917, p. 6) ends thus: 'Mrs Simpkins was very widely known throughout the Bay of Plenty and much respected for her kindly disposition and her many generous acts in times of distress.'

2. [Male, no name] (c.1834) The Tapsells' second child, a boy, was stillborn. He was buried behind the Maketū trading station in a small plot surrounded by a white picket fence. His body was dug up by Te Waharoa's men during

the sacking of Maketū for the sake of having the little coffin for a box.

3. Retireti (1836–1913; Retreat). Born on Mokoia Island. Married Ngatai o Maketū and had nine children (and one with another woman). Worked as a policeman. Retireti was the first Native Constable in New Zealand.

4. Perepe (1838–1913; Phillip). Born in Whakatāne. Married Ruta Manuahura in 1853 and had two children. Died in Maketū.

5. Ewa (1839–64; Eve). Born in Whakatāne. Married Dr Robert Hooper in 1855 and had two children. Died in 1864 at the Battle of Ōrākau after accompanying her husband and mother to the pā to provide medical assistance.

6. Īeni (1841–1911; Jens). Born in Whakatāne. Married Tūpaea's granddaughter Te Hake Te Aokore Warangi in 1862 and had five children (and one with another woman).

7. Tote (1842–72; Dorothy). Born in Whakatāne. Married Tamati Hutchinson and had three children. Lived near Thames and died in 1872.

8. Whetūmārama (1850–55; 'Bright Star'). Born in Whakatāne. Died aged five just prior to Christmas in 1855.

Tapsell also adopted at least one child — the daughter of fellow flax trader Taylor and his wife.

Throughout their years Hineitūrama was an excellent partner for Tapsell and assisted him in mediating between warring factions and in negotiating trading agreements. She was a careful, kind and thoughtful rangatira of the highest demeanour. Through her father she was of Ngāti Huia of Ngāti Raukawa and so had a close connection to Ōrākau. This connection opened up trade for Tapsell as well as allowing access to Hineitūrama's cousins Tūpaea, Te Rauparaha and Te Wherowhero. Their marriage was eventually solemnised and their children were baptised in Whakatāne in 1841 by the Catholic bishop Jean-Baptiste Pompallier (1802–71).

In Maketū the Tapsells often found themselves directly in the firing line between warring parties. They bore witness to numerous battles and accompanying acts of cannibalism and the preparation of mokomōkai (cured heads). Despite his role as a gun trader who provided muskets to the various iwi in return for flax, Tapsell often tried to act as a peacemaker in these conflicts, sometimes at great risk to his own safety.[45] This highlights the contradiction in Tapsell's activities: he was a trader keen to forge stable and peaceful alliances and create prosperity, but he also sold guns to various iwi bent on exterminating one another in the inter-iwi conflict that became known as the Musket Wars. In this Tapsell was far from unique; on the contrary, he was very much a man of his age manoeuvring through conflicts that were not of his own making, able to accrue profit on the back of them, while at the same time constantly faced with the danger of ruin and destruction.

Tapsell's relations with his Māori neighbours were not always harmonious. A disagreement with the chief Te Haupapa over payment for building a house led to Tapsell's stores being stripped and Te Haupapa and his people threatening to kill the trader. Only when Tapsell turned his home into an improvised fortress and armed himself with muskets and blunderbusses did Te Haupapa express regret and make peace with him. Further episodes of disagreement and cheating aside, the two became the best of friends.

Another argument that turned violent began when Tapsell scolded some Māori for roasting alive a dog that belonged to their enemy, his friend Hōri Tūpaea, as an act of utu. That night the culprits set Tapsell's cookhouse on fire and attempted to plunder his stores. Some suppliers tried to cheat in their dealings with Tapsell by placing stones in the bottom of baskets of flax to increase their weight and price or by demanding money for items once given to Tapsell as gifts. Nevertheless, Tapsell made great friends among

Phillip Tapsell's cartouche. The leather cartridge box for storing ammunition was taken from Tapsell at the storming of Te Tūmū pā in 1836. It came into the possession of Ngāi te Rangi who were allies of Te Waharoa and fought alongside him during the battle. The box was passed down through two generations and then gifted to Captain Gilbert Mair.

Gilbert Mair Collection, Auckland War Memorial Museum · Tāmaki Paenga Hira

39

his neighbours and he speaks admiringly of their acts of bravery, resolution, selflessness and generosity.

Not all of his descriptions of his neighbours' behaviour or of Māori rituals, beliefs and customs are written in flattering terms in Tapsell's memoirs, where he generally tries to present himself as a force for rationality and civilisation. He occasionally interfered in Māori traditions, for example tangihanga and mākutu rituals, which he considered nonsense or immoral. In one case he tried to prevent the whakamomori (customary suicide) of the grief-stricken widow of a Ngāpuhi chief killed in a battle. Having failed in his attempt, he tied a black ribbon around the hanging dead woman's wrist and dared one of his Māori crewmembers to retrieve it in the middle of the night in return for a coat. This may seem an unnecessary and disrespectful act, but perhaps Tapsell was trying to 'liberate' his employees from what he saw as the repressive superstition of tapu.[46] Despite these actions, he was often called on for his skills in medicine and surgery, particularly during the frequent battles when he would remove bullets from wounded warriors and apply ointments.

Not all of Tapsell's attempts at expanding his trading network met with success. He tried to extend his flax business to Mokoia Island in Lake Rotorua, sending his agent James Farrow there with a large number of goods for trade. Unfortunately the business did not flourish as Māori workers stopped preparing the flax and the various goods that were to be used to pay for it began to go missing. Tapsell had to shut the enterprise down. Later, however, he was invited by Waikato chief Murupara to set up trade in Matamata, where he employed a Mr Clementson as his agent.

In March 1836, Tapsell's time as a trader in Maketū came to an abrupt end when the papakāinga, pā and his station were sacked.[47] The spark to the events surrounding its destruction occurred when Te Hunga, one of Ngāti Hauā chief Te Waharoa's relatives, was murdered by Haere Huka, a Ngāti Whakaue chief. This single act brought a war between Ngāti Hauā with their allies Ngāi Te Rangi on the one side and Ngāti Whakaue on the other, which lasted nearly ten years.

Plundering and murder took place throughout the region and when the turn came to Maketū, Tapsell's agent Farrow was able to warn him that Te Waharoa was approaching with a heavily armed taua of over 1500 toa, but only moments before the attack started. The defenders of Maketū numbered probably no more than 60 and comprised Ngāti Whakaue under Te Haupapa and Ngāti Pūkenga under Nainai.[48] The details of the fighting, the killing and the subsequent cannibalism are related in detail in Tapsell's memoirs, as is the heroism of Te Haupapa, who stood alongside his friend to defend the trading post. Te Haupapa was shot and beheaded.[49] After a night of bloodshed,

Gateway of Maketū pā. Drawn in 1864 by Horatio Gordon Robley (1840–1930) and published in *The Illustrated London News* in 1867.

41

the heavily pregnant Hineitūrama and their daughter Kataraina were taken to safety in Te Tūmū by Hōri Tūpaea. Later they were joined by Tapsell who had to abandon the defence of their home. Tapsell's stores and goods were plundered by Ngāti Hauā and their allies, and his house and buildings were set alight. His losses were estimated to have been £4000. He was ruined. The Tapsells had lost everything.

The family spent nearly six months in safety on Mokoia Island in Lake Rotorua, where Hineitūrama gave birth to a son who they named Retireti (Retreat), in memory of the flight from Maketū. After the situation had calmed down enough, the family made their way to the coast and sailed to Sydney, where Tapsell settled accounts with Jones & Walker, who ended their contract with him.[50] He began working for Frederick Peterson and entered into a partnership with John Middlemas.

After the Te Tūmū wars, Maketū remained far too volatile a town to raise a family and the Tapsells had to settle further east in Whakatāne. Consequently, Tapsell lost all his interests in his own name in the Maketū region. Unfortunately, his fortunes did not much improve. His agent Clementson was drowned off Matatā and in 1844 the schooner *Falcon*, bound for Sydney, was wrecked in a storm off Maketū after having taken on board a load of flax. Tapsell saved only a few goods from the ship. Shortly afterwards he received news that Mr Peterson, his Sydney business agent, had been declared bankrupt and owed Tapsell hundreds of pounds.[51] Financial difficulties dogged Tapsell for the rest of his life.

Again, he built up a new flax-trading enterprise but business did not go well. Tapsell was forced to supplement his income with boatbuilding and working as a pilot. In 1864 Hineitūrama left

The *Falcon* memorial plaque. Found on the last surviving of Tapsell's cannons in Maketū, the plaque incorrectly states that he salvaged his cannons from the *Falcon* in 1840.

Author's photograph, 2015

TAPSELL
HINE·A·TURAMA
MARRIAGE TO PHILIP TAPSELL
BY BISHOP POMPALIER 1841
PERISHED WITH MANIAPOTO'S FORCES
· AT ORAKAU 1865 ·
AGED 46.
MOTHER OF KATARAINA, RETREAT
PHILIP, HANS, EWA & DORATHY

OF HER BONES N.Z. WAS MADE

The memorial for Hineitūrama. The stone lies next to Phillip Tapsell's grave in Wharekahu Cemetery, Maketū.

Author's photograph, 2015

Whakatāne to visit their daughter Ewa, who had married Dr Robert Hooper. By this time Tapsell's wife was in love with another man, her childhood friend Rōpata, and she had separated from her husband. Hineitūrama's journey proved to be fateful as she was caught in the bloody conflict between government forces and the Kīngitanga (Māori King Movement). She died with Ewa and Rōpata at the Battle of Ōrākau when British forces stormed the pā. As with all combatants killed in the assault, she was buried on the battlefield. Today a memorial stone for Hineitūrama stands next to Tapsell's grave in Wharekahu Cemetery in Maketū.

In 1866 Tapsell was once again faced with poverty. He petitioned the Governor for a pension as recognition of his role in the recapture of the *Wellington* four decades earlier.[52] The matter was referred to the government of New South Wales, but no more

Phillip Tapsell's grave. Tapsell was laid to rest in Wharekahu Cemetery to the accompaniment of cannon fire from the battery in Maketū.

Author's photograph, 2015

44

was heard of it. In his old age Tapsell lived with his daughter Kataraina and her husband George Simpkins on Moutohorā (Whale Island), where they ran a shop, and later with his son Retireti in Maketū.[53] He died, aged 83, on 7 August 1873 and was buried at Wharekahu Cemetery to the accompaniment of cannon fire from the battery in Maketū.[54]

The memoirs that tell the story of Phillip Tapsell's life are full of adventure, dangerous scrapes and action. Until the sacking of Maketū, the narrative is upbeat, coherent and fast-paced. However, the final 30 years of Tapsell's life after he moves to Whakatāne are dealt with only briefly and disjointedly. Te Waharoa's attack appears to have diminished not just Tapsell's business, but his spirit. There are anecdotes and descriptions of a few events, but the drive and pace of the narrative have disappeared and the story becomes tinged with sadness and disappointment.

OPPOSITE Kataraina and Phillip Tapsell. Photograph of father and daughter taken by John Low, Waikato.

1/2-005486-F: Alexander Turnbull Library, National Library of New Zealand · Te Puna Mātauranga o Aotearoa, Wellington

45

Whangaroa
Bay of Islands
Kerikeri Oihi Mission Station & Rangihoua pā
Paihia Kororāreka
Whangarei
Little Barrier Island (Hauturu)

BAY OF PLENTY

Tairua
Thames Mayor Island (Tūhua)
Pūriri
Waihi
White Island (Whakaari)
Mōtītī Island
Tauranga
Te Tūmū Maketū
Whale Island (Moutohorā)
Matamata Matatā Whakatāne
Lake Rotorua Ōpōtiki
Rotorua Lake Rotoiti
Lake Tarawera

Te Urewera

Taupō

SEE INSET MAP

NORTH ISLAND

Port Nicholson

COOK
STRAIT

TASMAN SEA

Banks Peninsula

Akaroa

SOUTH ISLAND

PACIFIC OCEAN

Codfish Island

STEWART ISLAND

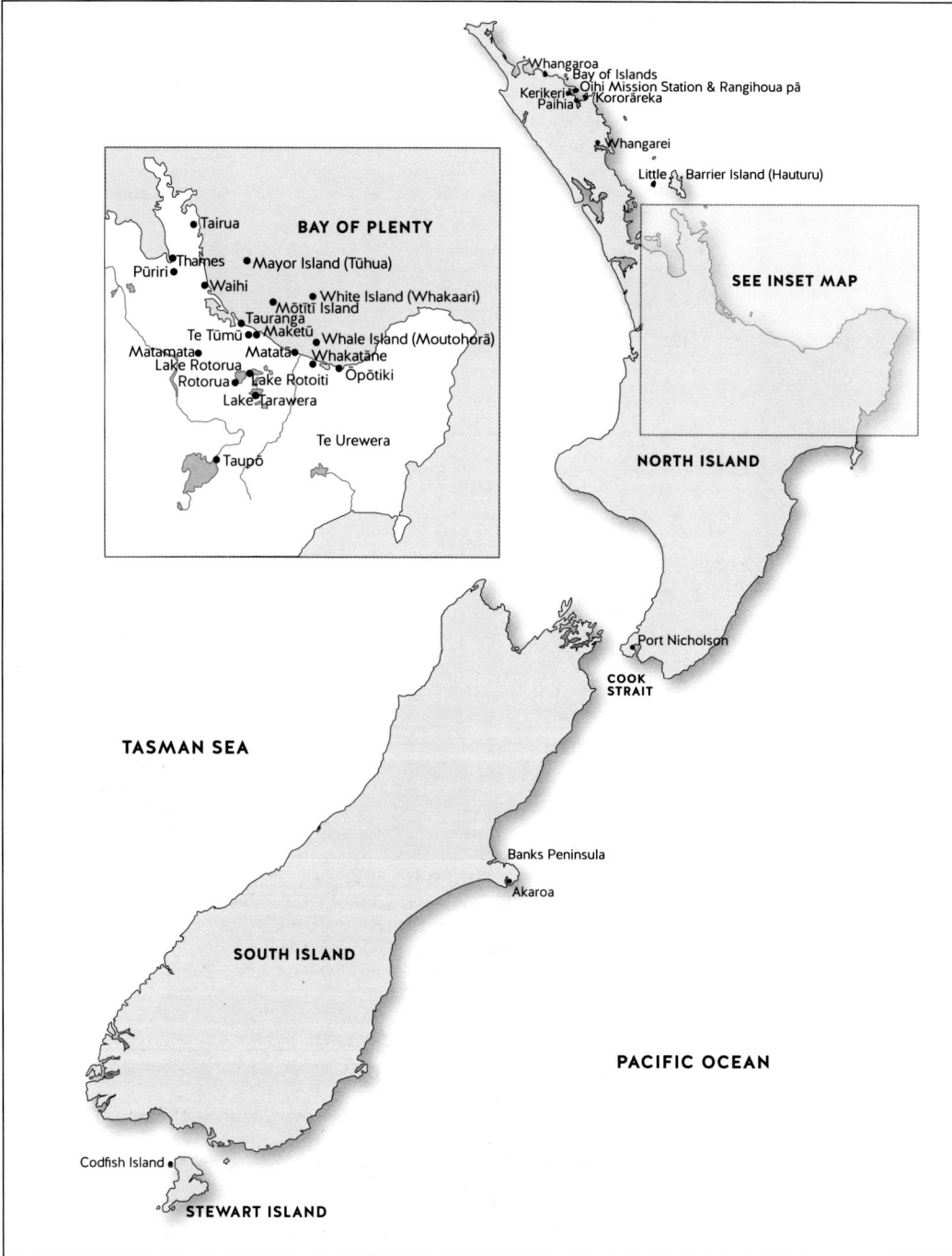

A map of Aotearoa New Zealand showing some of the places
mentioned in the text. The inset map illustrates the places that were
of importance to Phillip Tapsell during his life in the Bay of Plenty.

NOTES

1. Tasman had named it 'Staten Landt', but the Dutch cartographers of the mid-seventeenth century coined the name 'Nova Zeelandia' based on the province of Zeeland in the southwest Netherlands.

2. Although most of the foreigners who settled among Māori were of British or Irish origin, some were from continental Europe and North America. Pacific Islanders and men of Indian and African-American origin also assimilated as Māori.

3. Trevor Bentley, *Cannibal Jack: The Life and Times of Jacky Marmon, a Pākehā-Māori* (Auckland: Penguin, 2010), p. 15.

4. Trevor Bentley, *Pakeha Maori: The Extraordinary Story of the Europeans who Lived as Māori in Early New Zealand* (Auckland: Penguin, 1999); Trevor Bentley, 'Images of Pakeha-Maori: A Study of the Representation of Pakeha-Maori by Historians of New Zealand from Arthur Thomson (1859) to James Belich (1996)', unpublished PhD thesis (Hamilton: University of Waikato, 2007); Bentley, *Cannibal Jack*.

5. Bentley, *Pakeha Maori*, p. 10.

6. James Belich, *Making Peoples: A History of the New Zealanders from Polynesian Settlement to the End of the Nineteenth Century* (Rosedale, NZ: Penguin, 1996), pp. 132–33; Bentley, *Pakeha Maori*, pp. 37–38, 118.

7. Belich, *Making Peoples*, p. 132; Bentley, *Pakeha Maori*, passim (see book's index); Robert McNab, *Murihiku: A History of the South Island of New Zealand and the Islands Adjacent and Lying to the South, from 1642 to 1835* (Wellington: Whitcombe and Tombs, 1909), pp. 317–19.

8. James Cowan, *The Adventures of Kimble Bent* (London: Whitcombe and Tombs, 1911).

9. John 'Jacky' Marmon (*c.* 1798–1880) was born in Sydney to Irish convict parents. He went to sea as a young man, but tired of colonial life, he escaped and settled among Māori in New Zealand. His memoirs were serialised and first published in *The New Zealand Herald* (beginning 9 October 1880, p. 6) and later in a much longer version in *The Auckland Star* (see advert in *Auckland Star*, 18 November 1881, p. 3). See also Bentley, *Cannibal Jack*.

10. Bentley, 'Images of Pakeha-Maori', pp. 75, 168.

11. Bentley, 'Images of Pakeha-Maori', p. 178.

12. This year of birth is based on censuses and other archival evidence available in Copenhagen. A souvenir programme produced for celebrations in Maketū of the bicentenary of Tapsell's birth, *1778–1978: The Descendants of the Union of a Viking of the North to That of a Viking of the South* (Maketū: Reunion Committee, 1978) has his year of birth as 1778, and the booklet *Whanau-a-Tapihana Reunion 1830–2004* (Maketū: Reunion Committee, 1978) has his year of birth as 1777. James Cowan, in his *A Trader in Cannibal Land: The Life and Adventures of Captain Tapsell* (Dunedin: A.H. & A.W. Reed, 1935), p. 17, writes that Tapsell was born in 1779, while Preben Dich, in his *Blandt hvaler og kannibaler. Hans Falk — en dansk eventyrer i New Zealand* ([Lyngby]: Holkenfeldt 3, 2006), p. 1, correctly states his year of birth as 1790. Tapsell's tombstone says that he 'died at the age of 94 years on the 6th of August, 1873', i.e. that he was born 1778–79. His age on various whaling voyages found in the British Southern Whale Fishery database (whalinghistory.org), that ultimately goes back to the information provided on his falsified papers, puts his year of birth at 1786 or 1797.

    By the time Hans was born, the couple had already had one child. Their first child was also christened at the Church of Our Saviour in Copenhagen on 17 August 1787 and also received the name Hans Homan: 'Hans Homan — Jens Hansen Arbeidsmand og Giertrud Johanne Homan, Fad*dere* Madam Lassen *Madam* Clemensen, Herr Lassen Fuldmægtig, Herr Tenvig(?), M. Bøye Schow Fiskebløder, Herr Juul Bødker' (Hans Homan — Jens Hansen, labourer, and Gjertrud Johanne Homan. Godparents: Madam Lassen, Madam Clemensen, Mr Lassen, clerk, Mr Tenvig, M. Boye Schow, dried-fish seller, Mr Juul, cooper), *Vor Frelsers Kirkes Døbe-Protocol fra 1763–1796 incl.* (Church of Our Saviour, Baptism Register, 1763–96 Inclusive), p. 208. Sadly, the couple's first child, Hans, passed away while still a small child (according to the records of the Church of Our Saviour, Jens Hansen reported the death of a son called Hans on 1 June 1788 and 11 February 1789). When the couple had their next baby, they re-used the name Hans in memory of the child that they lost. This was common practice.

13. 'Anno 1785 af 16. Februar Er effter kongel*ige* allernaadigste Tilladelse Ungkarl Jens Hansen og Jomfru Giertrud Johanne Hansdatter Hoeman Copolerede hinanden i Huuset af

Velædle Hr. Dom Provst Schultz.' (16 February 1785: In accordance with royal, most merciful permission, the bachelor Jens Hansen and the maiden Gjertrud Johanne Hansdatter Homan were married to one another in the house of the very honourable chapter dean Schultz.) *Ægteskabstillysningbog for Roskilde Domkirke 1678–1793* (Betrothals, Banns and Marriages for Roskilde Cathedral 1678–1793), 16 February 1785.

14. 'Jens Hansen Arbejdsmand og Gjertrud Johanne Homan en Søn Hans Homan; Faddere Mad: Lassen. Mad: Sünckenberg; Kjøbmand Høvisk; Bogholder Lykke; Fuldmægtig Larsen. Dåb.' *Protocoll over Fødte og Døde i Vor Frelsers Menighed paa Christianshafn fra September 1759 til 1800 inclusive* (Register of Births and Deaths in Our Saviour's Congregation in Christianshavn from September 1759 to 1800 inclusive), p. 119; cf. *Vor Frelsers Kirkes Døbe-Protocol fra 1763–1796 incl.* (Church of Our Saviour, Baptism Register, 1763–1796 Inclusive), p. 227.

15. 'Huustømmersvend Jens Falck [...] boende til leje i 311 i Laxegaden [...] Hans Hustrue Giertrud Johanne Homand [...] død 12de Maj 1798 [...] efterlader sig Egteskabet 2 Sønner Hans 10 Aar gammel og Niels Christian 4 Aar gammel.' *Københavns Skiftekommission, Forseglingsprotokol, Klasse 5, 1799* (Probate Commission of Copenhagen, Sealing Protocol, Class 5, 1799), p. 390b. Note that Hans' age is incorrectly given here.

16. 'Den 26de October bleve antegnede til at lyses for Enkemand Jens Falk, constitueret Vandmester og Enken Marie Dorothea, Enke efter forrige Skibstømmermand Arentsen [...] copulerede 22de November', *Helligaands Kirke (Helliggejst Kirke), Trolovelse 1763–98, Vielse 1763–1817* (Church of the Holy Ghost, Engagement 1763–98, Marriage 1763–1817), p. 144.

17. The 1801 census entry for Lavendelstræde 87.89 145: 'Jens Hansen Falk Huusbond 40 Vandmester / Marie Esmark hans Kone 40 / Begge i 2det Ægteskab / Hans Falk Huusbonder 10 ugift / Niels Falk 6 ugift / Søner af 1e Ægteskab.' *Folketælling 1801. Band 18. København Vester Kvarter I* (Population Census 1801. Vol. 18. Copenhagen Western Quarter I), p. 116.

18. The British Southern Whale Fishery database (whalinghistory.org).

19. Between 1809 and 1826 he visited the country at least six times on whaling voyages.

20 On the *Boyd* massacre and its consequences, see Wade Doak, *The Burning of the Boyd: A Saga of Culture Clash* (Auckland: Hodder & Stoughton, 1984).

21. Tapsell sailed three times from England to the South Seas on the *Catherine*: 1813, 1816 and 1819.

22. The *Sydney Gazette and New South Wales Advertiser*, 24 September 1827, p. 2: 'We perceive that Mr. Tapsell, late Chief Officer of the Sisters, whaler, Captain Duke, and to whose exertions was principally to be attributed the recapture of the brig Wellington, has now the command of the schooner Darling.' On the recapture of the *Wellington*, see below.

23. *The Monitor*, 24 September 1827, p. 7: 'Arrivals: On Friday the Schooner *Darling*, Tapsell Master, from Tongataboo, July 16, and New Zealand August 19. Passengers — Mr. Weiss and family; Charles Tindall and Ellen Masterson. Lading — Missionaries' property.'

24. About this time, Tapsell met Jacky Marmon, the Pākehā-Māori mentioned in the previous section, for the first time: 'It was after this [1811] I fell in with Tapsell, who was carpenter aboard the Catherine, a whaler also.' *New Zealand Herald*, 9 October 1880, p. 6; Bentley, *Cannibal Jack*, p. 108.

25. Of course, Tapsell's memoirs, noted down and then revised and published in a serialisation in the *Daily Southern Cross* by Edward Little, were shaped with an audience in mind — they are not intended as private reminiscences, but rather as an eventful page-turner for publication. The attention paid to the blood and gore of warfare, to slavery and to cannibalism may well have been intended by Little to captivate, titillate and horrify Pākehā readers. Indeed, we see the same marketing ploy in the titles of later books about Tapsell: James Cowan's *A Trader in Cannibal Land* (1935), Preben Dich's *Among Whales and Cannibals* (2006), and Kåre Bluitgen's *Hans Falk in the Land of the Cannibals* (2010).

Cannibalism in traditional Māori society of the past remains an emotive and charged topic in the present: any discussion inevitably draws a range of responses, including displeasure, anger and allegations of misrepresentation. The most detailed account of traditional Māori cannibalism is Paul Moon, *This Horrid Practice: The Myth and Reality of Traditional Māori Cannibalism* (Rosedale, NZ: Penguin, 2008). The book was the first attempt to provide a survey of the history of cannibalism among the Māori and caused a furore in some academic circles. See, for example, the review by John Bevan-Smith: '[Review] Paul Moon, This Horrid Practice: The Myth and Reality of Traditional Maori Cannibalism', *New Zealand Journal of History*, 44.2 (2010), pp. 203–205; Paul Moon's response: 'Correspondence', *New Zealand Journal of History*, 45.1 (2011), pp. 146–147; and Ruth Laugesen's summary: 'Close to the Bones',

New Zealand Listener (online), 227 no. 3694 (26 February 2011). For a different early European perspective on cannibalistic practices than that found in the Tapsell manuscript, see William Jennings, 'The Debate over kai tangata (Māori Cannibalism): New Perspectives from the Correspondence of the Marists', Journal of Polynesian Society, 120.2 (2011), pp. 129–48.

26. There is some chronological confusion in Tapsell's account at this point: the Battle of Te Ika-a-Ranga-nui was in 1825, not 1822.

27. Of course, many Pākehā men lived with Māori women as man and wife without having a Christian wedding. William Darby Brind, who was captain of Tapsell's ship the Asp, lived in several such relationships. One day in 1830 when several young, high-ranking Māori women, who were rivals for Brind's affections, exchanged insults, fighting broke out between hapū (subtribes) within Ngāpuhi on the beach at Kororāreka in an event since known as the Girls' War. Tapsell and Hineitūrama lived together as man and wife for many years without being married. On Tapsell's marriages, see Ernest E. Bush, 'The Three Wives of Philip Tapsell', Te Ao Hou. The Maori Magazine, 74 (1973), pp. 11–13.

28. When he returned to the Bay of Islands in 1829, Tapsell learnt that Maria Ringa was dead; Donald Murray Stafford, Te Arawa: A History of the Arawa People (Auckland: Reed, 1991), p. 193.

29. 'The Life and Adventure of John Marmon, the Hokianga Pakeha Maori; or Seventy-Five Years in New Zealand', Auckland Star, 4 February 1882, Supplement, p. 1; Bentley, Cannibal Jack, pp. 151–52.

30. Phillip Tapsell first met Jacky Marmon around 1811.

31. Tapsell's version of the capture of the Wellington also appears in James Cowan, Hero Stories of New Zealand (Wellington: Harry H. Tombs, 1935), pp. 22–30; see also Cecil and Celia Manson, The Affair of the Wellington Brig: A True and Terrible Tale (Wellington: Millwood Press, 1978), in which the role of Tapsell is highlighted. In Part 3 'Contemporary accounts of Phillip Tapsell's life', you will find contemporary newspaper accounts praising Tapsell, as well as a version of the events provided by Tapsell 40 years after the event. Other accounts, in which Tapsell's role is mentioned only briefly if at all, can be found in The Australian, 'Piracy by Prisoners and Re-capture', 10 February 1827, p. 3; The Sydney Gazette and New South Wales Advertiser, 'Piratical Seizure of the Brig Wellington', 16 February 1827, p. 2, and 'Further Particulars of the Piratical Seizure and Re-capture of the Brig Wellington', 17 February 1827, p. 5.

32. Samuel Marsden's account of the marriage can be found in Part 3 'Contemporary accounts of Phillip Tapsell's life'.

33. On Jones & Walker, see Janette Holcomb, Early Merchant Families of Sydney: Speculation and Risk Management on the Fringes of Empire (London: Anthem, 2014), pp. 107–108.

34. On the flax trade and the role of Pākehā-Māori, see William Carl Schaniel, 'The Maori and the Economic Frontier: An Economic History of the Maori of New Zealand, 1769–1840', unpublished PhD thesis (Knoxville: The University of Tennessee, 1985), pp. 256–72.

35. Maketu Minute Book VI, p. 41; quoted in Stafford, Te Arawa, p. 196. Cf. F. Dillon Bell, Maori Deeds of Old Private Land Purchases in New Zealand, From the Year 1815 to 1840, with Pre-Emptive and Other Claims (Wellington: George Didsbury, 1882), pp. 591–92:

> 272. Richard Jones, of Sydney, Esq., Claimant.
>
> 100,000 (one hundred thousand) acres, more or less, being one-half of the track of land named Mackatoe, situated in the North Island of New Zealand, about twenty miles east of Tawranger Harbour, commencing from a point called Town Point. [Boundaries not stated.] Alleged to have been purchased on the 8th November, 1830, by Mr. Philip Tapsell, acting on behalf of the claimant, from the Native chiefs Tesbie Kickeru, Toke Peutorea, Bonire, and Tebipe. Consideration: Various articles of merchandise to the value not stated. Nature of conveyance: Instrument in writing, dated 8th November, 1840.

See also the judgment delivered in the Native Land Court regarding the Paengaroa block and quoted in Stafford, Te Arawa, pp. 193–95.

36. Stafford, Te Arawa, p. 192.

37. Indeed, Tapsell's importance for Te Arawa in procuring muskets was a decisive factor for local iwi when choosing alliances during times of conflict. Stafford, Te Arawa, p. 211.

38. Alister Matheson, 'Tapsell's Big Guns', Historical Review: Bay of Plenty Journal, 37.1 (1989), pp. 1–12; Paul Tapsell and Quentin Tapsell, Whanau-a-Tapihana Reunion 1830–2004 (Maketū: Reunion Committee), pp. 16–17; Paora Tapsell, 'Te Haupapa', in The Lives of Colonial Objects,

ed. Annabel Cooper, Lachy Paterson and Angela Wanhalla (Dunedin: Otago University Press, 2015), pp. 24–31. His storehouse doubled as guest accommodation (*The Early Journals of Henry Williams, Senior Missionary in New Zealand of the Church Missionary Society, 1824–40*, ed. Lawrence M. Rogers (Christchurch: Pegasus Press, 1961), pp. 200–201):

> *Wednesday, 2 [November 1831]*. [...] A little after one arrived at Maketu much wet from having to wade through the swamps at the close of the journey. Not much fatigued. Mr. Tapsel asked us in to refresh ourselves. In the evening intended to have proceeded on, but as it commenced raining deferred my march until the morning. *Thursday, 3*. Much disturbed all night by fleas, as our beds were laid in Mr. Tapsel's store in which a large dog was generally kept.

39. 'Anno 1832, d. 26 October [...] Vandmester Jens Hansen Falck [...] som 25 Oktober døde [...] efterladende Hustru Marie Dorothea Falck, fød Ismarck [...] fra foregaaende Egteskab efterladende sig 1 Søn Hans Homan Falck, omtrent 40 Aar *gammel*, Skibscapitain og boende på Neu Zeeland [...] I sit sidste Egteskab efterladende sig ingen Børn.' *Landsover- samt Hof- og Stadsretten, Københavns Skiftekommission, Forseglingsprotokol 1832–1833, Protokol 2 1–193* (National, Royal and City Court, Copenhagen Probate Commission, Sealing Protocol 1832–1833, Protocol 2 1–193), p. 133 (no. 75). It is noteworthy that Jens' other son, Niels Christian, is not mentioned in the obituary and may already have been dead.

40. In 1820 Waikato travelled to England with Hongi Hika and Thomas Kendall and met King George IV.

41. The missionary Henry Williams describes Tapsell's reaction to and role in this conflict in his journal. See *The Early Journals of Henry Williams*, pp. 224, 234–37.

42. Rumours spread that Tapsell and his family had been killed during the raid (*The Early Journals of Henry Williams*, pp. 174–75):

> *Sunday, 3*. [April 1831] After service went to Waitangi. Report among the natives of the death of Mr. Tapsel that he had been killed and eaten in the neighbourhood of Tauranga, together with his wife, the sister of Warepoaka and others. He had been put there by the House of Jones and Walker of Sydney for the purpose of collecting flax. The natives in considerable agitation in consequence of the various accounts from the Southd. of the number recently killed.

43. It is likely that the European(s) in the pā who attempted to take Tapsell's life were Franks and/or Clark, two traders from Tauranga. See Stafford, *Te Arawa*, p. 212. The incident reflects the huge rivalry between the traders and the lengths that some would go to in order to extend their control throughout the area and increase their profits.

44. A child who died and was buried in Maketū is mentioned in the memoirs (see p. 153). On Tapsell's children, see Paul Tapsell and Quentin Tapsell, *Whanau-a-Tapihana Reunion 1830–2004* (Maketū: Reunion Committee), pp. 10–15; and Russell Caldwell, *Tapihana: Brothers in Arms* (Christchurch: Iwi-Link Management, 2004).

45. In June 1833 Tapsell wrote on behalf of his people to Henry Williams to request missionaries to be sent in order to ensure peace (*The Early Journals of Henry Williams*, pp. 317-18):

> *Saturday, 8*. Fine. Rec'd two letters from Mr. Tapsel, a flax agent residing in Maketu, the man who opposed us so strenuously last year when at Tauranga with the natives. At the latter part of his first letter, which was written just at the conclusion of making peace, he says, 'My people bid me write to you to send them a Missionary; if you should approve of that I hope you will send one to Tauranga, Wakatane, and the River Thames; as it would be the means of keeping peace amongst them.' This is the testimony of one who has been living several years amongst this people, and has tried the power of his abilities, and the strength of his European knowledge in keeping this war in agitation, but has found it ineffectual. What he expresses in his letter I doubt not but is his sincere opinion that the influence of Missionaries will alone stay this destructive work.

46. This stands in stark contrast to reports that Tapsell sometimes declared himself tapu. The manuscript may well present a more 'one-dimensional' Pākehā Tapsell than was actually the case. Although baptised a Lutheran, Tapsell does not seem to have been particularly preoccupied by Christianity during his life — at least in the form of religious institutions — a fact borne out by his arguments with missionaries. He also was happy to live with Hineitūrama for many years without actually having a Christian wedding, finally tying the knot in a Catholic ceremony. His children underwent Catholic baptism at the same time. In

the manuscript he does say that he has all his prayers in his head (p. 236), that the Bible is 'a good book' (p. 244), and that his God protects him (p. 247). Toward the end of his life he turned to religion and became an avid reader of the Bible. This newfound piety is described in his obituary; see Part 3, 'Contemporary accounts of Phillip Tapsell's life'.

47. Ron D. Crosby, *The Musket Wars: A History of Inter-Iwi Conflict 1806–1845* (Auckland: Libro International, 2012 [1999]), pp. 302–307.

48. Crosby, *The Musket Wars*, p. 305.

49. See Part 3 'Contemporary accounts of Phillip Tapsell's life'. To this day Tapsell's only surviving cannon, now located on the shore next to the Te Arawa monument in Maketū, is known as Te Haupapa. See the illustration on p. 37 and Tapsell, 'Te Haupapa'.

50. He took his wife and children to Sydney with him on this trip (*The Australian*, 6 June 1837, p. 2):

    Arrivals. Yesterday, the bark *Lynn*, Shaw master, from New Zealand [...] Passengers: Mr. Ferraby, Mr. Tapsell, four New Zealanders and two children', *The Sydney Monitor*, 17 March 1837, p. 2. Cf. also: 'Departures [...] June 4. — The Schooner *Harlequin*, Anderson Master, for New Zealand. Passengers — Mr. and Mrs. Tapsell, Mr. Banks, and two children, and Mr. Hitchcock.

    While in Sydney, Tapsell appears to have also made an agreement with David Scott & Co. of Sydney (*The Sydney Monitor*, 21 April 1837, p. 3):

    CAUTION. The Public are hereby cautioned from Purchasing any New Zealand Flax from Phillip Tapsell, late agent at New Zealand, to Messrs. R. Jones & Co., but now residing in Prince-street, Sydney, he having Sold his Flax to us, and received an advance in money on the same. DAVID SCOTT & CO. Lower George-street, April 21, 1837.

    See also later similar notices in the same, the *Sydney Herald* and the *Sydney Gazette and New South Wales Advertiser*.

51. Indeed, in a letter from 1845 Tapsell describes himself as being 'rather in low circumstances'. See the illustration on p. 191.

52. See Part 3, 'Contemporary accounts of Phillip Tapsell's life'.

53. Retireti had rebuilt the family homestead in Maketū in the late 1850s when he returned as an adult, married Ngatai o Maketū and took up residence as a member of Ngāti Whakaue and Ngāti Pikiao through his mother Hineitūrama. In this way the family could maintain and assert their Te Arawa rights to Maketū in Māori native title and beyond his father's lost claim. Today, the majority of Tapsell lands have been lost through alienation, but the mana of Te Tāpihana has remained intact over Maketū.

54. Notice of Phillip Tapsell's passing (*Daily Southern Cross*, 9 August 1873, p. 3): 'TAURANGA, Friday. Old Phillip Tapsell died at Maketu on Wednesday night at 10 o'clock, after a fortnight's illness. A great tangi will be held to-day. It is believed he was 96 years of age.' See Part 3, 'Contemporary accounts of Phillip Tapsell's life' for obituaries and a description of the funeral.

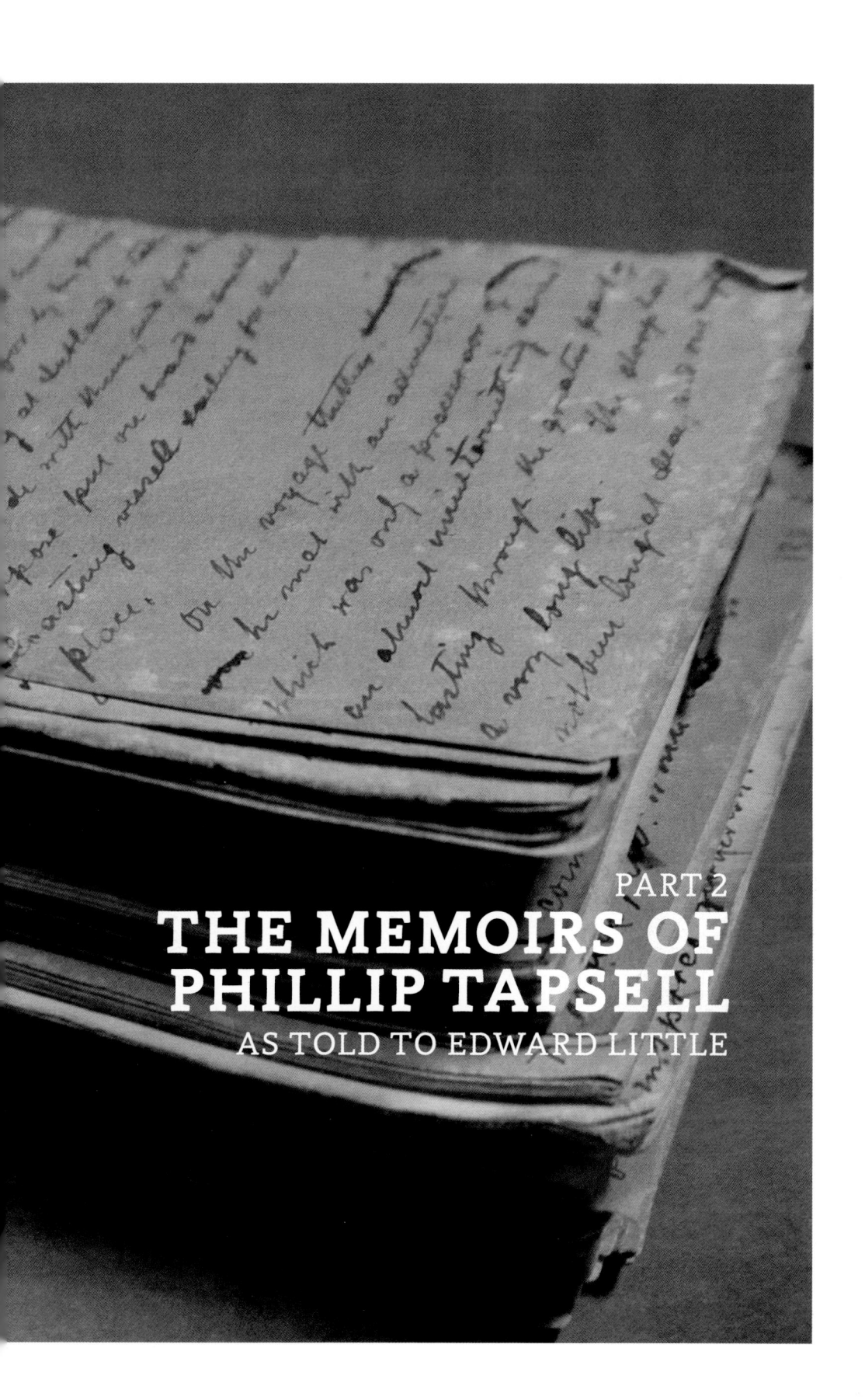

PART 2
THE MEMOIRS OF PHILLIP TAPSELL
AS TOLD TO EDWARD LITTLE

1

Birth[1]

HANS HÖMMAN FALK, better known in New Zealand as Phillip Tapsell, the subject of the following biographical sketch was born in Copenhagen somewhere about the year 1777,[2] the eldest son of Jens Hansen Falk, an important public functionary in that city.[3]

The boy on the burning deck

AT THE EARLY AGE OF EIGHT his mother dying, he was sent for by his grandparents living at Jutland to take up his abode with them, and for this purpose put on board a small coasting vessell sailing for that place.

On the voyage thither, he met with an adventure which was only a precursor of an almost unintermitting series lasting through the greater part of a very long life. The sloop had not been long at sea, and one night while young Falk was slumbering peacefully in his berth, he was awoken by a sense of suffocation caused by dense fumes of smoke which filled the cabin. Scrambling with difficulty up the companion way, he reached the deck, and found the fore part of the vessel on fire, the bulwarks, rigging, and sails, all in flames, the taffrail being the only part they had not reached.[4] The terror and dismay of young Falk may be imagined when he looked around for the crew and not a soul was to be seen. The boat was also gone. They had all taken flight and forgotten him! The rapid reflections of so young a voyager in such a crisis may be imagined, but cannot be described. There is little doubt that he wished himself at home again in Copenhagen, and safe under his father's roof. But the exigencies of his situation did not permit of delay. Two courses were open for him. Before him were the blazing planks and rigging, and a cruel death by fire. He looked over the side, and the cool water, glistening in the moonlight, seemed the easier end of the two. He made up his mind to the latter alternative, and was about to plunge into the sea, when his ear caught the sound of a voice hailing him. It was the captain in the boat, which was approaching and at no great distance. The crew had discovered their mistake, and were returning. They were soon alongside, and several brawny arms stretched out to receive him as he leaped over the side, and was placed in safety amongst them. The boat was small, and very leaky. There were, in addition to the crew, three or four passengers, and they had no provisions with them. For three days were they out at sea in this frail and diminutive craft, without food, and bailing continually. At length they were picked up by a coasting vessel from Jutland and landed safely at Copenhagen.

He was again persuaded to sail in another vessel for Jutland, by the assurance that she could not burn as she was made of copper, the fact being most probably, that she was sheathed with copper, an unusual circumstance with coasting vessels of that time.

She did not take fire, but landed the young voyager in safety at Jutland, where he remained with his grandfather and grandmother for two years, going to school during that time, at the end of which they both died, and Hans was sent by his uncle back to Copenhagen, where he was put to school till his fourteenth year, when he was bound apprentice to the sea, and he served his time in the Miditerranean and East County trades.[5]

Youthful errors

THE PARENTS OF HANS being in comfortable if not affluent circumstances, there was no necessity for his following the sea as a profession, but the necessity was brought about by the following conduct on his part, which he now relates with great candour:– While at school, he fell into the company of bad boys, and learnt to play cards, an amusement which required a supply of money that he could not legitimately command; and the young scapegrace had recourse to the pocket-book of his father, which he abstracted from the pocket of that parent while he took his afternoon nap. Being detected by his step-mother on one occasion, the consequences so alarmed him that he never repeated the offence, and, foreswore cards forever afterwards.

The occurrence made home distasteful to him, and, having partiality for the sea, though against his father's wish he determined upon trying a seafaring life. (*Daily Southern Cross*, 1867)

In 1801, after the Battle of Copenhagen, in which Admiral Nelson seized the Danish fleet,[6] Hans shipped as boatswain in a Hamburg vessel bound to Riga, which he left there, and then sailed as mate in an American brig bound to Boston. Instead of proceeding to Boston however, she went onto London, where the brig and cargo were sold, and where he engaged as boatswain and boatsteerer on board a whaling ship commanded by Captain Jonathan Clarke, bound for Timor.[7]

Changes his name

AT THIS PERIOD, England being at war with most of the European powers, no foreigner was permitted to sail as an officer in the merchant service, and as the great demand for men in the navy rendered it impossible to procure an entirely English crew, the foremast hands in most vessels consisted of people of all nations.[8] Falk therefore, in engaging as a petty officer on board the whaling vessel, found it necessary to adopt the English nationality, and assumed the name of Phillip Tapsell, passing as a Manxman, under which character the slight accent in his pronunciation was not easily detected.[9]

First whaling voyage

CAPTAIN JONATHAN CLARKE was an American, belonging to Nantucket, and, until the vessel proceeded to sail gave his crew no opportunity of becoming acquainted with his real character, maintaining while on shore a reserved and effeminate mildness of behaviour that proved a most effectual disguise.

While the vessel was taking in stores at the city-canal, he would occasionally come on board, generally dressed in a suit of black, with all the appearance of a preacher, which character his meek demeanour and subdued tone of voice well supported. No one would for a moment imagine that the clerical looking and lamb like individual stepping diffidently about the deck, and only occasionally exchanging a remark with those around, was one of the most profane and ferocious reprobates that disgraced the merchant service, even at a time when humane captains were the exception, and tyranny and cruelty were the rule. He would quietly approach the sailors at work, and address them in gentle accents after the following manner: — "Well, my man, how are you getting on?" Till the crew were disgusted with his sanctimonious behaviour. And several of them thought of leaving, for they did not like to sail with a personage, who, judging from appearances, was more fit to deliver a sermon at a street corner than to command a lot of rough salts like themselves. When off Dover, and the pilot had left the ship, he threw off the mask. He had been pacing the quarter-deck for some time without speaking, but presently the crew were astonished to hear him roar out in true nautical style, "Brace forward the yards."[10] The order was obeyed, and all hands were called aft. "McGuinness," said he, addressing the first officer, "You are the chief mate, and I am the Captain. Remember that." They never had cause to forget the injunction.

A Tartar Captain

THE VESSEL ARRIVED at Timor without any occurrence of any incident worthy of notice, and commenced whaling.[11] The tyrannical and cruel character of the Captain was now manifested without disguise. Altercations were of continual occurrence, and violence on the part of the Captain repeatedly resorted to. Differences between him and the chief mate were so frequent that at last, falling in with an English Frigate, he sent the latter on board on the ground that he did not consider his life safe while in the same ship. Being a man of great physical strength, he had often recourse to blows and the use of weapons until there was not a man on board who had not been wounded by him. This treatment at length became unendurable, and seven of the crew, including Mr Tapsell, determined to leave the vessel at the first opportunity, and for this purpose packed up all their effects for removal at a moment's notice.

57

Escape from the ship

WHEN ABOUT TWO HUNDRED MILES from Boru, a Malay settlement in Timor, the opportunity for escape arrived unexpectedly.[12] Mr Shaddock the new chief mate, who had succeeded McGuinness, and who, like the Captain was also an American of Nantucket, one night during his watch on deck, informed Mr Tapsell that he was very sleepy, and requested the latter to look out for him while he lay down for a short time, which the latter consented to do. When the coast was clear, the conspirators were apprised of the fortuitous circumstance, and no time was lost in putting all the chests into the waste boat which hung in the davits.[13] The tackle was well greased, so that it moved without creaking, and the boat was lowered into the water without giving any alarm. Previously however, some of the hands had been aloft and, that is called, 'racked' the braces,[14] so that they could not be worked from below, nor the yards be moved in any direction.

The preparations had so far succeeded, as they thought, without the knowledge of any one on board, but Mr Tapsell suddenly encountered a boy on mideck,[15] who said to him, "I know what you are going to do." Mr Tapsell desired him to be silent, and say nothing till the boat was well clear of the vessel, which he promised, and faithfully performed. The boat was at a considerable distance before the alarm was given, and lights could be seen moving backwards and forward on board, indicating that a search was being instituted.

The surprise and anger of Captain Clarke when he found that the braces could not be worked may be imagined, and before the obstacle could be discovered and removed, the boat and crew were well beyond reach.

Next morning, the vessel fell in with the Grand Sachem, also out on a whaling voyage, to the Commander of which Captain Clarke related his misfortune, adding that he did not know where to look for his missing boat.[16] The Captain of the Grand Sachem being familiar with the geography of that neighbourhood, suggested Boru as the place for which the runaways would most likely steer, and offered to accompany Captain Clarke and pilot him there.

Meanwhile the boat's crew, well provisioned and provided with navigation instruments, compass and chart, taken from the ship, made the best of their way for Boru. They were two nights at sea and during the third, a very heavy rain fell, which drenched them completely, and saturated their clothes. It was before daylight on the third night that they sighted Boru, pulled into a cove between two mangrove swamps, and hauled the boat up, spreading their clothes out on the bushes to dry. Unfortunately for their safety, amongst the garments so displayed, was a new shirt of a bright scarlet color.

When the two ships hove in sight they conjectured them to be East Indiamen, putting in for wood and water, and agreed to ship on board if the opportunity offered.

The two captains landed at Boru, and proceeded at once to the chief functionary of the place, called the Sultan, to whom Captain Clarke made his complaint, offering a large reward for the capture of the men. Accordingly a party of soldiers were sent in search, who, while marching round the Beach, were attracted by the sight of the red shirt hanging out to dry, and advancing upon the place, came suddenly upon the party of sailors. One of the soldiers addressed them in broken English, informing them that the two ships which had arrived were East Indiamen who were short of hands, and willing to give very high wages. This was just what the men wanted, yet, for fear of treachery, it was arranged that one of the number were to go first, and if every thing were right, to hasten back again. The man was so long of returning, that Mr Tapsell and another walked towards a point from which the two vessels could be seen, and on examination through the telescope found them to be their own ship and another. They had scarcely made this discovery before Mr Tapsell saw the whale boat with the remainder of the crew approaching. In his heart he cursed their stupidity for thus exposing themselves to the view of the ship, when the boat came towards the shore, and a Malay jumped out, armed with a musket, which he pointed at Mr Tapsell, on which his companion took to his heels and fled into the bush.

One of the boats' crew called out to Tapsell, advising him to surrender, for that resistance was useless as they were all bound.

The Malay who had landed, then made signs that Mr Tapsell should suffer himself to be bound, but he refused, and was permitted to get into the boat with his arms at liberty. He was then told of the manner in which the crew had been captured. A strong party of Malays had surrounded the encampment, remaining concealed, while a number came forward, bringing bamboos containing wine, which they offered the sailors to drink, and of which they, by no means reluctant, partook so heartily that in a short time they became drunk, and were easily overpowered and bound.

Capture

WHEN THEY WERE BROUGHT BEFORE THE CAPTAINS in presence of the Sultan, the former, addressing them said;

"I suppose you know what I can do to you? I can take you on board of a man of war at Albino and have every man of you hung for piracy on the high seas.[17] But I am willing to overlook everything that has taken place, if you will go on board again, and do your duty as before."

This they all refused to do, at the same time narrating their grievances to the Sultan, and showing the wounds they had received from the hands of the Captain.

The Sultan then informed them that the Captain should not take them away against their will, and that they might remain with him if they chose. He treated them with great kindness, put them under no restraint, and furnished them with a house and plenty of provisions. Indeed he endeavoured to persuade Tapsell to remain there, and take up his abode with him, offering him many advantages if he would comply.

Captain Clarke, who knew that he could not make a voyage without the men, came daily to urge his request that they would come on board, resorting to entreaties, and fairly cried with disappointment at their determination. At last, they yielded to his importuning and consented to go on board, the captain giving a written undertaking to hold them harmless from any consequences of their illegal act. This was signed in the presence of the Sultan, and witnessed by Captain Donoman of the Grand Sachem.[18]

Scurvy treatment[19]

AT THIS TIME several of the hands on board the ship were laid up with scurvy, and the inhuman captain caused four or five of the worst patients to be buried up to the middle in the earth, for the purpose, as he said, of drawing the scurvy out of them. In this position the poor creatures were left for a night, uttering fearful screams, which were audible from the vessel, and sounded like the despairing cry of persons on a wreck. They were not long afflicted with scurvy after this treatment for they died in two or three days.

The vessel had not been long at sea when the brutality of the captain produced another disturbance leading almost to mutiny. Once, when out in the boat the captain made fast to a whale, which rose suddenly, and, striking the boat, tilted it up, and threw Tapsell over the gunwale into the sea. The captain, without waiting a moment to take him in, followed the whale, and left him swimming for his life amongst thousands of Tiger sharks the most voracious kind that exist. So numerous were they, that he touched them at every stroke as they swam by his side and followed in his wake. He was perceived by one of the boats belonging to another ship and rescued from his perilous position, and by and by, a boat from his own vessel approaching, he leaped into the water and was taken in.

The admiral

WHEN THE SHIP was full about to return homeward, the Captain put five of his men on board The Echo a vessel carrying a letter of marque commission insisting that they should be taken home for trial, but the Captain of the Echo, putting into Table Bay, and not wishing to carry them further, gave them a quiet hint to escape, which they were not long of doing, and, were soon after picked up by the press gang, and lodged on board the Lion, a seventy-four gun ship, then in the Bay.[20]

Thus there was only Tapsell remaining on board out of the seven who had run away with the boat, and another, who on the passage homeward, having a quarrel with the captain, and a man of war brig speaking the vessel, hailed her, and expressed his wish to enter the navy. A lieutenant then came in a boat and took him off, having first compelled Captain Clarke to give him an order for his share of the voyage.

So now Tapsell only remained when the vessell called at the Cape of Good Hope. There the Captain, hearing that five of his men were on board the Lion, and having Tapsell, the sixth, with himself, made sure of hanging them all, so went off at once to the Admiral for the purpose of making his statement.[21] But he met with a reception he did not expect. The Admiral, after hearing what he had to say, replied, "Had you brought them confined to me at first, they would have been punished, but you coaxed them on board to help you to fill your ship, and now you want to get rid of them". He then directed the steward to open the door as an intimation that the interview was over, and Captain Clarke was obliged to retire baffled in his object. Men for the navy were at that time very scarce, and the five referred to, all being good seamen were too valuable to be lightly given up.

On arrival in London,[22] Captain Clarke at first refused to pay Tapsell his share of the voyage, but the latter placed the matter in the hands of a respectable solicitor, and soon forced the Captain to disgorge, besides having to pay all law expenses connected with his application.

This voyage lasted three years and seven months.

The crimp system/Gates, the crimp[23]

IT WAS AT THIS TIME that Mr Tapsell first made the acquaintance of a man named Gates, a crimp and boarding house keeper, who proved to be one of the most infamous of a class of persons who were characterized in their dealings by iniquity of the most heartless kind.

When a vessel came home from a voyage it was the custom of the crimp to meet her at Gravesend,[24] and having ascertained the amount of money coming to each sailor, to prevail upon one (or more) to return with him to London and take up his abode in his house. Being wartime, and men in great demand, it was not uncommon for a sailor to be pounced down upon by the press gang immediately on his arrival from a voyage and carried away for an indefinite period of service in the navy, and it was also customary by mutual arrangement between the press gang and the crimp, that the latter should be permitted to take a sailor under his protection until he had fleeced him of all he possessed, when the crimp would give information to the gang who would come and take poor Jack away. The crimp's first steps on getting hold of a 'homeward bounder', as returned seamen were termed, was to obtain from him an order for the pay due to him, and also a bill of sale on his effects, and luggage, giving him small advances from time to time, until he considered the unfortunate seaman had gone far enough, when he would inform the gang that he was done with, and they would, to the affected surprise of the crimp, make their appearance and drag him off. In this way the crimp and the press gang "rowed together". But crimps were also in collusion with one another, and one would often swear a fictitious debt against a sailor, and get him arrested and lodged in Newgate,[25] — arrest for debt was very easy in those days. Another crimp would visit the prisoner, condole with him, offer to pay his debt, — which was nil — and give him a berth in a fine ship; his gain thereby, being a bonus of seven pounds 'crimpage', as it was called, paid by owners for every seaman the crimp might procure. The sailor would most likely jump at the offer of liberty, and the crimp's object be gained, whereas, if the sailor had been at large, and engaged himself without the intervention of the crimp, he could have pocketed the seven pounds in addition to a bonus of five pounds paid to each man on entering a ships books.

It was with the aforesaid Gates one of this disreputable fraternity that Mr Tapsell lodged on his return from his first whaling voyage.

NOTES

1. Edward Little's published serialisation of Tapsell's reminiscences appeared in the *Daily Southern Cross* in 1867. In places in this publication, newspaper versions of events containing section headings or even entire episodes that are missing in the original manuscript from the Alexander Turnbull Library are reproduced. Section headings are indicated with italics as in this case, while quoted blocks of text are credited with the name of the newspaper and the year of publication.

2. Tapsell's year of birth was 1790. On the confusion about his year of birth, see Part 1, 'The Pacific Viking', Hans Falk: the child.

3. The sources inform us that Jens Hansen Falk was a labourer (Danish: *Arbejdsmand*) and a water and sanitation official (Danish: *Vandmester*). See Part 1, 'The Pacific Viking', Hans Falk: the child.

4. The taffrail is the curved upper part of the stern of a wooden ship.

5. 'East County trades' refers to the trade with the countries around the Baltic Sea, particularly Estonia and Latvia, which at the time were part of the Russian Empire.

6. The First Battle of Copenhagen (Danish: *Slaget på Reden*) was fought on 2 April 1801 between the Danish fleet and the British fleet under Sir Hyde Parker and Horatio Nelson. The British won a hard-fought victory. It was after the Second Battle (or Bombardment) of Copenhagen (Danish: *Københavns Bombardement*) in 1807 that the Danish fleet was seized by the British navy under Admiral James Gambier.

7. Jonathan Clarke of Nantucket was captain of the *Eliza* (264 tons) when it departed on a whaling voyage to Timor on 19 February 1810 (not 1801) and returned 16 September 1812. It was reported whaling off Timor in January 1811. Although Tapsell is listed as First Mate in the British Southern Whale Fishery database (whalinghistory.org), crewmembers McGuinness and Shaddock, who appear later in this episode, do not appear in the database.

8. During the Napoleonic Wars (1803–15), Britain's enemies included France, Spain and Denmark-Norway. Due to shifting alliances, Britain was at times also at war with Austria, the Ottoman Empire, Persia, Prussia, Russia and Sweden.

9. According to historian James Cowan, he is said to have chosen the surname Tapsell due to its similarity to the word 'topsail'. Tapsell is, of course, not a Manx name. In addition to Phillip, he sailed under the name Tom and Thomas. On Tapsell's various names, see Part 1, 'The Pacific Viking': Phillip Tapsell: the sailor.

10. A yard is a spar on a mast from which the sails are set, and a brace is a rope used to control the angle of the yard to enable the ship to sail at different angles to the wind. The verb 'to brace' means to move or turn a sail by means of the braces.

11. On whaling in the Straits of Timor, see Robert Harrison Barnes, *Sea Hunters of Indonesia: Fishers and Weavers of Lamalera* (Oxford: Clarendon Press, 1996), pp. 329–36.

12. 'Boru' is Buru Island (Dutch: *Boeroe*), the third largest island within the Moluccas (Maluku Islands, Indonesia). The *Eliza* was reported to be sailing off Timor in January 1811 (Source: British Southern Whale Fishery database at whalinghistory.org).

13. Davits are the cranes on the side or stern of a ship used to suspend and lower a boat into the sea.

14. The verb 'to rack' means to bind two ropes together by weaving material between and around them.

15. The mid-deck or middle-deck is a ship's deck between the upper and lower decks.

16. The *Grand Sachem* was a whaling ship (236 tons) built in Newburyport, Massachusetts. It left Cork to go whaling in the South Seas in May 1809 (returned November 1811) under Captain George Dunnaman of Nantucket.

17. Albino is possibly a mistake for Ambon (Dutch: *Amboyna*), the largest town within the Moluccas (Maluku Islands, Indonesia). It was the seat of the Dutch resident and military commander of the Moluccas.

18. Captain George Dunnaman of Nantucket. See also note 16.

19. Scurvy is a disease resulting from the lack of vitamin C that, due to lack of fresh produce in their diet, was very common among sailors in the eighteenth and nineteenth centuries. The understanding of the disease as a nutritional deficiency and its cure (the consumption of fresh citrus fruit) was anything but universal in the nineteenth century and many crackpot remedies persisted.

20. The *Echo* (409 tons, ten guns) under Captain John Whiteus of Nantucket received a letter of marque on 4 February 1807. A letter of marque and reprisal was a government licence that authorised its bearer (a privateer) to capture enemy vessels and bring them to Britain. Essentially, it was a form of licensed piracy. The Impress Service ('press gang') was created to force men with seafaring experience between the ages of 15 and 55 to serve on naval vessels. Refusal to comply was severely punished. It operated throughout the British Empire here, at Table Bay, Cape Town, South Africa. The HMS *Lion* was a full-rigged, 64-gun ship launched in 1777 at Portsmouth Dockyard.

21. The penalty for mutiny at the time was regulated by the Mutiny Act of 1803, which made mutiny punishable by death.

22. Tapsell arrived back in London in September 1812.

23. A crimp is a person who entraps or forces men into service as sailors through trickery, violence, or intimidation. Crimpage was driven by a shortage of experienced sailors and an economic incentive that saw crimps paid for each sailor they got on to a ship. The practice, also known as shanghaiing, flourished in the port cities of England.

24. Gravesend is an important port on the south bank of the Thames estuary in Kent, England.

25. Newgate is the infamous prison in the City of London. The terrible conditions and grim history are described in Stephen Halliday, *Newgate: London's Prototype of Hell* (Stroud: The History Press, 2007).

2

Mr Tapsell's next voyage was as boatswain and boatsteerer in the whaling ship New Zealander, commanded by Captain Parker.[1]

Massacre of the Boyd

THE VOYAGE OUT was without incident, and the season having arrived, the vessel proceeded at once to the whaling ground off East Cape, where several other ships were also cruising, and all were busy catching whales when a vessel from the Bay of Islands in New Zealand brought intelligence of a frightful massacre of the crew of a vessel called the Boyd.[2] Of this tragedy it will be necessary to give an outline. The ship Boyd was on her way to India from Sydney, and the Captain being desirous of procuring spars for the use of the navy, resolved to put in at the Bay of Islands for that purpose. Before leaving Sydney, Mr Marsden of Paramatta had entrusted to his care a Maori boy, the son of Tipahi, a great chief, under the impression that he might be serviceable to the captain in obtaining spars.[3] On board the vessel was a soldier's wife and child[4] on their passage to India, the first of whom managed to ingratiate herself with the young chief by little acts of kindness which he did not forget, while the captain, unfortunately considered in necessary to flog the youngster.[5]

On the vessel's arrival at the Bay, Tipahi went on board to welcome his son, and after a long cry, questioned him about his treatment while away.[6] The lad answered that Mr Marsden had used him well, and the soldier's wife been very kind to him, giving him food when he would otherwise have been short. Tipahi was satisfied, and said that this was very well, but on enquiring how the captain had treated him, and being informed that he had been flogged by that person, he scowled, and said:–

"Well, he is coming for spars, I will pay him for it."

The captain's object being known, Tipahi offered to conduct him to a place where good spars could be obtained, and the captain with a boat's crew, well armed, went ashore for the purpose. Tipahi led them a distance into the woods, where the captain saw some fine timber, with the appearance of which he expressed himself satisfied, but Tipahi assuring him that much better could be found in another place, they accompanied him as he desired. He led them by an unnecessarily circuitous route on purpose to fatigue them, so that when they at last came to the spot, they were glad to seat themselves on a large fallen log to rest. This had all been arranged beforehand by Tipahi, who stood in front of them engaging their attention by conversation while a Maori armed with a tomahawk took his place behind each European, waiting for a signal from their chief, which in due time was given, and the heads of the unfortunate strangers were almost simultaneously cleft open. The bodies were then stripped, the savages investing themselves with the garments, and, thus attired, they returned to the beach, from which they could see that the ship was crowded with natives, who, it is believed, observing their chief with his party clothed in the dress of Europeans, knew that the murder of the boat's crew had been accomplished, and the massacre of the remainder of the ship's company commenced. It was over in a few minutes, all on deck being speedily dispatched, a few took to the rigging, where they remained until Tipahi, who had come on board and stood on the quarter deck, called out to them to unbend the sails,[7] come down, and he would protect them.[8] They complied with his command, went aft to claim his protection, and were instantly tomahawked. The woman and her child were spared.[9]

The murderers crowded into the cabin for plunder, and dragging out a keg of powder, stove in the head. They then took down muskets from the stand, and commenced snapping the locks over the powder, a spark falling into which, it exploded, blowing the after part of the ship and a great number of Maoris into a thousand fragments.[10]

Retribution

THE INTELLIGENCE of this atrocity having, as has been said before, been conveyed to the cruising ground by a whaling ship at anchor in the Bay when the massacre occurred, it was unanimously agreed by the commanders of all the vessels there, seven or eight in number, to leave the ground and sail at once for the Bay. This they did, abandoning the whales they had caught, and crowding on all sail arrived together and came to anchor off Rangiu.[11]

Three boats from each ship were manned with full crews, well armed, and pulled for the island to which Tipohi and his tribe had retired, surrounding it on every side.[12] The crews thus landed, and attacking the natives wherever they could be seen, shooting great numbers, burning their houses and destroying their crops. A few made their escape in canoes, Tipohi, though wounded by a shot from Captain Parker, managed, with the assistance of two women, to swim to the opposite shore. The greater part of the natives were killed; and so the massacre of the Boyd was promptly avenged.[13] This piece of business transacted, the ships returned to the cruising ground where they were very successful, and whales very plentiful.

The New Zealander returned to London at the end of three years, a full ship, Mr Tapsell was paid off, and sailed as passenger in a Danish brig to Copenhagen, where he spent some time in the society of his friends and relations.

The Battle of Copenhagen[14]

HE WAS IN COPENHAGEN in 1807, at which time the British landed troops and made an attack on the city, finishing by removing the Danish fleet and naval stores from the docks and Dockyards there.

The English troops were landed between Elsinore and Copenhagen and reached the suburbs of that latter city about three days after landing.[15] Having constructed batteries they opened fire on the city which was returned, though without doing any serious damage on either side, very few being killed, and those by accident by the falling of buildings which could hardly escape where hot shot and shell were flying about. The Danish troops were not ordered out, nor did the inhabitants leave the city. The farmers in the suburbs pursued their ordinary avocations, and did a thriving trade with the English soldiers by whom they were not molested, and who paid well for every thing they got. The firing lasted about twenty-four hours, when it suddenly ceased and the English fleet made its appearance, landing crews of seamen, who at once commenced to fit masts to and rig the Danish fleet, the hulls of which were lying in the docks. In an incredibly short time, the masts were stepped; rigging fitted, sails bent, and the vessels towed out to sea. All the naval stores were removed, and the fleet departed, when this was done, the troops broke up their camp and marched away, embarking at their former place of landing. The whole affair was over so quickly, and with so little injury to either side as to leave the impression that the attack had been a make believe, and the capture and removal of the Danish fleet, according to a prearranged plan in which some show of resistance had to be maintained.

Turns privateer

AFTER THIS WAS OVER, many Danish privateers were fitted out, and Mr Tapsell got command of a cutter carrying ninety men and two guns, a stern chaser, and bow chaser, with four swivels on each side. He had been out only a week, when he fell in with, and captured an English brig loaded with lintseed.[16] When bringing her to Copenhagen, he was chased by a man of war brig which gained upon him, so he ran the prize ashore near Drago,[17] and the man of war following, stuck fast in the shallows, but getting off, left the prize to her fate, and went away. Mr Tapsell succeeded in getting off the captured brig and bringing her safely into Copenhagen, where she was well sold.

When this prize was boarded her captain shed tears, but the privateers captain did not molest any personal property belonging to the captain or crew, who were permitted to take it ashore, themselves being detailed as prisoners of war.

Is boarded

AFTER THIS, Mr Tapsell got command of the Cortadla a large privateer ship,[18] with which, when fitted out, he lay for some time under the batteries at Elsinore while the English fleet lay at anchor within sight on the opposite side at Helsingfors.[19]

The Cortadla was provided with boarding nets, which were always hoisted after dark to prevent surprise. It may be explained that a boarding net is composed of stout rope and constructed so as when raised, to enclose the deck of the vessel, and the lower part of the rigging as high as halfway to the truck,[20] thus guarding against a surprise, and preventing access to the deck from outside unless by cutting through the netting, which operation would delay the boarding party and give the defenders time for preparation.

One moonlight night about twelve oclock, the sound of oars was heard by the watch on board the Cortadla, and on looking out, three boats full of men were seen approaching. These were challenged, and not answering satisfactorily, alarm was given. By the time all hands had come on deck from below, the enemy were in the boarding nets, attempting to cut their way through, and, as may be imagined, offering an easy target for sword or pistol to the defenders by whom many were killed. Five or six succeeded in gaining the forecastle, but were speedily overpowered. One of the Cortadla's crew, standing beside Mr Tapsell on the quarterdeck, was shot in the shoulder, and fell. Mr Tapsell in a hand to hand conflict received a sword cut across the abdomen from which the intestines protruded, and he fell to the deck. But the boarders were beaten off with heavy loss, and retired, after the order had been given to "jump into the boats".

Mr Tapsell was conveyed below, and his wound dressed by the two doctors belonging to the ship, the operation being so excruciatingly painful that he several times entreated the surgeon to put a pistol to his ear and blow his brains out. The doctor smiled, and told him it would be all right soon.

It was not considered safe for the Cortadla to remain another night in the same place, as in all probability she might be visited by a stronger party, who would not be so easily repulsed; so at daybreak next morning, she was got under weigh, and in a few hours was out of sight of the fleet.

Frozen in the ice

MR TAPSELL LAY ON HIS BACK for some weeks without being permitted to stir, but had completely recovered when they fell in with three prizes, one Russian and two Dutch, all large ships, loaded with hemp and tallow, on their way to Karlskronen to wait for the English convoy.[21] The Cortadla was in possession of her prizes two or three days and in the East Sea on her way to Denmark with them in company,[22] when the frost set in, continuing the next day, and after the third night she was hard and fast, firmly imbedded in a sea of ice, with the three prizes, all similarly circumstanced, in sight in different parts of the horizon. In this situation they remained a month, sending down the topmasts, and making snug to winter there. But at the end of the month the ice giving signs of breaking up, Captain Tapsell caused a hole to be broken alongside for the purpose of taking soundings, at first they found eighteen, and shortly after, seven fathoms of water, by which Mr Tapsell knew that the ice was setting in for the shore, so he ordered the boats to be got out away from the side of the vessel, and filled with necessary articles. Shortly after, the ship touched the ground, and heeled over with the pressure of the advancing ice, which cut into the timbers so that when she righted again, she was found to be half-full of water. The ice was now breaking up rapidly, and it was judged necessary to run for the Swedish coast, which was then just visible in the distance. All hands therefore lent assistance in pushing the boats over the ice, which broke up behind them as they ran. It was literally a race for life, for delay would have been destruction. When they reached the shore, they found a strong body of Swedish soldiers waiting to receive them, by whom they were immediately seized, and conveyed to an old castle at Karlskronen, where they were detained for about a week, during which time many gentlemen came to see them from motives of curiosity always leaving small presents of money to enable the prisoners to procure better food than the gaol supplied. The conduct of the gaoler and his son was very harsh and cruel, the latter often striking the prisoners with a whip.

Taken prisoner

THEY WERE NEXT REMOVED into a prison in the country at Gluckstadt,[23] a distance of about forty miles from Karlskronen, where they fared rather better than before, being allowed to walk outside the walls in view of the sentry. Mr Tapsell was permitted to extend his walks through the town in company with a soldier. At length he began to meditate on escape, and one night, with a two fellow-prisoners, seized the opportunity when the sentry's attention was otherwise occupied, to give him the slip, and get away into the fields at some distance from the town. They there made their way to the coast, remaining concealed during the day, travelling at night, and subsisting on a small stock of provisions they had saved from their prison allowance.

69

When they arrived near Karlskrönen they saw a ship lying at anchor, and a boat moored to the beach. Always ready in expedients, Mr Tapsell's determination was at once made to board the vessel, cut the cable, and make his way as well as he could to the Danish coast, which was not very distant. Accordingly when the night was pretty far advanced, they emerged from their hiding place and stole down to the water's edge, where the boat was lying as before said.

One of the party had 'knocked up' during the journey from Gluckstadt,[24] and had to be supported by his companions to enable him to walk.

They reached the boat, not a person was to be seen. All was still, the moment of escape appeared to have arrived, and Mr Tapsell with one foot on the gunwale, was about to step into the boat, when they were suddenly surrounded by a number of horse soldiers, by whom they were at once captured, and lodged in the guard house at Karlskronen, in which the captain of the troop had his quarters, and before whom the prisoners were brought.

"Tapsell," said he, "I am sorry that I have got you, but now that I have, I must keep you".

To which Mr Tapsell replied that of course he knew his own duty. After which they were dismissed, the Captain sending Mr Tapsell a good supper and a glass of grog.

Next morning, they were brought before the Governor who addressed them sternly;–

"Do you know what your people do with ours when they take them?

"Treat them well", was Mr Tapsell's answer.

"No, they cut their heads off", said the Governor.

"I think you are mistaken", replied Mr Tapsell.

"What!" thundered the Governor. "Do you say that I am a liar? Take him away, and give him nothing to eat."

He was removed, and kept without food till the following morning, when the sounds of cart wheels in the street could be heard. Mr Tapsell thought he could hear the rattle of a chain. "I think there is something for us", said he to his companion. And so it proved. They were to be conveyed to Gluckstadt, and intended to be chained together, but a great crowd of sailors in the street exclaimed so loudly against such treatment of prisoners of war that the Governor was compelled to make a virtue of necessity and permit them to go unshackled, merely observing to them that he was sure they meant to go quietly. But this was only a blind,[25] for at the next halting place, the chains were put on, and there were no sailors to interfere in their behalf.

From there they were taken to Gluckstadt, where instead of being put amongst their companions as before, they were thrust into a filthy dungeon with the worst description of felons, thieves and murderers, and where lice were crawling up and down the bars of the windows. They did not remain long here however, for the inhabitants of the town petitioned on their behalf, and they were removed to other and better quarters though the prison fare was very indifferent.

A Sister of Mercy

THERE WAS AN OLD WOMAN who used to visit the gaol selling tobacco and other small luxuries, to the prisoners besides disposing of whisky 'on the sly' to such as could afford to pay for it, whose sympathies became warmly enlisted in favor of Mr Tapsell. She had two daughters at service in Copenhagen, and a son at sea, and it is possible that the circumstances of Mr Tapsell being both a sailor, a Dane, and a prisoner, excited her interest and compassion, which his good looks and frank bearing did not tend to weaken.

This kind old body, on learning how coarse the fare of the prisoners was, regularly brought Mr Tapsell a comfortable breakfast, dinner, and supper, with a glass of grog at night. So punctual were her visits, that the soldiers on guard, when they saw her coming, used to call out, "Tapsell, here is your mother coming." To this he would reply, "Ah! indeed, she is a mother to me."

His imprisonment lasted about eleven months, at the end of which an exchange of prisoners took place, before which time however he had written to his father at Copenhagen for a supply of money to enable him to procure some needful comforts. The answer, with a remittance, arrived the day after the exchange was made, and the prisoners were on their way to the coast. Before they left Gluckstadt, the good old woman came to take farewell of her protegé, presenting him at parting with a large case bottle of whisky for his refreshment on the road, and entrusting to his care two letters for her daughters in Copenhagen.

The liberated prisoners were conveyed in wagons to Helsingfors,[26] where they were shipped to Elsinore, from which place they travelled by coach to Copenhagen, where Mr Tapsell once more was in the enjoyment of liberty, home and friends.

NOTES

1. There is a mistake here. The sources show that Tapsell was indeed on board the whaler *New Zealander* that departed London on 8 November 1808, but that the vessel was under the command of Captain William Elder. Captain William Parker was in command during Tapsell's voyage on the *Eliza* that left London 1810. Given that the *New Zealander* returned to port after the *Eliza* had left, it seems likely that Tapsell switched ships abroad. An illustration of the *New Zealander* is used on the frontispiece of James Cowan's *A Trader in Cannibal Land* (1935).

2. The *Boyd*, a 395-ton brig under Captain John Thompson, put in to Whangaroa Harbour in December 1809 to secure a cargo of kauri spars for the British navy. As utu (retribution) for wrongdoings by Europeans, local Māori massacred sixty-six of the seventy aboard, looted the ship and then unintentionally blew it up. See Wade Doak, *The Burning of the Boyd: A Saga of Culture Clash* (Auckland: Hodder & Stoughton, 1984).

3. From 1794, Samuel Marsden (1765–1838) lived in Paramatta, a settlement founded in 1788 and situated about 25 km from Port Jackson (Sydney, NSW). Known as 'the Parramatta chaplain', Marsden became the senior Anglican minister in New South Wales in 1800 and purchased land to establish New Zealand's first mission at Rangihoua Bay in 1815. The Māori boy referred to here was Te Ara, also known as Tara or George, the son of Piopio (a Māori chief from Whangaroa) and brother of Te Puhi. 'Tipaha', also spelt 'Tipohi' in the manuscript, was Te Pahi (?–1810), chief, Ngāpuhi (iwi). Tapsell, like many of his contemporaries, wrongly accuses Te Pahi of the massacre, presumably confusing him with Te Puhi (Te Ara's brother) or Piopio (Te Ara's father). The source of confusion goes back to the first written account of the massacre by Alexander Berry. See Doak, *The Burning of the Boyd*, p. 115.

4. The mother and child were Ann ('Nanny') Morley — a former convict who was married to the ex-soldier and then Sydney publican Joseph Thomas — and her baby.

5. Te Ara seems to have been either falsely accused of stealing some spoons (that had in fact been accidently tossed overboard by the cook) or caught concealing an axe in his clothes. For this he was scourged with a cat o' nine tails. See Doak, *The Burning of the Boyd*, pp. 94–95.

6. Tipahi is a mistake for Piopio, the father of Te Ara.

7. That is to unfasten or untie the sails.

8. Chief Te Pahi arrived the following morning in a canoe, entering the harbour from the Bay of Islands. He did manage to rescue the sailors from the rigging and put them ashore. However, as the men fled along the beach, Te Pahi was held powerless while the men were killed by the Whangaroa people.

9. In addition to Ann Morley and her child, two others were spared: Thomas Davis, a 15-year-old cabin boy who had befriended Te Ara on the voyage, and Elizabeth (Betsy) Isabella Broughton, a two-year old girl whose mother, Anne Glossop, a former convict and mistress of government servant William Broughton, was killed. The four survivors were rescued in January 1810. See Alexander Berry's *Account of the Destruction of the Ship 'Boyd' Wangaroa, N.Z. 1810–12*, also *Settlement of Shoalhaven, N.S.W., 1882* in qMS-0163 at the Alexander Turnbull Library for an eyewitness account of the rescue of the survivors and the ship's papers (pp. 1–7), the revenge against the chiefs by mock execution (pp. 7–10) and the fate of the survivors (pp. 26–28).

10. According to Te Ara's testimony to Samuel Marsden: 'My father Piopio and five others were blown up. My father had got part of the powder on deck with some muskets. He was trying one of the flints in the musket to see if it would fire. A spark caught the powder in one of the barrels. All that were near were killed.' *The Letters and Journals of Samuel Marsden*, ed. John Rawson Elder (Otago: A.H. Reed, 1932), p. 88; Doak, *The Burning of the Boyd*, p. 102.

11. There is an illustration of the pā or fortified settlement at Rangihoua ('Rangiu') on p. 29. In his book, *A Narrative of a Nine Months' Residence in New Zealand in 1827; together with a Journal of Residence in Tristan d'Acunha, an Island Situated between South America and the Cape of Good Hope* (London: Longman, 1832), author/artist Augustus Earle describes Rangihoua as (pp. 169–70):

> The village of Ranghe Hue, belonging to Warri Pork [Wharepoaka], is situated on the summit of an immense and abrupt hill: the huts belonging to the savages appeared, in many places, as though they were overhanging the sea, the height being crowned with a mighty par [pā]. At the bottom of this hill, and in a beautiful valley, the cottages of the missionaries are situated, complete pictures of English comfort, content, and prosperity; they are close to a bright sandy beach: a beautiful green slope lies in their rear, and a clear and never-failing stream of water runs by the side of their enclosures. As the boats approached this lovely spot, I was in an extasy of delight: such a happy mixture of savage and civilised life I had never seen before.

12. The island here is probably Te Puna (now known as Te Pahi Islands), Bay of Islands, where he had his pā. The attack took place on 26 March 1810.

13. About 60 of Te Pahi's people were murdered by the whalers during this act of 'revenge'. See Angela Ballara, 'Te Pahi' from *The Dictionary of New Zealand Biography. Te Ara — The Encyclopedia of New Zealand* (http://www.TeAra.govt.nz/en/biographies/1t53/te-pahi).

14. The beginning of the nineteenth century was a difficult time for Denmark. The involvement of the Dano-Norwegian kingdom in the Napoleonic Wars was nothing but a series of national disasters. Siding with France gave Denmark a number of powerful enemies — Britain, Germany, Russia and Sweden — which led to a series of humiliating and catastrophic defeats for the Nordic nation. The most appalling was when the British bombarded the capital city during the Second Battle of Copenhagen in 1807 in an attack that killed hundreds of civilians and injured many more. As a final act of humiliation and revenge, the British Navy then confiscated ('Copenhagenised') the entire Danish fleet. On the bombardment, see Thomas Munch-Petersen, *Defying Napoleon: How Britain Bombarded Copenhagen and Seized the Danish Fleet in 1807* (Stroud: Sutton, 2007). Tapsell's unique version of events is in sharp contrast to his contemporaries' and later historians' descriptions. Perhaps Tapsell thought it best to play down the destruction, so as not to upset his readers, subjects of the British Crown.

15. Elsinore (Danish: *Helsingør*) is in northern Sjælland, Denmark, about 45 km north of Copenhagen. The town overlooks the Øresund Strait between Denmark and Sweden and lies opposite Helsingborg in Skåne, Sweden.

16. The fibres of linseed or flax (*Linum usitatissimum*) are used to make linen.

17. The small port of Dragør ('Drago') lies on the southeastern tip of Amager, about 12 km south of Copenhagen, Denmark.

18. The *Cort Adeler* ('Cortadla') was the largest of the Danish privateer ships used by Danish sailors against the English. The frigate was financed by a group of stakeholders and listed by the ferryman Jens Lind in Helsingør. On 20 August 1808, it fought off an attack by approximately 150 English soldiers. See the illustration on p. 14–15, 24. On 11 January 1809 its fate was sealed when it became stuck in ice off Copenhagen. See 'Kaperfregatten "Cort Adeler" angribes i Snekkerstenbugten', *Handels- og Søfartsmuseet paa Kronborg: Aarbog* (1942), p. 106. Unfortunately, Tapsell's tale of being given command of the *Cort Adeler* (aged just 18!)

and his subsequent imprisonment cannot be verified by either Danish or Swedish sources. Furthermore, it would have been impossible for Tapsell to have been imprisoned for a year (i.e. until 1809), sail to Riga, Malta and finally to London to then be onboard the *New Zealander* as first mate departing London 8 November 1808. It may be that Tapsell read or heard about the *Cort Adeler* and its fate and created his own version of events, giving himself a starring role.

19. Helsingfors is the (former) Danish name for Helsinki and is clearly a mistake here for Helsingborg in Skåne, Sweden. The town overlooks the Øresund Strait between Sweden and Denmark and lies opposite Helsingør on Sjælland, Denmark. The Swedes were allied with the British against Napoleon (and thus, Denmark) at the time.

20. A truck is a circular or square wooden cap fixed to the top of a mast.

21. The coastal city of Karlskrona ('Karlskronen') lies in Blekinge, Sweden, and has long been an important base for the Swedish navy.

22. The East Sea (compare the Danish name for the body of water, *Østersøen*, 'the East Sea') refers to the Baltic Sea. The name may be an example of Danish influence in Phillip Tapsell's English.

23. There is no such place with this name in Sweden. The name is German and translates as 'joy town'. A village with the Swedish version of this name, Lyckeby, does exist in Blekinge, just 8 km inland from Karlskrona, but although it once had a castle, it had been torn down at the beginning of the seventeenth century. See K. Arne Blom and Jan Moen, *Försvunna städer i Skåneland* (Lund: LiberFörlag, 1983), pp. 118–26.

24. 'Knocked up' was slang for exhausted, tired out.

25. A 'blind' is being used here figuratively to mean a pretence to conceal one's real plan.

26. Helsingfors is a mistake for Helsingborg, Skåne, Sweden. See note 19.

3

AT COPENHAGEN Mr Tapsell shipped as mate on board a Dutch ship bound to Riga, where he loaded with hemp and flax and proceeded to Karlskronen to wait for a convoy to run through the Belt.[1] After the convoy started under the protection of English men of war, several vessels were cut out of the fleet by Danish gunboats, some of which were set fire to.

After arrival in London, Mr Tapsell sailed as mate in a brig loaded with Government stores for the English troops stationed at Malta.[2]

An Algerian pirate[3]

WHEN OFF THE ISLAND, and within a few hours sail of the harbour, a long, low looking craft, with a row of brass swivels on each gunwale,[4] and full of men, came suddenly alongside. She was rigged with latteen sails,[5] and slipped through the water like an eel, so noiselessly, that she was under the brig's side before the crew were aware of her approach. She was crowded with villainous cut throat looking rascals who, to judge from appearances, were ready for any deed of atrocity, and whose close proximity was anything but desirable.

One of the gang, who appeared to be the chief, hailed the brig in broken English, asking her name, destination, and cargo, his comrades, or subordinate desperados, glaring at the pacific merchantman with the expression of hungry tigers longing to dip their fangs in the blood of a prey already within their reach. The appearance of a man of war at the entrance to the harbor, evidently preparing to come out, most probably deterred them from making any attempt, and without ceremony or salutation the ill looking craft slipped away as she had come, passing by the brig as if the latter had been at anchor, and rapidly left her far behind. When the brig got inside the harbor, Mr Tapsell was informed that the people on board the man of war had observed the pirate, and were ready to come out immediately if any attack had been made.

The brig returned to London with a cargo of rags, broom, silk and sulphur.[6] At this time Mr Tapsell was sailing under a protection from the Swedish Consul, and so was not in danger from the press gang.[7]

Mr. Gates again

ON ARRIVAL IN LONDON he took up his quarters at the house of Gates the crimp, where were several other mariners. Judging from results, it would appear that these were mostly "outward bounders", whose account with Mr Gates was soon to be closed, for one morning, as Mr Tapsell returned from a 'cruise' about town he found all the lodgers gone, and was informed that "the gang" had been there, and taken them away.

The effects they had left behind, together with sundry little balances of cash undrawn becoming the lawful spoil of the not very conscientious Gates.

All were taken, but one, a Swede, a crony of the estimable crimp, and of him, for want of a better, Mr Tapsell during his stay, made a companion, taking him with him out walking, and bearing the cost of all their excursions. During one of these, they called at the house of another crimp, where the landlady, addressing Mr Tapsell, said, "I suppose you will give Gates an order for your pay",[8] to which he responded, "If I get him down to Gravesend I will handspike him."[9]

This was repeated by the treacherous Swede to Gates, who gave Mr Tapsell to understand that it had come to his knowledge, and how, on which the latter took the first opportunity of seeking an explanation from his companion.

"Well, you cannot deny that you said so," retorted the mischiefmaker.

"No, I cannot," answered the indignant Tapsell, giving him a tremendous blow with his fist that sent the man's head through the window, after which he beat him till he was quite tired, and then went away. On the following morning, Mr Gates said to him,

"I understand you have lately become a bully in my house. I think that twelve months in Newgate would do you good."

No more was said, and shortly afterwards Mr Gates in his usual manner, invited Mr Tapsell to walk with him. This he had done frequently before, he did not like going out alone, because he was liable to abuse from sailors he had robbed, whom he might chance to meet. The two accordingly went out together, taking the direction of the police station at Shadwell office.[10] On the way, Mr Tapsell could not avoid thinking of the remark made by Gates in the morning, and had a vague idea that the direction in which they were walking was at least a coincidence. At length they arrived opposite Shadwell office, where was a tavern which possessed amongst other attractions the advantage of being a sponging house.[11]

"Go in there," said Mr Gates, pointing to the tavern, "and call for something to drink. I have a little business to transact across the way, and will return directly."

Mr Tapsell assented, and when he had seen Gates enter the Shadwell office, walked into the bar, which had two entrances, one of which opened into a bye street leading to the Thames. He did not call for anything to drink, but passing from one door to the other, made the best of his way to the river. Here he called a waterman's boat and was soon put across to the other side, where he lost no time in going to a merchant named Burnett, and engaging as chief mate in the whaling ship Catherine,[12] which was chartered to take women prisoners from Cork to Sydney, and afterwards at liberty to proceed on her whaling voyage.

The fitting up for the accommodation of the prisoners were so remarkably comfortable and good that visitors used to come from all quarters to inspect her.

After taking in the prisoners, who, together with children, numbered about a hundred and twenty, the Catherine lay some time in the Cove waiting for a convoy.[13]

Besides her was another whaling ship called the Three Bees, under engagement to take out men prisoners to the same destination.[14]

The women on board the Catherine were of various degrees of criminality, from the murderer down to the simply vagrant, for vagrants were transported in those days. Amongst the former class was a woman that had murdered the wife of another man, who, to requite the obligation, had murdered her husband, and afterwards married her. They were both tried convicted and sentenced. The man was hung, but the woman, being pregnant, had been reprieved. Prior to her embarkation she had undergone an imprisonment of six or seven years, and she was now on her way to New South Wales, transported for life. The image of her murdered victim never left her thoughts. She would start up in the night, and clutching her companion convulsively, point to a portion of the apartment, exclaiming, "There she is, there she is, do you not see her?"

The companion of course, would see nothing. But the belief in her being really haunted became general after an occurrence which, even if arising from superstitious fear, was, to say the least of it, a curious coincidence.

It was the rule that all the women were to be in their quarters below by a certain hour, and after that hour, one evening, one of the crew observed a female figure standing in the waist of the ship.[15] Wondering who could have broken the rule on this occasion, he advanced towards the figure, but before he could discern the features, it disappeared. He hurriedly made his way to the steerage,[16] where, on coming to the light, he was observed to be deadly pale. He took ill immediately after, and was never properly well during the voyage. The remarkable portion of the incident was that the figure was visible to him precisely at the same moment that the murderer was the real or imaginary witness of a spectral appearance.

It is probable that a true version of the character of their offences could not be obtained from the prisoners themselves. Men convicts will rarely — except in confidence amongst themselves — confess to a worse crime than poaching. Nevertheless one of the women asserted that she had been sentenced for being late in the streets in consequence of being accidentally shut out of her dwelling.

The convoy being at last ready, a very large fleet of vessels sailed out of the cove of Cork.

When the Catherine reached Sydney, the Three Bees was there before her, and had landed her prisoners. The women were still on board the Catherine when the other ship took fire accidentally. Smoke was observed from the shore issuing from various parts of the deck. She was at once boarded by some of the officers, who, on removing the hatches, found the hold to be in a sheet of flame. The fire being in too advanced a stage, nothing could be done to save her, and she was left to her fate. All the vessels in harbor slipped their cables and moved round into Watson's Bay, where they were safe in the event of an explosion.[17] The guns of the Three Bees being loaded, went off as the fire reached them, one of the balls passing through a room in the dwelling house of Captain Piper, and striking off the corner of a desk at which he was writing.[18] At last the fire reached the magazine, which blew up with a magnificent explosion, some heavy shears used for stepping the mainmast being lifted up high in the air,[19] and then driven deeply into the ground, where they stood as firmly as if they had grown in the soil.

During the Catherine's stay in Sydney harbour the doctor was accidentally drowned while having an altercation with one of the women prisoners who gave him a push which caused him to fall overboard. In his fall he caught hold of the woman, and both went over the side together. The doctor sank, and never rose again, but the clothes of the woman buoyed her up, and she was rescued.

The Catherine went from Sydney to the Bay of Islands where she fitted out, and then sailed for the whaling ground, where they were very successful, returning a full ship to London in three years from the time of their departure, ten months of which were occupied in the conveyance of the prisoners.

Mr Tapsell sailed again in the Catherine on another whaling voyage, putting into the Bay of Islands as before, and laying in a stock of wood, water and potatoes.[20] The vessel then sailed for what is known as the Middle ground,

77

between Lord Howe's Island and New Holland, and afterwards touched at Norfolk Island, which had sometime before this been occupied by free settlers from New South Wales, removed by order of the Government in consequence of the alleged prevalence of vices of the most revolting kind.[21]

They were removed in such a hurry that they were not permitted to take with them implements furniture or household goods, great quantities of which lay in piles on the beach. Their houses were destroyed, and even the Governor's dwelling partially broken down. The Catherine's boats took several loads of tools, grindstone, nails, spades, hoes and other farming implements which proved of great value for trade in the Bay of Islands, and enabled them to purchase ample supplies of pigs and other provisions required.

Mr Tapsell availed himself of the opportunity to examine this beautiful island, which appeared to have been extensively cultivated by its last occupants. Goats were very abundant, and flocks of fowls were flying from tree to tree.

Bananas, plantains, oranges and lemons were in profusion, and even coffee was in the berry was gathered from the tree in sacks by Mr Tapsell and his party.

This beautiful island, for fertility and climate is susceptible of being converted into a comparative Elysium,[22] where the products of nature would without labor supply the immediate wants of man, where ease and abundance might be enjoyed, and toil be unknown, where men might revel in the joys of life without a struggle for bare existence, cast care, anxiety and boding apprehension to the winds, and abandon themselves to an indolent, luxurious contemplative delight, disturbed only by the effort necessary to pluck the fruits scattered by nature with a lavish hand. This island, by a strange contrariety of purposes, was at two separate periods inhabited of the worst specimens of the human race. The free settlers of infamous memory, and subsequently the thrice convicted felons who had become too bad for gaols which civilized men might look upon, whose double distilled iniquity poisoned the atmosphere they breathed, of which island it might be said, by a parodying of the words of Bishop Heber:-[23]

Fanned with spicy breezes,
A lonely, lovely isle,
Where every prospect pleases,
And only man is vile"

Mr Tapsell had a narrow escape while rambling through one of the plantain valleys. He had been previously cautioned to beware of certain natural wells scattered through the island, and was walking carelessly along accompanied by a little dog, when he heard a sound as of a cannon shot in the distance, and pausing, heard it repeated, but on taking a pace or two forward, he was amazed to see a large circular hole many feet in diameter, almost concealed by rank vegetation growing round the edges.[24] It was so deep that he could not see the bottom, but from its depths he could hear the splashing of his little dog in the hidden waters, every stroke of whose paws echoed from the hollow caverns down below like the report of a distant gun. The loss of the dog was his salvation. A few more careless steps forward, and he would have been plunged into a living tomb.

The Catherine touched also at Curtis's Island, the Captain with two boats put ashore for wood and the vessel with Mr Tapsell on board stood off the land.[25] The latter found that a current setting in shore, rendering it necessary to keep the vessel well off the land, and though the men in the boats complained of the distance they had to pull with the wood, he persevered in keeping his distance. But the next day he was sent ashore with the boats and the captain brought the vessel closer in, with a view of easing the labor of the men. The party on shore were suddenly startled by the report of a gun, and on looking up, saw that the Catherine was ashore. The boats pulled off instantly to her. A quantity of cargo was thrown overboard, an anchor got out, and after much labor she was warped off,[26] but so damaged as to render it necessary to proceed to the Bay of Islands to repair damage.

79

Kai tangata[27]

ONE DAY WHEN AT ANCHOR in the bay, a canoe came alongside with a number of large kits[28] containing freshly killed meat from which blood was streaming. Mr Tapsell enquired from the native who had accompanied it what the kits contained, who told him is a confidential whisper that it was "tangata", in other words, human dead bodies, cut up into joints ready for the oven. He was so disgusted that he ordered the astonished native into his canoe without loss of time.

Another time, one of the sailors, having missed a jacket which had been hanging up in the rigging, complained to Mr Tapsell, who asked the man whom he suspected of taking it. The man indicated a native in a canoe then alongside. He was recommended to overhaul the canoe. The native showed fight and brandished his spear. "He's got your jacket, douse him", said Mr Tapsell.[29] No sooner said than done, claret flowing freely.[30] The blood being observed by a number of natives in a war canoe towing astern, they began to scramble up each side of the quarter. A cry from the man in the rigging, "They are boarding us." "Out with your muskets, then", was the answer.

At that time it was customary to have arm chests in all the tops, in which a quantity of muskets were kept always loaded.[31] The men seized the weapons, and speedily a number of muzzles were pointed towards the deck, which the savages no sooner beheld than they leaped over the side with the greatest precipitation. Mr Kendall,[32] the missionary who was below at the time, came on deck, and told Mr Tapsell that the latter had done very wrong, as now the natives would go and plunder his house. Mr Tapsell replied that it was not likely he was going to permit them to take the vessel and perhaps murder all on board. Mr Kendall then requested to be put ashore at his own place.[33] This Mr Tapsell objected to, as endangering the boat and crew, but offered to land him a short distance off, whence he could walk over to his own premises. With this he was obliged to be contented, and being landed crossed the hill and found a crowd of natives busy pulling down his fence. He immediately took off his coat, and mixing with the crowd, began to pull down the fence too. The natives in surprise said to him, "What are you doing?" "Why, you have begun, let us all finish it," replied he. The natives seemed struck with the novelty of the idea, and immediately set to work and restored the fence.

Meantime Shonga,[34] a great Chief, who had been in the cabin of the Catherine while the disturbance was taking place, hearing the noise, came on deck, and seizing the carpenters' adze, threatened to split the head of any man who ventured to come on board, and on being informed of the cause of the disturbance, took a stout rope, with which he flogged the offending Maori unmercifully, then calling for a line, he made it fast to a large pig which the man had brought in his canoe, and told the sailors to haul it on board, which they did, and so received utu for the stolen jacket.[35]

The Catherine requiring a new mainmast, one was provided by the natives who brought down the immense sparr, some sixty or eighty feet long, for payment of a musket.

While the vessel was getting ready to sail, a great expedition under Shonga, Wharepoaka, Titara, Tareha, Pomera, and Rewa, was preparing for a warlike excursion on the tribes to the South, with something like a hundred war canoes, many of great size.[36] The Catherine and the expeditionary fleet left the Bay together.

By a singular coincidence, Mr Tapsell on his next voyage twelve months after, entered the Bay with the same fleet when they returned in triumph.[37]

Napoleon at St. Helena

ON HER VOYAGE HOME, the Catherine sighted St Helena and was about to call there when the captain was apprised by a message from the Admiral there, that the ex-emperor Napoleon Bonaparte was a prisoner in the island, and vessels were not allowed to approach within gun shot, but that whatever they required, should be conveyed to them from the shore.[38] The Catherine requiring water, a supply was quickly brought off in the man of war boats. Other articles were procured by telegraphing to the agent on shore.[39] This rigorous exclusion from communication with the outer world was said to have been rendered necessary in consequence of an attempted rescue of Napoleon by an American vessel.[40]

The Catherine returned to London where Mr Tapsell and the crew were paid off.

Mr Gates for the last time.

ON THIS OCCASION Mr Tapsell accidentally met Mr Gates in the street. He was handsomely dressed with abundance of gold rings and chains about his person. He accosted Mr Tapsell; "That is my mother-in-law", said he, pointing to a showily dressed woman walking in advance of him. "I am doing well now, not as before, when I kept a boarding house."

"I am glad to hear it," answered Mr Tapsell. He never saw Mr Gates again, but some time afterwards read in the newspapers that he had been hung for the murder of a poor limeburner, under the impression that he carried a large sum of money, but after the crime was committed, found only a few coppers on his person. After conviction, Gates confessed to the murder of a lieutenant in the navy on his way to join his ship at Deptford,[41] when he was attacked by Gates and his gang. The officer defended himself with great bravery with the aid of a stout stick, and would have succeeded in beating off his assailants, but the stick breaking, they overpowered him and cut his throat.

NOTES

1. The Great Belt (Danish: *Storebælt*) runs between the islands of Fyn and Sjælland in Denmark. The wide channel is the principal shipping route between the North Sea and the Baltic Sea.
2. From 1800, Malta was under the protection of the British and officially became a dominion of the British Empire in 1810. It was used as a way station and naval base.
3. Barbary piracy was rife in the Mediterranean during the nineteenth century. See Robert C. Davis, *Christian Slaves, Muslim Masters: White Slavery in the Mediterranean, the Barbary Coast, and Italy, 1500–1800* (New York: Palgrave Macmillan, 2003).

4. The brass swivels were pivoted rests for guns making it possible to turn the firearms horizontally in any required direction.

5. A lateen is a triangular sail in a fore-and-aft direction, set on a long yard and mounted at an angle on the mast.

6. The shrub broom (*Genista tinctoria*), also known as dyer's broom or greenweed, was used to dye wool and cloth yellow. The shrub is native to much of Europe and Turkey.

7. It is remarkable that one moment Tapsell is imprisoned by the Swedes and the next he is sailing under their protection.

8. An order is a written direction to pay money made by a person legally entitled to do so.

9. To handspike means to strike with a handspike, which is a small crowbar or lever.

10. Shadwell is a district in East London on the north bank of the River Thames.

11. A sponging house is a house kept by a bailiff for the preliminary confinement of debtors.

12. The *Catherine* (325 tons) was launched in 1811 at New Bedford, Massachusetts, and was employed in whaling off Australia and New Zealand. It made one voyage transporting female convicts from Ireland to New South Wales in 1813.

13. Cork Harbour, Ireland. The port was originally called Cove (or the Cove of Cork) before being renamed Queenstown in 1850. It is now known as Cobh (Irish: *An Cóbh*).

14. The *Three Bees* (459 tons) was built in 1813 in Bridgwater, Somerset, and was employed as a convict ship. As described by Tapsell, it caught fire and exploded in Sydney Cove on 20 May 1814. For a report on the fire, see *The Sydney Gazette*, 21 May 1814, p. 2.

15. The waist refers to the middle part of the upper deck of a ship.

16. The steerage is the division of the after part of a ship that is just in front of the main cabin.

17. Watsons Bay (after the British sailor Robert Watson) lies on the eastern side of Port Jackson (the natural harbour of Sydney).

18. Captain John Piper (1773–1851) was a military officer and public servant who settled in Sydney in 1792. He was promoted to Captain in 1800.

19. Stepping the mainmast means fixing the mainmast upright in its step. See chapter 9, note 19.

20. What is here described as one voyage on the *Catherine* is actually two: one under Robert Graham that returned to England in May 1819 (departure date unknown) and one that left England in July 1819 to hunt whales off New Zealand and returned in May 1822. In his autobiography (*The Otago Witness*, 11 February 1882, p. 26; Bentley, *Cannibal Jack*, pp. 108–109), Pākehā-Māori Jacky Marmon describes an astonishing episode in 1820 involving Tom Tapsell (another name used by Hans Falk/Phillip Tapsell during his time at sea) about which we have no other knowledge:

   > That night I was surprised, when lying in my house smoking, to see a European come into the settlement, and under the clear light of the moon make straight for my house. All sorts of dangers came to my mind, but these were set at rest by him asking, in broken Maori, when I opened the door, if I would grant him a night's lodging, as he had lost his way. He seemed surprised when I answered him in English, and still more so when he found out I also was a European. He told me his name was Tom Tapsell, and that he had deserting from a ship in the Bay. Little did I think that in after years I was to know him so intimately. I made him as comfortable as I could for the night, and in the morning he proceeded on his journey to Whangaroa.

21. Middle Ground was the name of the whaling ground between Lord Howe Island and the New South Wales coast. The tiny Lord Howe Island (14.55 km²) lies in the Tasman Sea between Australia and New Zealand, about 600 km east of Port Macquarie (NSW) and about 900 km southwest of Norfolk Island. New Holland was a name used to refer to that part of the Australian continent that had not been annexed to New South Wales. However, here it seems to refer to the northern New South Wales coast. Norfolk Island served as a British convict penal settlement from 1788 until 1855, except for an 11-year hiatus between 15 February 1814 and 6 June 1825, when it lay abandoned. It was during this time that Tapsell visited the island.

22. In Greek philosophy and religion, Elysium was the paradisiacal location of the afterlife for the righteous, the heroic and those chosen by the gods. It is being used figuratively here to mean a place of perfect happiness.

23. Reginald Heber (1783–1826) was a parson, traveller and hymn-writer. He also served as the Bishop of Calcutta. The words referred to here are from 'From Greenland's Icy Mountains' (1819), a missionary hymn:

What though the spicy breezes blow soft o'er Ceylon's Isle;
Though every prospect pleases, and only man is vile?'

24. The adjective 'rank' is archaic and means rampant, thick, vigorous, luxuriant in growth.

25. Presumably, Curtis's Island is the small forested island off the coast of Queensland, some 475 km northwest of Brisbane, near Rockhampton. However, there is also an island of the same name near Tasmania (named in 1800) and one in the Kermadec group between New Zealand and Tonga (named in 1788). Neither of the latter two is forested.

26. To warp off means to move a ship by hauling on a rope or warp.

27. Kai tangata is Māori for human food, food made of human.

28. The kits or baskets, known in Māori as kete, are made from woven flax leaves.

29. To douse means to punch, strike, inflict a blow.

30. The word claret is being used here to mean blood.

31. Tops are the topsails or uppermost sails on a ship.

32. Thomas Kendall (1778–1832) was a missionary who arrived in New Zealand for the first time in 1814. He returned again in 1821 and worked as a teacher and gun dealer. He was dismissed by the Church Missionary Society in 1822 after beginning a love affair with his pupil Tungaroa (sister of Tapsell's second wife Karuhi). On Kendall's life, see Judith Binney, *The Legacy of Guilt: A Life of Thomas Kendall*, revised edition (Wellington: Bridget Williams Books, 2005).

33. This presumably refers to Thomas Kendall's house at Matauwhi, which he had built on the south side of the bay, away from the missionary station.

34. Shonga refers to Hongi Hika (c.1772–6 March 1828), chief and war leader of Ngāpuhi and a major protagonist in the first of the Musket Wars during which he overran much of northern New Zealand. See Ron D. Crosby, *The Musket Wars: A History of Inter-Iwi Conflict 1806–1845* (Auckland: Libro International, 2012), passim.

35. Utu is Māori for retribution, revenge.

36. The great expedition here was Hongi Hika's devastating campaign of 1818 against the iwi of the Bay of Plenty. See Crosby, *The Musket Wars*, pp. 56–57. Wharepoaka was an important chief at Rangihoua pā: the son of Rakau and the brother of Tungaroa (Thomas Kendall's pupil), Karuhi (Tapsell's second wife) and the chief Waikato (Hohaia Parati). He was prominent in the wars between Ngāpuhi and Ngāi Te Rangi at Tauranga and Te Tūmū in 1832–33. Titara refers to Titore Takiri, a noted chief of the Ngāpuhi iwi who took part in many expeditions to the south, leading those on the Tauranga area in 1832–33. He was the brother of Korokoro and Tuhi. See Crosby, *The Musket Wars*, pp. 250–52, 267–69; Eric Ramsden, *Marsden and the Missions: Prelude to Waitangi* (Sydney: Angus & Robertson, 1936), p. 25 n. 11; Alexander T. Yarwood, *Samuel Marsden: The Great Survivor* (Melbourne: Melbourne University Press, 1977), p. 217. Tareha was a noted Ngāpuhi chief who took part on most of Hongi Hika's raids. He led the siege against Te Waharoa of the Matamata pā in 1832. See Crosby, *The Musket Wars*, pp. 250–52. Pomera refers to Pōmare (Whetoi), Ngāpuhi leader in the southern Bay of Islands area. He led many raids in the north of the North Island and was killed about 1826 by Waikato at Te Rore. See Crosby, *The Musket Wars*, pp. 132–35, 166–67; Ramsden, *Marsden and the Missions*, p. 25 n. 11. Rewa, also known as Mānu, was a Ngāpuhi chief in the Bay of Islands who lived near Rāwhiti. He became a Catholic and opposed the Treaty of Waitangi. See Ramsden, *Marsden and the Missions*, p. 25 n. 11.

37. See p. 85 for Tapsell's description of the return of Hongi Hika's fleet to the Bay of Islands. However, note that this was several years later (not just one).

38. The island of St Helena (130 km²) is situated in the South Atlantic about 2000 km west of Namibia and 4000 km east of Rio de Janeiro. From 1658 St Helena was governed by the East India Company until it became a British colony in 1834. However, between 1815 and 1821 it was under the direct control of the British government as it was selected as the place of imprisonment for Napoleon Bonaparte. His spent his detention at Longwood House (6 km from Jamestown) from 1815 until his death on 5 May 1821.

39. That is optical telegraphing or semaphore.

40. There were several escape plans formulated for Napoleon, often with the support of his brother Joseph-Napoleon, in the USA. None of them was successful. On the various attempts to rescue him, see Emilio Ocampo, 'The Attempt to Rescue Napoleon with a Submarine: Fact or Fiction?' *Napoleonica. La Revue*, 11 (2011–12), pp. 11–31.

41. Deptford in southeast London was the site of the Royal Navy Dockyard.

4

THE EXPEDITION OF THE NGAPUHIS was a memorable one, and is spoken of to this day by members of the tribes who suffered from the slaughter with which it was attended as an event not to be lightly forgotten.[1]

The fleet first landed at the Thames where,[2] being armed with muskets, they easily vanquished the natives of that district, who had only their own rude implements of warfare to oppose in resistance, and fell before these, like grass before the scythe. Great numbers were killed, many prisoners taken, and abundant banquets off the bodies of the slain crowned the savage enjoyment of their cruel conquests. Tauranga was next invaded,[3] and the inhabitants there made the subjects of a wholesale carnage, a comparatively few being spared to grace the triumph of the conquerors, and furnish the materials of a feast on their return home. Maketu was next visited, and the canoes proceeded up the Kaituna River to the falls near Rotoiti.[4] The Ngatiwhakaue as the Arawa were then called,[5] hearing of the approach of the enemy, and knowing that they could not come by water into Lake Rotorua felt themselves secure from attack by making for the island of Mokoia,[6] where they took refuge, but they were suddenly surprised by the sight of the Ngapuhi in the Lake with their canoes, which the latter had dragged overland. The unfortunate Ngatiwhakaue with their tomahawks and spears like the other conquered tribes could make only a feeble defence against the death dealing muskets of their assailants, who slaughtered them without mercy, and captured many slaves, a few escaping in canoes to the shore.[7]

With their thirst for blood satiated, loaded with the spoils of victory, and with a numerous band of captives to exhibit as trophies of their valour and contribute to their festive board a dainty only fit for Mari warriors of renown, they bent their way homeward.

Another voyage

MR TAPSELL'S NEXT VOYAGE was in the "Asp", whaling vessel which arrived at the Bay of Islands as the victorious Ngapuhi, and came to anchor off Kororarika.[8] Shonga's party, with a great number of canoes, drew in line up abreast of Kiti-kiti a place known as Shonga's dockyard and all ran ashore together.[9] Mr Tapsell, seeing them arrive got out a boat and followed them to witness their proceedings. Their first act after leaping ashore was to knock off the figure heads of the canoes, and the next to take out the bodies of Shonga's two sons who had been killed. They then landed forty prisoners of war taken in battle, whom they had brought with them, and these were stationed in a row and at a given signal all tomahawked.[10] They met their fate with stoic indifference and never betrayed uneasiness of suffering by the movement of a muscle. Some were killed with one blow, and others required several blows to dispatch them. The bodies were then cleaned, cut up, and put into ovens, which soon sent up a steam having the odour of roasted pork. When the cooking process was over, the warriors fell to upon their hideous meal, which they devoured with greediness and apparent delight, the women keeping aloof, for they are not allowed to eat human flesh.

Some sacrifice being required in satisfaction of the loss of Shonga's two sons, a wife of the latter, who was blind, called for her slave boy to approach her.[11] The boy came, expecting to receive protection from his mistress, but she seized him by the hair of the head, and thrust him under water, placing her foot upon him and keeping him down till he was drowned. Mr Tapsell did not wait to witness the remainder of the proceedings.

Fate of an unfaithful wife

POMARE, ONE OF THE CHIEFS, on his return with his party to his own place at Kororareka, was there informed of the infidelity of his wife, upon which he caused all his warriors to sit down in a circle, in the centre being himself and his recreant spouse, whom he stripped naked, exposing her to the view of all present, after which he deliberately killed her with his tomahawk, and then ate her.

(*Daily Southern Cross*, 1867)

A short honeymoon

IT WAS ON THIS OCCASION that he was married to a native girl named by Mr Kendall, the ships in harbor firing a salute at the termination of the ceremony.[12] This was the first marriage that ever took place in New Zealand, and Mr Tapsell was the first person who clothed a Maori woman in a European dress. The captain of the vessel ridiculed the idea of giving civilized garments to a cannibal such as she,[13] but Mr Tapsell assured him that the day would come when such as she would "walk in silk attire" and rejoice in apparel of satin and velvet. A plentiful banquet was provided on board the "Asp" in honor of the occasion, with bucketsful of grog for all hands. After dining with Mr Kendall, Mr Tapsell, with his bride, set out for a walk in the bush; resting for a moment, Mr Tapsell feeling tired he fell asleep, and when he awoke, his bride was gone. He searched for her some time in vain, and supposing she had returned to the house of Mr Kendall, he proceeded thither, but she had not been there. Making sure that she must be on the ship, he went on board, but could obtain no tidings of her. As the vessel was about to sail, he abandoned the search, and the Asp was leaving the harbor when her brother came on board to take farewell of his sister. When informed that she had run away, he was at first incredulous, but after being assured by some Maoris that such was the case, he became very angry, and threatened to kill her with his tomahawk. He was however dissuaded from that intention by Mr Tapsell, and left the vessel, which proceeded on her way home.

The woman died soon after.

When off Cape Horn, a large whale was captured, which was an unusual circumstance in that particular locality. The prize was very opportune, as it gave them sufficient oil to fill the vessel. Mr Tapsell left the Asp in London, where he spent some months in recreation.

Sells his voyage

IT WAS THE CUSTOM of the owners of the 'Asp' to refuse to have any dealings with Jews, who at that time carried on a great part of the trade that was done with the sea-faring community; and, with this object, this owner used to send the ship's husband to meet the vessels at Gravesend with money to make advances to the officers and men, which they might require till the accounts of the voyage were made up. But it so happened that, after such advances had been made to the 'Asp's' crew, and while she was discharging in

the London docks under the charge of the chief mate, Mr. Tapsell, a Jew whose store was situated in that neighbourhood, and whom Tapsell passed every day, constantly besieged him with offers to trade; expressing a wish to purchase his "voyage," as the term is, meaning his share of the voyage. At last, wearied with his importunity, and reflecting that his oil casks had leaked a good deal during the voyage, Tapsell came to terms with him for £550. When the cargo was landed, and the oil gauged, the accounts were made up, and Tapsell had the curiosity to go with the Jew to the office of the owner, where the men were to be paid off, himself waiting outside, while the Jew went in to receive the money. When he came out Tapsell asked him what luck he had had, but he raised his hand with a gesture of dissatisfaction, and hurried away without speaking. He afterwards said that he had lost £70 by the transaction.
(*Daily Southern Cross*, 1867)

Fair and false

DURING HIS SOJOURN in the metropolis, he fell in with a handsome woman who owned a grocer's shop and was in easy circumstances, whose charms won their way to the susceptible heart of the hardy sailor. It was true, she had a slight cast in one eye, but that only gave an interesting expression to her countenance, while her luxurious and glossy curls shaded a face that lighted up with animation and dimpled with happy smiles at his approach. He had now, he thought, discovered the individual who was to complete his felicity on earth, and resolved to put that important question which men find so hard to ask, and which sets the tender hearts of women in a flutter. To do this successfully, opportunity is required, and a favorable one not occurring, he resolved to make one. He asked her to accompany him to the theatre. She consented, and they were both seated in the full glory of the dress circle, when the lady was tapped on the shoulder by the box keeper, who requested her to remove her bonnet. This she indignantly refused to do, until her admirer called her attention to the fact that all the ladies in the boxes were without bonnets. She then retired to the cloak room and presently resumed her seat as before by the side of her swain, whose ardent glances she tenderly returned. The interest of the play engaging her attention, she was obliged occasionally to avert her face from her companion whose gaze now for the first time fell upon the top of her head, which to his consternation he discovered to be quite bald. The interest of the play was gone. A tumult of miserable conjectures distracted his mind. The glossy locks adorning her face which he had had so much admired, were false. The eye with the interesting cast might for aught he knew, be made of glass. The teeth, that glittered like pearls when she spoke or smiled, might be the cunning workmanship of a skilful dentist. His confidence in humanity was overthrown. Life was unreal, artificial, hollow. He longed for the play to terminate as he had never longed before. Never did a play appear so dreary and tedious as this, and when at last the curtain fell, he gave a sigh of relief, joyfully accompanied the lady to her home, bid her an affectionate good night, and never saw her more.

The character of a man about town, without other object than pleasure seeking is rather expensive to maintain, and after several months stay in London, Mr Tapsell found his Exchequer at a low ebb, under which circumstances he wrote requesting a supply of money from his father who remitted him a hundred pounds through a merchant in the city,[14] on application to whom Mr Tapsell was very kindly received, pressed to dine at the merchant's house, and made to promise that he would not fail to leave intelligence of his future movements. He gave the promise, and accepted the invitation but never went near the merchant again. At the same time he received a letter from his brother containing an order on Captain Patterson Stewart of the English navy for two hundred and fifty pounds,[15] but on application at the Office of the Admiralty, he learned that Captain Stewart was then absent on a foreign station.

Mr Tapsell next engaged as Chief mate on the 'Sisters', and took a gang of riggers to fit her out at Dover where she was lying.[16] When this was completed he brought her to the city canal, and took in stores for a whaling voyage. She was on her way to the Bay of Islands when Captain Duke, the commander, expressed his intention to go to Hobart Town, giving as a reason his desire to obtain a supply of potatoes which were better and cheaper there than in New Zealand. Accordingly the vessel put into the Derwent,[17] and Captain Duke landed a quantity of goods which he entrusted to an agent there to dispose of for him, by which transaction he lost a large sum of money.

The Catherine was sent in charge of Mr Tapsell to Oyster Bay for the purpose of Bay — or sight whaling as it is called.[18] A Colonel Meredith,[19] had in addition to a cattle and sheep run, also a whaling station at this place, and the competition which ensued between his men and the crew of the 'Sisters' prevented either party from being successful, the jealousy of one inducing them if possible to deter the other from catching fish.

While the Sisters was lying in Oyster Bay, a noted bushranger named Brady with his gang paid the neighbourhood a visit.[20] Colonel Meredith being absent at Hobart Town his wife and daughters were one morning early alarmed by the entrance into their bedrooms by a man no other than the

88

notorious Brady, who to their relief, told them not to be alarmed as he did not intend to do them any injury, but he exhibited a cat — a whip of many thongs, used for flogging prisoners — which he informed them was intended for the Colonel if he had been at home, in return for the cruelty with which he was said to treat his Government servants, after which he departed peacefully. He and some of his gang were observed for some days from the deck of the 'Sisters' and a strict watch kept on board that vessel for fear he might think of taking a passage by her.

The whaling in the Bay proving unsuccessful, the Sisters was brought round to Hobart Town where she lay for a short time, during which on one occasion Mr Tapsell paid a visit to a friend living a short distance from the town, and was returning in the evening when he arrived near a wayside public house opposite to a wood on the other side of the road. As he approached, a man suddenly emerged from the wood and stared at him with fixed attention. This man was dressed in a bottle green coat with long boots and breeches, and had altogether a sporting appearance. Beyond the fact that he himself was clothed in a suit of black and displayed the customary appendages of a gold watch chain and seal Mr Tapsell was not aware of any thing in his appearance justifying so rude a gaze. But the conduct of the stranger appeared still more singular when he placed his finger to his mouth and gave a loud whistle. Being fatigued, Mr Tapsell entered the inn which was close at hand, and seating himself at a table, called for refreshment.

89

The man whom he had seen on the road almost immediately followed him in, and took a chair at the opposite side of the table gazing intently at the other occupant of the room. Presently the hostess brought in the refreshment, and looking for a moment at Mr Tapsell, said, "I suppose you don't remember me?" "I cannot say that I do", answered he. "I am Kitty Lynch that came with you in the Catherine from Cork."[21] Then turning to the man in the green coat she said to him "Walk out, Sir". He obeyed without a word. When he had gone, she remarked to Mr Tapsell, "You must stay here tonight, Take my advice." She said no more on the subject, and Mr Tapsell took the hint, remaining to breakfast the following morning. He was convinced afterwards that he had escaped a snare, and that the woman, whom he had treated well when a prisoner in the Catherine, had in recollection of former kindness, interposed to prevent him from falling into the clutches of the man he had seen who probably brought much business to the house while pursuing a criminal course of life.

The vessel left Hobart Town sailing for the cruising ground. Captain Duke at this time gave way to habits of intemperance keeping his bed under the plea of sickness and Mr Tapsell for a good while believed him to be suffering until he was informed by the Steward of the real cause of his illness and that it was his custom when the chief had reached the deck to jump out of bed and fill a tumbler with brandy from a keg in the corner of his stateroom. This he would hastily swallow and then return to his couch.

On hearing this, Mr Tapsell removed the keg to his own cabin and placed it under lock and key. The Captain rising as usual to help himself to a dram, found that the liquor had been removed. He called the steward and demanded to know by whom it had been removed. The steward informed him, on which he sent for Mr Tapsell who was then aloft looking for whales. When he made his appearance, the captain said, "You have taken away the liquor from here. Do not deprive me entirely of it." Mr Tapsell replied that he would keep it until he was sufficiently well to take charge of the ship, adding that the captain would certainly kill himself if he continued to indulge as he had done. The former had just reached the deck when the captain ran upstairs after him and ordered all hands to be called aft, when he said, "Men, have I ever done you any injury? I ask you because I am going to die. I have not many minutes to live. Oh Tapsell", he continued, "if you had only done this before, you would have had the thanks of all my friends." Mr Tapsell replied that he hoped to have their thanks yet, that the captain would get over this and soon be quite well.

Mr Tapsell then allowed him small quantities of brandy occasionally, medicinally, until he was restored to health when the custody of the brandy and the charge of the ship were restore to him.

A circumstance occurred which probably hastened his recovery. The vessel was one day caught in a white squall and laid on her beam ends,[22] the sudden fright attending which brought him on deck and occupied his attention after he got well rapidly, after which he intimated his wish to go into the Bay of Islands and the vessel accordingly sailed for that station.

NOTES

1. Ngāpuhi is a large iwi centred around Hokianga, Bay of Islands and Whangarei. The description of the expedition fits the expedition of 1823 when Hongi Hika dragged his war canoes overland to attack Te Arawa in Rotorua. Ngāpuhi used muskets bringing about a devastating slaughter. On this expedition, see Crosby, The Musket Wars, pp. 120–35.
2. Thames is the former name (bestowed by James Cook) of the Waihou River that flows 150 km north from the Mamaku Ranges into the Firth of Thames.
3. Tauranga in the Bay of Plenty was founded in the thirteenth century and is situated at the traditional landing site of the Tākitimu and Mātaatua canoes. Tauranga developed rapidly during the first half of the nineteenth century due to the growing trade in flax.
4. Maketū in the Bay of Plenty is situated near Tauranga at the traditional landing site of Te Arawa canoe. Maketū developed rapidly during the first half of the nineteenth century due to the growing trade in flax. The Kaituna River flows from lakes Rotorua and Rotoiti northwards for 45 km to the Bay of Plenty (near Maketū). Lake Rotoiti, called Te Rotoiti-kite-a-Īhenga in Māori, is one of a chain of lakes in the Okataina caldera and lies on the northern shore of Lake Rotorua. It drains into the Kaituna River.
5. Ngāti Whakaue is an iwi from the Rotorua district belonging to Te Arawa, a confederation of iwi and hapū that trace their descent to the Arawa canoe that landed at Maketū. These

include Ngāti Whakaue and Ngāti Pikiao mentioned in Tapsell's memoirs.

6. Lake Rotorua, located in the Bay of Plenty, is the second largest lake in the North Island. Mokoia is a small island (1.35 km²) located in the lake.

7. Slavery was an important component of Māori society. Taurekareka (slaves) were usually captured during battles and spent their lives doing heavy physical work or fighting (under their masters' supervision). Furthermore, slaves could be used for marriage (particularly highborn female captives), for prostitution, in peace negotiations or as food. Some captives never became slaves but were instead killed as revenge by the wives who had lost their men in battle. By making all Māori British subjects, the Treaty of Waitangi (1840) effectively banned the practice as slavery had been abolished in the British Empire since 1807.

8. The *Asp* (346 tons) sailed July 1822 under Captain William Darby Brind for whaling off New Zealand. In December 1823 she was at the Bay of Islands with 1200 barrels of whale oil. The ship arrived back in England in May 1825. Kororāreka (Russell, Bay of Islands), also known as the Hell Hole of the South Pacific, functioned as New Zealand's capital from 1840 to 1842, after which the capital was shifted to Auckland (and in 1865 to Wellington).

9. 'Kiti-Kiti' refers to Kerikeri, about 20 km northwest of Russell and 80 km north of Whangarei. Shonga's dockyard was an English name for Hongi Hika's fort, Kororipo pā, located on the Kerikeri inlet known as Te Waha o Te Riri (The Inlet of War).

10. Hongi's treatment of the captives on returning to the Bay of Islands was a traditional action to sustain the mana of those who had been killed on his own side and to exact revenge.

11. Hongi Hika's senior wife, Turikatuku, was blind most of her adult life. Note this different description of events from a reader's letter to the editor of the weekly news in the *Daily Southern Cross* (12 May 1869), p. 4:

> Sir, — I have been reading "Tapsell's Life" in your columns with much interest, for I knew him well. He was a fine-made man, and I believe it was greatly if not entirely owing to his courage and promptitude that the brig "Wellington" was taken in the Bay of Islands from the convicts, I was living there at the time. His is no doubt a remarkable life, but his biographer makes a few mistakes in his account of events. For instance, the inhabitants of an island in the Bay of Islands who were cut off by the whalers on the coast, in revenge for the massacre of the crew of the "Boyd," were quite innocent of any participation in that deed. The chief Te Pahi was a mild inoffensive man, not even connected with the Whangaroa natives. Nearly every one on the island was killed by the whalers, and when I left the Bay, some years back, it had not yet been inhabited.
>
> The name of the Whangaroa chief was Te Puhi, but I do not think he was the principal actor in the "Boyd" affair.
>
> Again, he states that the "early missionaries had a blacksmith who manufactured axes. &c., and sold to the Maoris at an enormous percentage." Now, it is well known that money has only of late years been in circulation amongst the Maoris. The children of the missionaries as late as 1824 did not know what a shilling was like, and possibly did not know the names of our coins from a sovereign down to the penny. Their fathers were men who adventured their lives for the natives, and were many times in danger of being killed. Many times they were in great straits for want of the common necessaries of life, and, but for the seasonable help from occasional visits of whalers, would often have been in deplorable case.
>
> Again, the great Hongi (called in your paper Honga) never had more than two sons, one killed at Kaipara (Charlie), and one now living at Whangaroa. He had three daughters, one of whom I know is still alive. She was the widow of Honi Heke (Johnny Heke), and since his death has married a Hokianga chief. I was present at the landing of the war party mentioned by Mr. Tapsell. The two young men were near relatives of Hongi's, — names, Tete and Pou. I saw several people killed, and knew of their diabolical orgies, but Hongi's blind wife did not kill her young slave. I saw the wives of Tete and Pou kill five unfortunates. The canoe in which the bodies were brought home was broken up, but no others.
>
> I should not have taken this notice of the history of Tapsell if the characters of a few simple-minded worthy individuals had not been touched. There are Maoris and whites still living who can vouch for the truth of these statements. — Yours, &c, A 50-Years Resident.

12. Tapsell's marriage to Maria Ringa was the first solemnised marriage in New Zealand. See the illustration on p. 27. Thomas Kendall had converted Maria and officiated at the wedding

91

without the approval of his fellow missionaries. See Damon Ieremia Salesa, *Racial Crossings: Race, Intermarriage, and the Victorian British Empire* (Oxford: Oxford University Press, 2011), p. 79.

13. The captain of the *Asp* was William Darby Brind. Born in Birmingham in 1794 and died at the Bay of Islands in 1850.

14. This is the second time the manuscript mentions Tapsell contacting his father for money. The sum he received, £100, would have been a substantial sum for a city sanitation supervisor.

15. Tapsell's younger brother was Niels Christian Falk (born c.1794). See Part 1, 'The Pacific Viking': Hans Falk: the child. Captain James Patterson Stewart had sailed along the coast of Denmark and been involved in attacks on Danish vessels in 1812. See William James, *The Naval History of Great Britain. Vol. 5* (Cambridge: Cambridge University Press, 2010 [1st edition 1859]), p. 325.

16. The *Sisters* (282 tons), a whaling ship from USA. Robert Duke (1796–1845) was a shipmaster and whaler who together with his brothers acquired the *Sisters* in 1822. See Janette M. Holcomb, 'Captain Robert Duke, (1796–1845): A Biographical Case Study of Investment in the Colonial Whaling Industry', *The Great Circle*, 32.2 (2010), pp. 9–30.

17. The Derwent rises in the Central Highlands of Tasmania and flows 200 km southeast to empty through Hobart into Storm Bay, the Tasman Sea. The *Sisters* arrived in Hobart Town on 8 April 1826.

18. 'Catherine' is clearly a mistake for the *Sisters* here. Oyster Bay is on the east coast of Tasmania. The *Sisters'* crew caught whales for three months, killing five large whales and producing 48 tons of oil that was shipped to London on the *Henry*.

19. George Meredith (1777–1856) was born in Birmingham, England. He arrived in Hobart Town on 13 March 1821 and subsequently settled at Oyster Bay.

20. Matthew Brady (c.1799–1826) was transported to Van Diemen's Land in 1820 for seven years for stealing food in Manchester, England. After being transferred to Macquarie Harbour penal station on Sarah Island, he escaped. Together with his gang, he spent the next two years (1824–16) roaming the island before being captured and hanged.

21. Kitty or Catherine Lynch (b. 1784) was a children's maid from Limerick. When she arrived in Australia on the *Catherine* (1813) she was 30 years old. She was awarded a certificate of freedom on 31 August 1819.

22. Beam ends are the sides of the ship. In other words, the vessel is listing more than 45° and may be in danger of capsizing.

5

Rescue of the "Wellington", 1827

THE SISTERS HAD NOT BEEN many days in the Bay of Islands, when one day a strange sail hove in sight, bearing for the Bay. It was the custom at that time for the Captains of vessels in the harbour to meet strangers outside and pilot them in, and Captain Duke together with Captain Clarke of the Harriett — the only other vessel in the Bay — went out for that purpose and returned with a brig which they brought to anchor within a cable's length inshore of the Sisters.[1] A strange vessel in so unfrequented a locality as the Bay of Islands then was, was naturally an object of curiosity, amongst others, to Mr Tapsell who examined her long and attentively through the telescope. When Captain Duke came on board he enquired what vessel it was and received the information that it was the brig Wellington from Sydney to Norfolk Island with prisoners come into the Bay for wood and water.[2]

"I think there is something not right about her", said Mr Tapsell, "There are a great many people on board, and they all seem to be quarter deck hands."

"Oh no, it is all right", said Captain Duke, "I saw the prisoners below."

But Mr Tapsell's misgivings were not altogether removed, and he continued to watch her narrowly all the day.

There were an unusual number of people on the deck, some of whom were walking about, some standing in groups talking earnestly, one or two carrying muskets, and all apparently on a footing of familiarity. The more he looked, the stronger his suspicions became until at last he arrived at the conclusion that she had been run away with. A person named Walton, the reputed commander was invited to dinner on board the Sisters together with Captain Clark of the Harriett.[3] After the cloth was removed, Mr Tapsell rose as if to leave the Cabin, and addressing the visitor, said, "Walton, you have run away with that vessel". Walton seemed thunderstruck and quite trembled as he replied, "I have, I could not help it." "That will do for me", said Tapsell, and went on deck. By and by, both Walton and Captain Duke came on deck, the former of whom walked backwards and forwards alone, while the latter came to Tapsell, and said anxiously, "What shall we do with this man? We had better let him swim on board".

"Swim on board! No, that will never do, after you have invited him here to dinner. Better to wait till his boat comes for him, or else put him on board."

All this time Walton was pacing the deck by himself, and Captain Duke very uneasy at his presence on board. After dark a boat full of armed men came from the brig and pulled round the Sisters. Mr Tapsell seeing that the men were armed told them to keep off the side, when they enquired for Captain Walton. "I know of no Captain Walton", said Mr Tapsell, "but a man named Walton is on board." Walton was then desired to get into the boat, which he did. The next day a gale of wind blew, and Mr Williams the missionary came on board, to communicate some information he had obtained about the brig.[4] It appeared that some of the hands had been ashore purchasing powder from some white men living in the Bay which was a suspicious proceeding when they could have procured it cheaper and in larger quantities from the whaling ships, and also that Mr Fairburn, one of the missionaries, having gone on board the Wellington and returning past the door of the Captain's cabin had a note signed Harwood slipped into his hand stating that the brig had been seized by the prisoners and that he the captain was then confined in his berth.[5] Mr Williams said that he had mustered all the Maoris he could and endeavoured to prevail upon them to attempt the capture of the pirates, but they were afraid, and kept behind the rock, out of sight. After a long conversation with Captain Duke and Mr Tapsell, Mr Williams left the ship saying to the latter as he went over the side, "I hope you will not let her go", to which Mr Tapsell replied, "she shall not go."

That night a gale of wind set in so strong that it was found necessary to let go a second anchor, but the weather moderated in the morning and the wind died away. Captains Duke and Clarke went on board the Wellington, and preparations were made to take her out. The second anchor was hove up, and the first hove short on, the hands were aloft loosing the foretopsail and shuting it home ready to get underway.[6] Mr Tapsell, seeing this from on board the Sisters, called all hands aft, and told them that it would be disgraceful to permit the brig to go away when they knew that a guard of soldiers were prisoners were in irons in her hold who would all certainly be murdered when the vessel got out to sea. The crew answered unanimously "You speak and we will obey." He then gave orders for some to get the hawser up and clap a spring on the cable,[7] and the rest to mount the guns and get the small arms ready for action, which was done. When Walton in the Wellington saw this, he said to Captain Duke, "You are here to see me out of the harbour, and now you are preparing to give me a broadside. I shall now detain you and Clarke on board." Captain Duke protested that he knew nothing about the preparations, that whatever Tapsell was doing was for his own protection in case the brig should drop alongside the 'Sisters'. He gave his word of honour that the Wellington should be allowed to go: on this assurance, captains Duke and Clarke were permitted to leave the brig.

"What are you doing?" Exclaimed Duke when he came on board the 'Sisters'. "I am making preparation to prevent the rogue from going out," answered Tapsell. "What can we do?" "Consider", said Captain Duke, there are eighty-five desperate characters on board. Tapsell replied that such people proved cowards when they were tried. "But I have given my word of honour that she shall go out." said Duke. "And I have given my word of honor she shall never go out." replied Tapsell. "Captain Clarke will have nothing to do with it" urged Duke. "No", said Captain Clarke, "I will have nothing to do with it." Mr Tapsell then asked if Captain Clarke would permit him to ask the officers and crew of the Harriett, and he consented, on which Mr Tapsell went off in a boat to that vessel, but the mate of the Harriett replied that he had a wife and family and would not interfere.

On Tapsell's return to the 'Sisters' and reporting the result of his mission, Captain Duke said, "No one but a madman would have anything to do with it." To which Mr Tapsell replied, "Then I will act the madman's part"

Captain Duke, perceiving the determination of his chief mate, after a while offered no opposition to the preparations, allowing them to proceed, and occasionally giving a direction.

On the following day which was Sunday, the ensigns of the Sisters and Harriett were hoisted, and Mr Tapsell pointed and fired a gun from the quarter deck of the latter vessel which carried away the Wellington's fore topmast. The next shot cut her mainmast half through about two feet from the deck, and after a while the Harriett took up the firing delivering four or five rounds. About a dozen shots were fired altogether.

Captain Duke entering into the spirit of the action and encouraging the men to "fire away."

Shortly after the commencement of the cannonading, to which the Wellington never replied, the mutineers all bolted down below, and, not reappearing, firing was ordered to cease, Mr Tapsell manned a boat and went on board armed with a brace of pistols and dagger concealed, giving orders to the boat's crew to keep off the side of the brig. Walton was on the deck to receive him. On informing the latter that he had come to take possession of the Wellington, Walton said, "I give up the vessel, I will unship the rudder,[8] unbend the sails, or do anything you wish." Tapsell replied that there was no necessity for doing that, but the soldiers must be ordered up on deck their irons knocked off, and ammunition given up. When this was done, Walton invited him into the cabin to partake of refreshments, and Mr Tapsell was complying, when he observed a crowd of men with cartouche boxes on and with muskets in their hands seated round the table. He drew back remarking that he did not require so strong a guard, on which they were ordered to leave, which they did, but shortly after returned and stood in the doorway. Walton placed wine and spirits on the table desiring Mr Tapsell to help himself. Fearing poison he expressed his willingness to do so after Walton himself had partaken, which done, they returned to the deck and Captain Harwood was restored to the command of his vessell.

Meantime Captain Duke, had been negotiating for the custody of the prisoners till the Sisters was ready to take them on board, with several Maori Chiefs who seeing the result of the engagement had emerged from their place of concealment, and were induced to undertake the charge by bribes of muskets, so that when the mutineers, who really only numbered some thirty of the prisoners, the rest whom they could not trust being kept in irons by their comrades, they were distributed amongst the Maori chiefs, one taking two, another three and so on, and becoming responsible for their safe custody. The next day was occupied in getting the 'Sisters' ready to receive the prisoners, two of whom escaped while being brought on board.

Some Maoris went in pursuit, and returned with information that the two had escaped to Paihia, where Mr Williams was,[9] and that they had drawn their knives who attempted to be captured. On which Mr Tapsell proceeded in a boat to the place indicated, seized one of them in a hut, the other making his escape by cutting through the raupo.[10]

On his return with the prisoner, the sentry informed him that during his absence a great noise had been heard in the hold and he could see the prisoner's arms in motion as if they were sawing their irons; whereupon they were mustered and examined, and their handcuffs found to be nearly cut through. They were then ordered to be flogged, and the first of the number, a young man named Drummond,[11] after receiving two or three blows, offered to reveal the plot which had been matured for the recovery of the vessel, which was, that when Mr Tapsell's attention was occupied in getting the vessel under way he should be seized, his throat cut and his body thrown overboard. Captain Duke was to be spared. After this, a blacksmith attached to the mission was employed to make fresh irons, in which one of the missionaries, who could do smith's work, assisted him. When these were made, the convicts were all handcuffed with their arms behind them.

The same night Mr Tapsell heard groans proceeding from one of the

Watchways, and on enquiry as to the cause, heard a voice in answer say, "It's nothing sir, it'll soon be over." There was another groan, and all was silent, nor was the sound repeated. In the morning, to Mr Tapsell's surprise, all the prisoners had their arms before them as at first. He was curious to know how this had been managed, and enquired from the prisoner Drummond, who was kept on deck for fear of the vengeance of his comrades who had threatened to tear his heart out for the revelation he had made, when he effected the transposition with the greatest ease, slipping through his manacled limbs like an eel.

All being ready, the Sisters and Wellington sailed together for Sydney keeping company all the way, each carrying a signal lantern at night to make known to the other her situation.

A very strict watch was kept during the voyage which was an anxious one for Mr Tapsell, who went constantly armed, and dared hardly take his rest for several days and nights successively so that frequently on his watch he used to fall asleep and continue to walk the deck while he slept.

Reception in Sydney

IN THE COURSE OF TIME the two vessels arrived safely at Sydney alongside the wharf where Captain Nicholson, Superintendent of Dockyards came on board the Sisters.[12] "Who is the mate here?" demanded he. "I am, in the room of a better", replied Mr Tapsell. "Well, get the irons knocked off these prisoners," said he authoritatively. "Indeed I shall not", answered Mr Tapsell, "I have had trouble enough to bring them here safe, and if you want their irons knocked off, you must get it done yourself." Assistance was procured, the irons removed, and the prisoners taken on board the hulk. They were subsequently tried for the offence, nine of them hung, and the remainder transported Norfolk Island.[13]

The captain's revenge

DURING THE PRELIMINARY INVESTIGATION before the magistrates, Mr Tapsell attended, though not called on to give evidence, and was one day returning from the Court and passing a tavern called the Rose and Crown when he was hailed by Captain Duke who was seated within.[14] On entering the room the latter asked him if he had seen the newspapers at the same time tossing some towards him.[15] Mr Tapsell looked them through, and found that his conduct was highly eulogized while that of Captain Duke received unqualified censure.

"Tapsell," said the latter, "We have not always pulled together, we have sometimes had words, but my temper is like the wind, that blows over and is gone."

Mr Tapsell replied that it was the same way with himself.

"Well then," said Duke, "I want to know if you will contradict the statements contained there."

"No, I will not", was the answer, "that is nothing but a true account taken from the log book."

No more was said, and they separated, but on the following morning all hands were called aft and Tapsell broken[16] before the men whom the Captain directed to obey him as a chief officer no longer, adding to Tapsell "There is the shore for you or you can remain in your cabin, which you choose." Tapsell answered that he preferred to remain on board, as his life would not be safe on shore amongst prisoners and their friends.

Timely arrival of the rainbow

ACCORDINGLY HE REMAINED and the Rainbow man of war commanded by the Honorable Captain Rous opportunely arriving the following day, he went on board and lodged a complaint.[17] Captain Rous received him kindly and recommended him to come on board the Rainbow and remain, which he did.

Treachery and violence

ON THE OCCASION of one of his visits to the shore he fell in with another of the women prisoners he had brought out in the Catherine. She bore the Milesian cognomen of "Judy Cafferty, and then kept a public house on what was known as 'The Rocks' in Sydney.[18]

Mr Tapsell on entering found the place full of people, mostly Irishmen. After a short stay he was rising to go, when the landlady made the apparently unnecessary remark, "Why are you in such a hurry?" You are quite safe here." To this he replied that it was necessary for him to be on board the man of war before eight oclock at night.

He took his way to the wharf by way of the Custom House the steps to which were almost perpendicular, and was about to descend when he received a violent blow under the ear which sent him headlong to the bottom, where he lay for some time insensible, how long, he did not know. On recovering consciousness, his first act was to pass his hand over his head to ascertain if he were bleeding, but no blood was to be seen, his next, to ascertain if he had been robbed, but his watch, chain and money were safe, so he came to the conclusion that he had been the object of a treacherous attack, and that his assailants had left him for dead.

Sails in the man of war

THE HONORABLE CAPTAIN ROUS (now Admiral) was a good friend to Mr Tapsell, and wrote on his behalf to Governor Darling,[19] in consequence of which communication Captain Nicholson came on board to ascertain if he were qualified to take charge of a Government vessel. The examination proving satisfactory, he promised him command of the Alligator,[20] then at Hobart Town, on her return, whose Captain was to be displaced in his favor. Meanwhile Captain Rous being about to sail round New Zealand requested him to act as pilot and sail with him. The offer was accepted and the voyage made. On the return of the Rainbow to Sydney Tapsell learned that the Alligator had been in and another Captain appointed. Captain Rous then offered him the situation of sailing master on board the Rainbow, which he felt himself compelled to decline, as he knew that the pay of that office would not enable him to keep on a footing of equality with the other officers of the mess, many of whom were sons of the nobility with ample finances at command to support an expensive mode of living. So the Rainbow sailed without him for India.

The schooner Darling was lying in the harbor bound for Tongatabu for the Missionaries, and as she wanted a captain, Mr Tapsell applied for and obtained the appointment.[21]

NOTES

1. John Clark was master of the *Harriet*, a 363-ton whaler, in 1825 (to New Zealand) and 1827 (to the Pacific).
2. In 1826, the *Wellington*, owned by Joseph Underwood of Sydney, was chartered by the governor of New South Wales to take 65 convicts to the penal station on Norfolk Island. See also Part 3, 'Contemporary accounts of Phillip Tapsell's life' for another version of the recapture of the *Wellington* by Tapsell.
3. John Walton had been a subaltern of the 48th Regiment and was sentenced in 1824 in Lancaster, England, to seven years' transportation for receiving stolen goods.
4. Henry Williams (1782–1867), a former Royal Navy lieutenant, was a pioneer missionary and leader of the Church Missionary Society in New Zealand during the first half of the nineteenth century. He settled in Paihia. His letters have been published by Caroline Fitzgerald as *Te Wiremu — Henry Williams: Early Years in the North* (Wellington: Huia, 2011).

He mentions Phillip Tapsell in five letters between 1831 and 1833. See Part 3, 'Contemporary accounts of Phillip Tapsell's life'.

5. William Thomas Fairburn (1795–1859) was a carpenter and lay preacher for the Church Missionary Society who arrived in Kerikeri in 1819 and later moved to Pūriri, Thames. Captain John Harwood was master of the brig *Wellington*.

6. The archaic verb 'to shute' means to shift or move.

7. A hawser is a large rope used for towing or mooring a vessel.

8. The verb 'to unship' means to detach or remove the rudder from a fixed position.

9. Henry Williams and his wife Marianne settled in Paihia, near Russell and Kerikeri, in 1823 and established a mission there.

10. Raupō is a tall swamp bulrush (*Typha orientalis*). Its stem was used as a strong building or decorative material and its leaves for roofs and walls. Its rhizomes and flowers were used as food.

11. Henry Drummond had been transported from Portsmouth on the *Ocean* in 1823. Aged just 15, he had been sentenced at the Old Bailey to 14 years transportation for pickpocketing.

12. Captain John Nicholson (1787–1863) was appointed harbourmaster and Master Attendant of Port Jackson in 1821.

13. In fact only five of them were hanged, even though 23 of the mutineers were sentenced to death by hanging (*The Australian*, 13 March 1827, p. 3):

> Five of the unfortunate men whom we had occasion to mention in our last as having been selected from amongst the number of others concerned in the late piratical seizure of the Colonial brig Wellington, to be the victims of justice, have terminated their existence on the gallows. The awful ceremony was gone through before eleven o'clock of yesterday forenoon, and deemed to operate with an equally imposing effect on the unfortunate sufferers, and spectators of all classes, of whom there was a greater assemblage than usual. [Thomas] Edwards, [James] Smith, [William] Leddington, [Richard] Johnson, and [Edward] Colthurst, were the five men to whom it has been thought, in consideration of their former offences, which would have drawn upon each of them the law's extremest rigour, had they not been permitted to reap the advantages of a conditional pardon, mercy could not be reasonably or justly extended.

14. The Rose and Crown was a public house on the corner of King and Castlereagh streets, opened for business in 1810 by Thomas Rose (d. 1837) and en route from the court on Phillip Street to the harbour.

15. See Part 3, 'Contemporary accounts of Phillip Tapsell's life' for examples of the newspaper articles about the capture of the *Wellington*.

16. Broken means flogged.

17. HMS *Rainbow*, a 28-gun ship, was launched in 1823. Henry John Rous (1795–1877) was a naval captain and later a member of parliament. From 1825 until 1829 he commanded the *Rainbow*, during which time he visited Australia and explored parts of northeastern New South Wales.

18. This is most likely Ann Caffrey (listed as Ann Caffray from Dublin on the convict list of the *Catherine*) who went by the name of Judith. She married John Hull (who was involved in the liquor business) in 1822. A notice in the *Sydney Gazette and New South Wales Advertiser* (11 October 1826, p. 3) suggests that the marriage was not successful: 'I hereby caution the Public against harbouring or trusting my Wife, Judith Hull, as I will not be answerable for any Debt she may contract after this Date. October 9, 1829 [sic]. John Hull.'

    During the nineteenth century, the Rocks on Sydney's harbourside were often frequented by sailors and had a poor reputation as a district for prostitution and notorious drinking establishments.

19. Ralph Darling (1772–1858) was governor of New South Wales from 1824 to 1831.

20. HMS *Alligator* was a 28-gun, full-rigged ship that was launched in 1821.

21. The schooner *Darling* operated in and out of Sydney, transporting goods such as whale oil and wood. In 1829, the schooner was seized in Botany Bay on suspicion of smuggling. Tongatapu is the main island of the present-day kingdom of Tonga.

6

Tongatabu

THE "DARLING" WAS A SCHOONER of about fifty or sixty tons. A Wesleyan Missionary with his wife and child were the passengers to Tongatabu.[1] A North-East gale setting in, the vessel made very little headway and was obliged to put into the Bay of Islands for wood and water, after which she got under way for her destination.

One day while Mr Tapsell was below in the cabin working his reckoning, he overheard the missionary address the man at the wheel:–

"Well, my man, how are you steering now?"

The man told him the course.

"Dear me," said he, "that is not the course for Tongatabu."

This was too much for the fiery Tapsell, who made two steps up the companion ladder, seized the offending missionary by the coat collar, and flung him forward, saying.

"How dare you contradict my course. Do you not know that to do so is mutiny? You had better not repeat such conduct or I shall confine you."

On their arrival at Tongatabu several of the missionaries residing there came on board and wished to take passage to Sydney, stating that if they remained they would all be murdered by the natives.

This statement was however contradicted by a chief who came afterwards by invitation to breakfast, and who, before sitting to table knelt down and offered up a prayer. He assured Mr Tapsell that no native in the island would hurt a hair of the heads of the missionaries.

Nevertheless, they expressed anxiety to leave the place with the Darling, and one of them, observing the Captain's stateroom in the afterpart of the cabin, enquired to whom it belonged. The steward informed him.

"I'll have that," observed he.

"No, indeed you shall not," said Tapsell, who was within hearing. "That is my cabin, and I would not give it up to my own owner, much less to you. There is the other cabin for you, and if that is not big enough, you will find plenty of room in the hold."

The one who had come a passenger from Sydney, remarked:–

"Tapsell is no friend to the Society."

"No, I am not, to such society as you," said the irate Tapsell.

"Well then, we will stay and be murdered," meekly observed the missionary.

"You can please yourself," was the laconic reply. "There is no compulsion. If that cabin is not good enough for you, there is plenty of room in the hold."

The end of it was that all the missionaries remained on shore, except the one who had come in the Darling who returned with her to Sydney.

It should be mentioned that Mr Tapsell turning his experience of the natives to account, had provided himself with a couple of boxes of large blue beads of which he made profitable use here, often purchasing a large pig for a single bead. In the course of a short time he had a large quantity of pork salted down for carriage to Sydney.

On arrival in Sydney he was informed by the owner that some serious charges had been laid against him at the Mission, and he would have to appear and answer them.

"Oh!" said Tapsell, "One story is very good till another is told," and on attending at the Mission House he made such representations of the private life and intemperance of the complainant that the latter was dismissed from the Society, and afterwards took employment in Sydney as a linen draper's assistant.[2]

On the return of the Darling from Tongatabu Mr Tapsell at this time applied to Captain Nicholson for employment, but was informed by that official that two lieutenants having come out from England would step before a sailing master. On which Mr Tapsell observed that he thought he had better leave the country as his life on shore would be in danger from prisoners and their friends. To this Captain Nicholson replied that he thought it would be the best.

After this, the same owner, Mr Street, gave Mr Tapsell command of a large schooner called the Samuel intended to take a sealing boat and a gang of sealers to Codfish Island together with slops and provisions to trade with other sealers engaged in that locality.[3] The "Samuel" rode cut a heavy gale at Codfish Island, and lost an anchor; and afterwards, returning northward, made for Port Nicholson in order to land a number of Maoris belonging to that place who were on board.[4] At the entrance to the harbour, Mr Tapsell found a strong ebb tide running out, and there being no wind, he could not go in, but was obliged to anchor. During the night, a dreadful gale set in, causing the cable to part, carrying away the boat that was towing astern, and rendering it necessary to send down the topmasts. But the ebb tide running out, and the wind blowing in, kept the vessel stationary so that there was time to get a gun up from below, and bend it on to the chain, and when the tide turned, he was able to run in to a sheltered part of the harbour. In the morning the gale had moderated sufficiently to permit of the Maoris being landed, and Tapsell made all haste to get the vessel under way for he feared that they might go away and say that the vessel was broken, come down in numbers, strip her and perhaps murder the crew, so little were they to be depended on in those days.

From Port Nicholson he went to the Bay of Islands where he remained on shore to purchase whaling gear, sending the Samuel home to Sydney in charge of the mate, as it had been arranged with the owner that a vessel should be sent for him to that Bay, when it was likely he had procured the necessary implements; and in course of time one arrived with a letter from the owner instructing him to take his passage to Sydney, where a ship was waiting for him to fit out.

About this time Tapsell fell in with the prisoner who escaped from Mr Marsden was on a visit to the Mission at the Bay, recommended Tapsell to marry a native woman who had for some time lived with the missionaries and bore an excellent character,[5] to which recommendation he replied that he had made the request of the missionaries to perform the ceremony and been refused, when Mr Marsden declared himself willing to perform the ceremony. They were accordingly married.

103

The Escaped Convict.[6]

SHORTLY AFTER THIS, five or six canoes came to Rangiu, where he was then living, his wife informed him that a white man was in one of them who was tattooed all over whom she thought was one of the prisoners that had escaped from the Wellington.[7]

Mr Tapsell on going to see recognized him the fugitive who had cut through the raupo and got away. He told the man he had no occasion to fear him as he had nothing to do with him now, fitted him out with clothes, and presented him with a quantity of tobacco.

Mr Tapsell sailed for Sydney, and found the ship Minerva waiting for him there.[8] He fitted her out and sailed for the Bay of Islands bringing a missionary with his wife as passengers, after which he proceeded on his whaling voyage, taking his wife on board with him. On reaching the old cruising ground near the Kingsmill Group he found the Minerva very leaky,[9] so much so, that on one occasion, the crew being about after whales nearly all the day, on their return found four or five feet water in the hold; all hands were set to work the pumps which after this were kept almost constantly going, mostly worked by a number of Maoris, slaves to Tapsell's wife whom he had brought on board.

The crew several of whom were old convicts now began to grumble and wanted to return, but Mr Tapsell was determined not to go back without oil; so the fishing went on for several months, the men grumbling all the time. It would have been a very good voyage as whales were plentiful but that being unable to procure gear from whaling vessels, he had to get it made in Sydney where no one knew how to temper the iron, which in harpoons requires to be of the very finest possible quality and when any strain was put on the harpoons they had these broke, so that many whales were lost. At last, having procured nearly fifty-tons of oil, he bore up for the Bay of Islands. In his course thither was a very dangerous reef known as Rack Reef where the Pandora — in search of Captain Bligh shortly before this — was wrecked.[10]

It was absolutely imperative that this reef should be weathered, and although a gale was blowing at the time, Captain Tapsell considered it necessary to crowd on every stitch of canvas,[11] and press the ship through the water so as to keep to windward of this terrible reef.

The crew remonstrated, but were told by their intrepid commander that they had to choose one of two alternatives; Either to carry on sail as they were doing till they had passed the reef, or to shorten sail, and permit the vessel to strike on rocks when every soul would be lost.

When by his reckoning he knew that he had passed the reef, he shortened sail, close-reefed to topsail, and went under easy canvas. The Bay of Islands was reached, and the Minerva anchored at Rangiu, where she was heeled over, and every endeavour made to find out the leak. Two carpenters at work stopped several places, but afterwards she leaked still.

A riot on board.

ONE DAY THE CAPTAIN being ashore repairing one of the boats, the mate was sent to borrow a Nautical Almanac for the use of the Minerva, and returned with a quantity of grog which he gave away to the hands until most of them were drunk and many of Maoris coming on board, the deck became a scene of confusion; The sailors began to push the natives over the side into the canoes, but the natives proving too many for them, the sailors broke into the Captain's cabin, got out the muskets and fired upon the natives, wounding one or two of them the carpenter at the same time flourishing his axe. All this would doubtless have ended in a massacre, but for the intervention of Tapsell's wife and her brother, Wharepoaka, who, with Tapsell himself came on board, and after some time succeeded in restoring quietness.

Two days after, a man of war came into the harbor and anchored off Kororarika, when Mr Tapsell ordered the anchor to be hove up, which the crew did very cheerfully, supposing the vessel was about to go to sea; and then he ran the Minerva alongside the man of war and lodged a complaint against the rioters. An officer came on board, five of the ringleaders were pointed out and taken off by the man of war for transmission to Sydney. Not long after Captain Tapsell, being anxious to procure more oil, took the Minerva off North Cape, and succeeded in capturing a large whale, which considerably increased the quantity he had on board. With this, he sailed for Sydney, and discharged the cargo of his ship.[12] After which, reflecting that another vessel lying alongside, the mate (Mr Creek) and second mate were employed on this duty, on leaving them to which, the Captain informed them that there was grog on the cabin table to which they might help themselves when they required it. This work being performed they went ashore, the Captain came off and got the anchor up, and was taking the vessel round to Cockle Bay,[13] when he perceived the mate coming off in a waterman's boat, and standing up in the stern sheets. When on board, he said mysteriously that he was being pursued for a debt and requested permission to hide himself in the Captain's cabin. To this consent was given. The Captain was engaged in the fore part of the ship when Mr Creek made his appearance in a state of frenzy. He danced about, ran round the cap stone, knelt down and prayed and behaved like a lunatic.[14] Leaving orders to have him looked after, Mr Tapsell went below to dinner, during which he saw through the cabin window the unfortunate man plunge into the water, evidently bent on self destruction, for, finding a difficulty in sinking, he tried to catch hold of his feet. A 'Government man' on board immediately jumped overboard and held him up until a boat was lowered and took them both in. He was then taken ashore and confined till the afternoon, by which time he had perfectly recovered, and was as sane as a man need be.

Gives up command.

THE VESSEL BEING DISCHARGED, and the accounts made up, Mr Tapsell reflected that the man of war would soon be in with the five of his crew, against whom he would have to appear, and, remembering that he had already acquired a bad name in Sydney in connection with the rescue of the Wellington, determined to leave the place, and get a passage home from the Bay of Islands. He accordingly gave up command of his vessel and sailed as passenger in the schooner New Zealander Captain Stewart for the Bay. When there, he made application to the Captain of the only whaler in harbour for a passage, offering to pay for it, but was refused, — for the alleged reason that the owner of the ship had given orders that she should take no passengers.

Mr Tapsell was then of the opinion that this was only an excuse, and that it was a plan arranged between Captain Duke and the other whaling Captains to refuse him a passage to England so that Duke might get home first, and tell his story his own way.

Trade in flax.

UNDER THESE CIRCUMSTANCES Mr Tapsell wrote to a Sydney firm named Jones and Walker, who had a Government contract for flax showing them the opportunity that existed for trading with the Maoris, and offering the advantages of his experience in conducting it.[15]

His offer was at once accepted, and the New Zealander on her return brought him a large quantity of muskets, powder, and other articles suitable for the trade, with instructions to the Captain to land him at any part of the coast he might think best. Accordingly, by the advice of his brother-in-law Wharepoaka, he proceeded to Tauranga, where he purchased from Hori Tupaia for four muskets an extremely large canoe, eighty feet long.[16] She was quite new, and not completely finished, being without the top streak, which was however made, and ready to lash on, and to get this done, he paid a hundred figs of tobacco.[17] Immediately on the ship casting anchor in Tauranga, Wharepoaka, whose wife was the daughter of a chief at Rotorua,[18] sent messages to her relations there, letting them know that Mr Tapsell had arrived, and for what purpose, and asking them to come down and see him. Amongst Tapsell's party were six or seven Ngapuhis, and ten or twelve women from Rotorua who had been taken prisoners in the last expedition and who were consequently slaves.

On receiving this invitation, Tohi, Wharetuhi, Pipi, Tipitipi, and Hori Haupapa came overland to Tauranga, and had an interview in which they enlarged on the advantages offered by Maketu as a place for Mr Tapsell to fix his residence.[19] It was therefore agreed that he should settle there, the large canoe and two or three others, were loaded with his goods and started Southwards. When opposite the island of Motiti,[20] Hori Tupaia was desirous of landing Mr Tapsell there, so that he might secure his trade all to himself, and some time was spent in vainly attempting to induce him to proceed to Maketu as agreed upon, until Mr Tapsell, getting angry, presented a pistol at his head, when he became convinced, the argument ceased, and the canoes went on their way to their proper destination.

Maketu in 1828.[21]

MAKETU WAS A DIFFERENT PLACE then 1828 to what it in now in 1869. Its physical appearance was not the same. The mouth of the river was so narrow that not more than two or three canoes abreast could enter at one time, while now, small coasting vessels can easily come in and out. The portion of the stream where vessels at present lie, was also very narrow and deep, while now, it is of considerable width; and the place where Tapsell had his first store is now continually under water. There were no inhabitants at that time, because it was a sort of Debateable ground, for which many tribes had fought, and the right of none was acknowledged.[22]

107

The purchase of Maketu.

WHEN THE PARTY ARRIVED at Maketu they occupied the first night in the bush somewhere about the place where Tapsell's store afterwards stood, and the next day a sort of hut was erected for his accomodation, the rest sleeping in the open air. In two or three days the people from Tauranga and Waikato began to arrive, those from Tauranga first, as they had followed the canoes along the beach, and in four or five days they had all mustered several thousands in number till Maketu was quite alive with crowds of human beings. The Rotorua people were afraid, and did not come, as a jealousy existed between them and the other tribes. When they were all assembled, and Tapsell had made known his object the chiefs went into committee to decide the ownership of the place. The deliberations were continued day and night for two or three days, with no appearance of an amicable termination, and at one time Wharepoaka told Mr Tapsell he was afraid it would end in a fight, in which case, he and the few Ngapuhi with him would fare very badly. But at last he brought the welcome intelligence that it was all settled, and given in Tupaia's favor, and that Mr Tapsell had nothing now to do but buy it from him. On which he sent for Tupaia and asked him if he would sell the place to which he answered in the affirmative. On the question being put as to the value he set upon it, he said he did not know, and Mr Tapsell laid out what goods he considered a fair payment; A case of muskets, a cask of powder, part of a cask of tobacco, some cartridge boxes and a quantity of pig lead.[23] With this, Tupaia was well satisfied, the bargain was completed, and the goods divided amongst principal chiefs, after which they all went away. Two or three days afterwards the Rotorua and Tarawera people came down and settled in great numbers,[24] their huts stretching along the beach and up the river Kaituna for a considerable distance until Maketu presented a scene of animation and activity in direct contrast to its former state of loneliness and desertion. All hands set to work to scrape flax, and the shell with which the operation was performed was heard going all the day, and sometimes all night, so eager were these people to prepare a commodity which they might exchange for the highly prized muskets and ammunition.[25]

This was how the Arawa first settled at Maketu.

NOTES

1. This is the missionary and preacher William Weiss and his wife and child. The New Zealand and Tonga district of the Wesleyan Mission chartered the schooner *Darling* to convey the Weisses to Tonga and to take supplies to the brethren John Thomas and John Hutchinson, then supposed to be in real want at their station in Hihifo, Niuatoputapu. References to this voyage can be found in J.G. Turner, *The Pioneer Missionary: Life of Rev. Nathaniel Turner, Missionary in New Zealand, Tonga, and Australia* (London: Wesleyan Conference Office, 1872), pp. 80–82; Andrew Thornley, *A Shaking of the Land: William Cross and the Origins of Christianity in Fiji · Na Yavalati Ni Vanua: Ko Wiliame Korosi kei na i Tekitekivu ni Lotu Vakarisito e Viti* (Suva, Fiji: Institute of Pacific Studies, University of the South Pacific, 2005), pp. 23–24.

2. If Tapsell is referring to Weiss, then this is incorrect, as he did in fact return to the mission in Tonga.

3. On the schooner *Samuel* and the seal trade, see Robert McNab, *Murihiku: A History of the South Island of New Zealand and the Islands Adjacent and Lying to the South from 1642 to 1835* (Wellington: Whitcombe and Tombs Ltd, 1909), pp. 341–55. Codfish Island, called Whenua Hou in Māori, is a small island located to the west of Stewart Island (Rakiura).

4. Port Nicholson is the historical name for Wellington Harbour, New Zealand.

5. Tapsell's second wife Karuhi was the sister of Wharepoaka, Waikato and Tungaroa. She had lived for many years among the missionaries. She died in 1832, just a few years after her wedding.

6. We do not know much about the fate of those mutineers who managed to escape from the *Wellington. The Australian* (9 May 1827), p. 3 has the following account of one such escaped convict:

    Harris, one of the prisoners who were being conveyed to Norfolk Island by the brig Wellington, at the time of her being pirated, but who escaped on shore at New Zealand, with others, previous to the re-capture of that vessel by the Sisters, was apprehended on Thursday last. Whilst the barque Faith was laying at the Bay of Islands, Harris contrived to ship himself as a seaman on board of her. His utter ignorance of any thing like seamanship soon becoming apparent, and the probability of his story being true becoming more doubtful every day, information of the man being on board was communicated to the police authorities. One of the assistant superintendents, with several constables, proceeded to Botany Bay on Thursday evening and laid violent hands on Harris whilst he was descending the rigging of the vessel.

7. The escaped convict had no doubt asked Māori to tattoo him with traditional motifs and designs, as it would act as a means of disguise — both helping him evade identification and possibly assuring him a warm welcome among Māori throughout the country.

8. The Sydney-based 155-ton brig *Minerva* was in poor shape: 'Yesterday arrived, from New Zealand, the Minerva, whaler, with 60 tons of oil, in a very leaky condition. She touched at New Zealand the 27th of last month [January]'. *The Sydney Gazette and New South Wales Advertiser*, 24 February 1829, p. 2.

9. The Kingsmill Group is a former name for the Gilbert Islands (Tungaru), now part of Kiribati.

10. Rack Reef is probably a garbled form of Wreck Reef (that is, the Great Barrier Reef). HMS *Pandora* (524 tons) was a 24-gun post ship of the Royal Navy, launched in 1779. On 7 November 1790, she sailed from Portsmouth commanded by Captain Edward Edwards to recover the *Bounty*, capture the mutineers and bring them to trial in England. The mutineers had already sailed off (eventually to settle on Pitcairn Island) when the *Pandora* arrived in Tahiti in March 1791, while the men who had not been loyal to the ring-leader Fletcher Christian remained and were captured. After collecting the men, the *Pandora* spent several months searching the ocean looking for the remaining mutineers. On 29 August 1791 she struck the outer Great Barrier Reef, claiming the lives of 31 crew and four prisoners. William Bligh (1754–1817) was commanding lieutenant on the *Bounty* during the breadfruit expedition that left Spithead for Tahiti at the end of 1787. In April 1789, the ship was taken by mutineers and Bligh and several other men were forced into the ship's boat. After sailing 6500 km they eventually reached safety in the Dutch settlement of Koepang (now Kupang, Timor, Indonesia). By the end of his career at sea, Bligh had risen to the rank of Vice Admiral of the Blue.

11. To crowd means to press, drive, hasten.

12. The ship's cargo is listed in *The Sydney Gazette and New South Wales Advertiser*, 3 March 1829, p. 2: 'IMPORTS. SHIPS' REPORTS. Feb. 21. Brig MINERVA, 155 Tons, TAPSELL, from the Sperm Whale Fishery, 135 casks sperm oil, 20 ditto head matter.'

13. Cockle Bay is one of the bays in Darling Harbour, located just to the west of the present-day Sydney central business district.

14. The capstan ('cap stone') is a horizontal wheel-like mechanism pushed by men walking round in order to wind up an anchor or hoist heavy sails.

15. Richard Jones (1786–1852, born in Chirbury, Shropshire) and William Walker (1787–1854, born in Fife) created a mercantile firm together with Edward Riley (1784–1825, born in London) in July 1820. Jones and Walker, as it was called, was one of the few firms involved with the flax trade in New Zealand. See Janette Holcomb, *Early Merchant Families of Sydney: Speculation and Risk Management on the Fringe of Empire* (London: Anthem Press, 2014), pp. 107–108 (on collaboration with Tapsell). On Jones and Walker, see *Australian Dictionary of Biography. Vol. 2*, ed. Douglas Pike et al. (Melbourne: Melbourne University Press, 1967).

16. Hōri Tūpaea (d. 1881) was the major leader of Ngāi Te Rangi, an iwi based in Tauranga. He resided at Otūmoetai pā until 1852 when he moved to Mōtītī Island, Bay of Plenty.

17. A fig is a twisted roll of tobacco (usually of the type called 'negro-head' or 'Barrett's twist') that has been packed tightly in layers. A fig measured about one inch across and eight inches in length. The fig had to be cut up and rubbed to make it ready for use. See [Louisa] Meredith, *Notes and Sketches of New South Wales during a Residence in that Colony from 1839 to 1844* (London: John Murray, 1844), p. 24.

18. Wharepoaka's wife was Te Rore.

19. Tohi Te Ururangi (d. 1864) was a renowned warrior and chief of Ngāti Whakaue (Te Arawa). He became known as Wynyard Beckham (Winiata Pekamu; cf. p. 122). His daughter Ngatai married Tapsell's son Retireti. Wharetuhi was likely a Te Arawa warrior(?). Pipi was Te Haupapa's brother and a Ngāti Whakaue chief (cf. p. 143). Tipitipi was a Ngāti Whakaue chief (cf. p. 125). Hōri Haupapa (b. c.1790), better known as Te Haupapa, was raised at Ōhinemutu pā and on Mokoia Island in Lake Rotorua. He became a warrior and chief of Ngāti Whakaue. See Paora Tapsell, 'Te Haupapa', in *The Lives of Colonial Objects*, ed. Annabel Cooper, Lachy Paterson and Angela Wanhalla (Dunedin: Otago University Press, 2015), pp. 24–31.

20. Mōtītī Island located in the Bay of Plenty, about 9 km off the coast of Papamoa.

21. It is more likely that Tapsell arrived in Maketū, at the mouth of the Kaituna River, towards the end of 1829 or in early 1830. See Enid Tapsell, *Historic Maketu. Hui Hui Mai!* (Rotorua: Rotorua Morning Post, 1940), p. 39.

22. The assertion that there were no inhabitants when Tapsell arrived suggests that this must have been the time when Ngāti Pūkenga were in Rotorua. See Enid Tapsell, *Historic Maketu. Hui Hui Mai!* (Rotorua: *Rotorua Morning Post*, 1940), p. 40.

23. Pig lead is unrefined lead cast in blocks ('pigs').

24. Tarawera is an area to the southeast of Rotorua.

25. Flax was scraped and worked with the shell of the pipi (*Paphies australis*), a common bivalve mollusc.

7

Mr. Tapsell's wife

MR TAPSELL'S SECOND WIFE, whom he had married at the Bay of Islands, was as has been said before, the sister of Wharepoaka, an influential chief of the Ngapuhis, and proved of great service to him as an interpreter in his negotiations with the natives, having acquired a very good knowledge of the English language during her stay with the missionaries. Personally, she was of very light complexion and so fair, that at Maketu she acquired the name of "the white woman". This light complexion was a characteristic of all her relations, for although her brother, Wharepoaka, had the full tattoo over his face, his skin between the blue lines, was as white as that of a European's.[1]

When they had been a short time at Maketu, Mr Tapsell, his wife, and Wharepoaka went to Rotorua, taking with them the slaves they had brought from the Bay of Islands, whom had been captured during the late expedition of the Ngapuhis southward. These they delivered up to their friends, giving them their liberty. The object of Mr Tapsell's arrival was explained to the natives. They were informed that he wished to trade with them for flax, and committees were immediately held, resulting in their agreement to commence scraping flax at once and for this purpose to take up their residence at Maketu. This universal willingness to prepare flax for market arose from a desire to obtain the much coveted muskets, of which they possessed very few, a circumstance which had rendered them an easy prey to the Ngapuhis, who were well provided.

Upon coming to a determination they sent messengers over the country as far as Cook's Straits to their relations there, telling them to come and scrape flax, and many of these came, bringing along with them an American negro, an Englishman, and a Lascar,[2] part of a crew sent by a Mr Ferguson to trade in flax,[3] who had all been murdered and eaten but these three, whom the natives brought to Mr Tapsell to be ransomed and the Lascar for a musket each. In narrating their sufferings they informed him that the natives had cooked the bodies of their companions and had offered them a portion to eat. The Englishman and negro stayed with Tapsell for some time, until a vessel arrived from Sydney and took them away; The Lascar remained for several years.

At this time Wharepoaka established friendly relations with all the tribes around with whom he had previously been at variance, so that Mr Tapsell was shortly on the best of terms with the Tauranga people, those of Waikato, Rotorua, Taupo, Tarawera, and almost every part of the island, and they began to scrape flax for him in all directions. Hori Tupaia, who proved the best friend he had, and the most honorable in his dealings, built a pa at Te Tumu, half way between Maketu and Tauranga, in order to be nearer the growing flax and nearer Mr Tapsell than at his own place.

Fish at Maketu.

WHEN HUNDREDS OF THE NATIVES at Maketu now set to work to making nets to obtain a supply of fish as provision for the numbers engaged in preparing flax, and the quantity of fish caught at this time was enormous. Tons and tons of fish were taken every day, and Mr Tapsell's share, set apart for his was an immense pile, infinitely more than he could consume, from which he used to select that he required, and give back the rest, which was then cured and sent to the natives living at Rotorua, who, in return, sent large quantities of potatoes carried by hundreds of women, like a string of pack-horses, who also brought the delicious cray fish procurable in the Lake, which the Lascar, whom Mr Tapsell employed as cook, with the aid of curry, converted into an exquisite dish. At that time there were no plantations in Maketu, and, besides the potatoes obtained from Rotorua, the natives had no other vegetable than the fern root,[4] which they prepared by beating, and made into a kind of bread. Mr Tapsell had brought with him a supply of flour, tea and sugar, and other European articles of diet, so that his table was always well provided. The abundance of fish at that time was in striking contrast to the present, when fish are quite a rarity, on account of the disinclination of the natives to give themselves the labor of taking them.

For a small payment the natives built Mr Tapsell a comfortable house at the foot of the cliff bounding the present pa of the Nga te Pikiao,[5] and in what was then a fine bush, but now, by the action of wind and tide, and the diversion of the stream, in the bed of the river; it was placed here for convenience in landing and shipping the flax.

The peace broken

WHAREPOAKA REMAINED HERE for about a year, and every thing went on very comfortably, the Maketu, Tauranga, and Waikato natives being on the most amicable footing, and going backwards and forwards constantly without molestation, until a band of the Ngapuhis, who had committed murder in the Bay of Islands and were in consequence outlawed, determined on a warlike expedition against the tribes on the East Coast.[6] They were remonstrated with by the other natives in the Bay on the impropriety of such a proceeding.

"Consider," said their advisers "that Wharepoaka is living there, and if you attack the other tribes they will kill him." But they answered that they did not care for Wharepoaka, whom they would take for a slave.

Accordingly they set out in five large canoes, full of men, with a swivel in the bows of one or two. They first landed at Mayor Island,[7] where they slaughtered all they could find, some escaping in canoes to Tauranga, where they imparted the intelligence, upon which messengers were sent to Waikato, and a great muster took place in Tauranga of fighting men of both tribes, who in their canoes prepared to go in pursuit of the marauders, on whom they purposed executing summary vengeance. Meanwhile the outlaws had proceeded to the island of Motiti where the work of wholesale slaughter was carried on as it had been elsewhere, numbers being killed, a few only escaping. Upon receipt of this information at Tauranga, the assembled natives launched their canoes, and set sail to beseige the island, which they surrounded. Many engagements took place, the Ngapuhis behaving with great bravery, until their ammunition was all done, when they still stood their ground, and were shot down as they stood, all but one, a son of Rewa, a chief in the Bay of Islands, who was taken prisoner and whom Mr Tapsell ransomed by payment of a musket from Tupaia's uncle, Hikaraia.[8]

There was great grief in Maketu when the news of this slaughter became known, most of the people killed being relations of Mr Tapsell's wife and Wharepoaka, the latter of whom became very uneasy, and anxious to return to the Bay of Islands to his own tribe, as he knew that utu would be required by them for the people slain, and a war be the consequence. So when Mr Tapsell's cutter, a vessel of forty tons — which collected flax on the coast — arrived at Maketu, she was sent to the Bay of Islands with Wharepoaka on board.

When she arrived, about five hundred fighting men embarked in canoes for Tauranga.[9] They pitched their camp about a gun shot from the pa at Otumoetai within Tauranga harbor.[10] When the Ngatiwhakaue, or Arawa, heard that the Ngapuhis were at Tauranga, a strong force went from Rotorua and Tarawera in canoes, taking up their position on the side of the pah opposite to that occupied by the Ngapuhi. Fighting lasted nearly all the summer, without inflicting heavy loss upon the beseiged, and several were killed on both sides.

Just at this time the wife of Mr Tapsell took ill, who wishing to see her brother before she died, Tapsell took her in his boat to Otumoetai, when the fighting was going on, put her on shore to her brother, and went himself into the pa to confer with Tupaia.

A treacherous pakeha

THERE WERE THEN TWO white men trading for flax, who lived near the pa at Otumoetai to one of whom Mr Tapsell was very well known. A chief coming into the whare where they were,[11] a whispered conversation was carried on between him and the European referred to with which proceeding Mr Tapsell was not pleased, and said as much to the man, who excused himself by remarking that trade was the subject of their conversation; but immediately after this, the man became profuse in his offers of hospitality, and pressed Mr Tapsell to occupy his bed, making his own on the floor which invitation the latter at first resolutely declined, but afterwards, yielding to the other's urgent request, consented.

The singularity of the invitation, after the whispered conversation, excited distrust in Mr Tapsell's mind, and prevented him from sleeping soundly, and about midnight, he was startled by the discharge of a musket at no great distance, followed immediately by the entrance of a bullet through the wall of the house a little above his bed, which was no doubt intended to dispatch him as he lay. The shot was not repeated, and Mr Tapsell remained in the same bed till morning, when he took breakfast with his host, to whom he related the circumstance, remarking that the person who fired the shot was "no friend to him". His entertainer expressed surprise, and said he could not imagine who had been guilty of such an act, but Mr Tapsell left with the impression which he retains to this day, that his host knew more about it than he chose to tell, and that jealousy of his trade was the motive of the treacherous attempt.

Mr Tapsell on this occasion brought a quantity of ammunition for the Ngapuhi and Arawa, to whom he was indebted for flax prepared by them, with which Tupaia was not very well pleased, though he did not manifest his displeasure by any act of hostility, and in the course of the day, Mr Tapsell took his wife on board and returned to Maketu.[12]

The Ngapuhi and Arawa, finding that they made no impression at Otumoetai, came to Maketu in their canoes, which they hauled up on the beach, and then marched to Te Tumu to fight with the people in Tupaia's pa there, where they killed a good many.

Maori dogs

ONE OF THE GREATEST NUISANCES in the domestic life of the Maoris at that time was the practice of keeping swarms of useless dogs, which were never fed, and which became as hungry and almost as fierce as wolves. Whenever a bitch pupped, all her offspring were supposed to live as best they could, for they never received a scrap of food from their masters, and, in consequence, those which survived such treatment grew up to be lean, hungry, snappish curs, compelled by necessity to thieve for their subsistence, and so fierce that they would assail a stranger in packs, and he would have difficulty in preventing them from tearing him in pieces. When Mr. Tapsell first settled amongst the Arawa, he could not stir out of doors without being followed step by step by a pack of half-starved wolfish animals, rendering it necessary to carry a stick for the purpose of self-defence, and when he was obliged to use it to repel the advances of one cur more forward than others, the rest would attack him furiously, and he would often have to stand at bay and do battle for some time with the brutes until rescued by their owners. But Mr. Tapsell summoned to his aid a trusty friend in the shape of a fine bull-dog, which he had brought from the Bay of Islands. This animal was of great size, immensely powerful, and so ferocious that he was required to be kept constantly on the chain, and him Mr. Tapsell occasionally released for short intervals, which he employed so well that it was seldom he did not tear the throats out of one or more of the swarms of mongrels that infested the place until they began to give Mr. Tapsell's place a wide berth, and when they did come round would approach stealthily and peep round corners to ace if their enemy were at large or not.

But the thievish propensities of these animals was a serious cause of loss. Hens were devoured while sitting in their nests, provisions stolen, and even casks of lard gnawed through and their contents devoured. As a remedy for this, Mr. Tapsell baited with meat a number of fish-hooks, which he hung on the fence surrounding his house, and by this means caught many unsuspicious tykes, whose brains he speedily knocked out, and thus he partially abated the nuisance.

It might seem wonderful why the natives should keep so many live creatures of no service to them, either as food or otherwise, but it appears they used to select the skins of some with a finer description of fur than others, with which to trim the mats of chiefs, and for this slender amount of utility they maintained or rather suffered to exist these droves of worthless creatures. It has been well said that all domestic animals degenerate by companionship with the savage. Even the dog loses its sagacity, honesty, and fidelity, and becomes cowardly, slinking, and treacherous.

(*Daily Southern Cross*, 1867)

Man Bating

ONE AFTERNOON Mr Tapsell saw them returning, dragging what he at first supposed to be posts of the pa where they had been fighting, but which, when they came nearer, proved to be dead bodies, which they brought across the river. One of the slain was a chief of the Ngaiterangi, a near relation of Tupaia's, a great favorite of Mr Tapsell's, with whom he did a considerable trade. He was the first who was cooked and eaten. They prepared him as the bodies of other animals are prepared for food. His head was severed, the body cut open, cleaned, and put into the oven to roast. It happened that he was a tall man, and thin, and after the cannibals had commenced their repast, they jumped up and danced, singing an improvised song derisive of this leanness of their victim and enlarging on the absence of fat on his carcase. The skin of a portion of his body which was elaborately tattooed they made into covers for their cartridge boxes. The other bodies, in number about ten, were then similarly treated, the intestines, as they were taken out, being thrown carelessly on the beach, where a pig of Mr Tapsell's commenced to make a meal of them. This was the first time that he had been compelled to witness the details of a cannibal feast, and the sight turned him quite sick. Getting down his gun, he immediately shot the pig, which a chief named Haupapa, wished to have, but Mr Tapsell threw it into the river, and the ebb tide carried it out to sea.

For a long time after this Mr Tapsell could not bear to eat pork, as scarcely a week occurred in which there was not a battle, and one or two people killed, who were of course eaten like the rest. After that, he always kept his pigs in a sty, so that they should not be able to get human flesh to eat.

Death of Mrs Tapsell.

ABOUT THIS TIME his wife died, who during her last illness entreated him to convey her remains to her own place at the Bay of Islands, and there have them buried, which he promised to do; so after her death, he placed her in a box, which he carefully caulked, and made as air tight as possible, covering it at last with a fine scarlet cloth.

At first there was a great disturbance among the Ngapuhis, to which tribe she belonged, because she had been permitted to die in the house, and had not been brought outside during her last moments.[13] For a while they were disposed to plunder the house of Mr Tapsell because of this infraction of an ancient custom, but Wharepoaka interfering, represented that the tribe and its laws had nothing to do with her, since she had married the white man, with which arguments they were at length pacified, came inside, and had a great lamentation. Before the coffin was closed, each relation took his ornaments from his ear, shark's teeth, and greenstones,[14] and laid them upon the corpse. Some deposited their greenstone meres, and Mr Tapsell, thinking something was required of him, took a valuable Turkish kreese which he wore, and placed it with the rest.[15]

Stabs a Chief.

THIS KREESE HAD BEEN SERVICEABLE on one occasion, when Mr Tapsell was landing a number of kegs of powder which were resting on the beach preparatory to being carried into the store. He gave orders for them to be carried up, but an old chief named Pongo, declared they should not be carried up, as he wanted them all placed in a row, so that he might count them. Mr Tapsell, however, was positive, which appeared to offend the old fellow, who, standing behind him, shook his mere menacingly over his head. Tapsell, turning suddenly round, perceived the gesture, whipped out his kreese in an instant, and with a sweep of his arm inflicted a slight flesh wound on the stomach of the obstructive rangatira,[16] who started back, crying out that he was wounded, on which a dead silence ensued, and the kegs were speedily carried into the store, the old chief never uttering a word.

Mrs. Tapsell's tomb

THE CASE CONTAINING THE BODY of Mr Tapsell's wife together with the ornaments referred to and his kreese, was kept in the flax house till the arrival of the cutter, when Tapsell himself accompanied it to the Bay of Islands where it was buried at Rangiu, Mr King performing the service over the grave.[17]

Before interment however all the relatives of the deceased took their ornaments back out of the coffin; Mr Tapsell wished to take out his kreese also but was prevented, and informed that it must be buried with the corpse. Before leaving the Bay, he caused a wooden monumental structure to be placed over, and a neat railing round the grave.

The tomb was situated on the top of a very high hill. At the time, crowded with people, but afterwards, deserted, as Wharepoaka, being much attached to his sister notified his wish that she should have the place to herself.

NOTES

1. Karuhi and her family were known for their fair skin and hair. Tā moko is the permanent marking of the body or face by Māori. Traditionally, the skin was cut rather than punctured using an uhi (chisel) struck with a mallet, and coloured using pigments. In the nineteenth century, under Pākehā influence, needles came to replace uhi.

2. In the nineteenth century a Lascar was a sailor from Yemen, Somaliland, India or Malaya who was employed on a European ship.

3. A Mr Ferguson also appears on p. 135. It could be the same man mentioned living near Port Underwood (Cook Strait) in Edward Jerningham Wakefield, *Adventure in New Zealand, from 1839 to 1844* (London: John Murray, 1845), Vol. 1, p. 107: 'In Ocean Bay, in which the swell causes a good deal of surf, we saw the timbers of some small vessels which were being built there, and found an old trader named Ferguson who had the reputation of never being sober.' Cf. also Bentley, *Pakeha Maori*, p. 208.

4. Fernroot, aruhe in Māori, was a staple article of diet. Its preparation required much labour with drying, roasting, scraping and pounding.

5. Ngāti Pikiao is an iwi belonging to Te Arawa.

6. This expedition in 1831 is described in Crosby, *The Musket Wars*, pp. 231–33.

7. Mayor Island (Tūhua) lies approximately 35 km north of Tauranga in the Bay of Plenty.

8. Hikareia, a chief and Hōri Tūpaea's uncle.

9. In February 1832, Ngāpuhi Wharepoaka, Titore Takiri and Arama Pi arrived at Otūmoetai pā with 600–800 warriors and an array of artillery including cannons.

10. Otūmoetai pā was one of the earliest pā to be modified to deliver and resist gun and cannon fire. The Ngāpuhi siege of Otūmoetai was the largest intertribal artillery battle of the Musket Wars.

11. Whare is the Māori word for 'house'.

12. Tapsell assisting the Ngāpuhi against Ngāi Te Rangi by providing them with ammunition marked a turnaround in alliances. In 1823, Ngāi Te Rangi had assisted Ngāpuhi under Hongi Hika in their attack on Te Arawa and Mokoia. Te Arawa had always resented Ngāi Te Rangi for helping Ngāpuhi by advising Hongi Hika to attack Te Arawa by using the Pongakawa Stream. Now Tapsell seized the opportunity for revenge. See Crosby, *The Musket Wars*, pp. 252, 267.

13. A tapu (religious restriction) is imposed over the place where someone dies. If death occurs outside, for example in a river, a rāhui (ban on trespassing against a tapu) is placed on the stretch of water to limit access for a period of time. Traditionally, if the death occurred in a house the building would have to be burnt down and later rebuilt by the family.

14. A form of green nephrite jade (pounamu) found in the South Island.

15. A mere is a Māori war club. A kris (or keris) is a dagger with a blade of a wavy form. The knife originates from Malaya but ornamentation with Turkish mountings was popular.

16. A rangatira is a Māori chief.

17. John Thomas King (1789-1854) was one of the first missionaries in New Zealand. He sailed with Samuel Marsden, Thomas Kendall and William Hall to the Bay of Islands in 1814.

8

Wharepoaka

WHAREPOAKA THE BROTHER IN LAW of Mr Tapsell was from the commencement a sterling friend. He was devoid of all those meannesses and greed which characterize so many of the Maori race. He never begged, but on the contrary was generous and liberal. He would call every now and then at Mr Tapsell's dwelling and enquire how the harness cask was filled,[1] and when informed that only two or three pieces of pork remained would depart, and presently return with a couple of fine grunters which some of his people would kill and cut up in a very short space of time.

His affection for his sister was very great, and his solicitude during her last illness extreme. The moment she expired, he ran out to the top of a high hill and called aloud to the Atua, praying him to direct the spirit of his departed sister on the right road.[2] There was a trace of the sublime in such an act. It did not accord with the then prevailing faith of Europeans then that such an intercession after death would [...]

A Maori prince

THE BROTHER OF WHAREPOAKA and Hongi, the great chiefs of the Ngapuhi availed themselves of an opportunity to visit Europe, and when there were presented to King George III with whom they had the honor of shaking hands, and who conferred on them titles of nobility, the relative of Wharepoaka receiving the cognomen of Prince Waikato, together with a very handsome gold mounted double barrelled gun upon which this name was engraved.[3]

The character of the New Zealander is never at any time remarkable for the abnegation of self, and this interview with Royalty had no tendency to promote humility in the minds of the two Maoris who frequently let Mr Tapsell know that they had attained a dignity to which he might in vain aspire. "Who are you?", one would say, "I have shaken hands with the King, and you would not be allowed even to see him."

Before leaving the Bay, three run-away sailors, an Englishman, and two Americans, came to Mr Tapsell and begged him to take them along with him, as they were very miserable. The natives there, claiming them as slaves, they were purchased from them for a musket each and brought in the cutter to the South.

Jealousy of traders

THE JEALOUSY BETWEEN THE EUROPEANS, and their anxiety to secure monopoly of the trade, were so great, that means were resorted to by one to injure the other, and even to take his life, less justifiable and scarcely less atrocious than those practised by the savages themselves. Thus, in one instance, as we have seen, a trader plotted to have Mr. Tapsell shot while asleep under the shelter of his roof and enjoying his hospitality; in another, three men whom he rescued from slavery contemplated kidnapping and maiming him for life, long after one in his own employ offered another a sum of money if he would "put Tapsell out of the way." Subsequently, a trader persuaded a number of chiefs to repudiate their debts to Mr. Tapsell, in order himself to secure the flax they had brought in payment; and another, during an absence of the latter in Sydney, industriously circulated amongst the natives a report that Tapsell had been hung, and would not return, and appropriated to himself (out of Tapsell's effects) an order for a large sum of money which he succeeded in converting. Such extraordinary and base conduct amongst a few traders living isolated amongst savages, and whose lives at times were not worth a moment's purchase, may well excite surprise; but it must be remembered that the hazardous nature of the trade prevented many from embarking in it, and merchants from being at all times nice in the selection of their agents, with some of whom an absence of law, and the prospect of enriching themselves at the expense of their neighbours, proved a temptation too strong to [be] resisted.

(*Daily Southern Cross*, 1867)

Tautara attacks Matata[4]

DURING MR TAPSELL'S ABSENCE from Maketu, Tautara, a chief of Whakatane, who had a bitter animosity against Rangitikina, the head chief at Matata, persuaded about three hundred of the Ngapuhis to start with him from Maketu in the middle of the night, unknown to Wharepoaka in order to make an attack on Rangitikina's settlement at Matata.[5] The alarm was given of the approach of the enemy, and by the time Tautara had reached the place, Rangitikina with his wife and family had escaped in a canoe to Whakatane.

Mr George White, who was then purchasing flax for Mr Tapsell, with his wife, a daughter of Rangitikina, were left behind, his wife taken prisoners, the Ngapuhis plundering the house and store of all the goods they contained, and burning a large quantity of flax which was ready for shipment.[6] Two women were also taken prisoners, and the party returned to Maketu.

When Mr Tapsell came back in the cutter from The Bay of Islands anchored in the river at Maketu, Mr White came off in a canoe, dressed in his shirt and trousers, the only clothing he was able to save when the Ngapuhis made their midnight attack. He communicated this disaster to Mr Tapsell and informed him that his wife was now a slave to the Ngapuhis, on which Mr Tapsell induced Wharepoaka to negotiate for her ransom with the man who claimed her as his property. The man consented, and she was purchased by Mr Tapsell for a double barrelled gun which had cost eighteen pounds.

121

Taking of the 'Hose'

THERE WAS ABOUT THIS TIME a brig called the Hose lying under Whale Island for the purpose of loading with pork, and the captain was killing pigs on shore.[7] In this vessel a boy named Cape, a son of Toihau, a chief of Whakatane, was on board, and his brother Narara coming alongside asked him how he had been used, to which he replied that he had been ill treated by the mate, who had thrown him overboard.[8] On receipt of this intelligence, Narara went ashore and mustered a number of natives who went off in two canoes and boarded the Hose, shooting the chief mate and several of the hands. The second mate climbed up the rigging, where a shot from below broke one of his arms. The captain on shore, observing that the vessel was in possession of the Maoris, launched his boat and pulled away as hard as he could for Tauranga, where he found the Prince of Denmark, of which Captain Clarke was commander, who no sooner was informed of the circumstance, than he set sail at once for Whale Island, and, a strong North west wind blowing at the time, he ran down the distance very quickly.[9] The natives in possession of the Hose, when they saw the Prince of Denmark bearing down upon them, took to their canoes and made for the main land, having first plundered the vessel of every thing, unbent the sails, and taken away the second mate as a prisoner.[10]

It would have fared very badly with him but for a chief of the Arawa named Tohi, now known as Beckham who interfered to save his life and took him under his protection, ultimately conveying him to Tauranga, where he delivered him up to Captain Clark, who on asking what he demanded as payment, was answered that no payment was required; nevertheless, he made the Chief a present of a fowling piece.

A strong dose

SHORTLY AFTER THIS HAD OCCURRED, Captain Stewart called with the New Zealander at Whakatane,[11] where Narara came on board, and was presented with a glass of grog in which more than a hundred drops of laudanum had been put with a view of killing him, but the dose was too strong, and defeated its object, the chief throwing it up when he got into the canoe. On the next trip, Narara came off again,[12] and when alongside a Maori woman called Kokopet living on board, called out to him to keep away, or the white man would kill him.[13] "Oh, no," said he, "the white men are too fond of me for that," came on board, and went into the cabin as before, for a glass of grog, of which he was very fond. The Captain gave him the grog, and then told him to go into his canoe, as the vessel was about to get under weigh. He accordingly went on deck, but was suddenly seized with a presentiment, which made him very uneasy, for instead of going boldly over the side, he crouched down at the gang way. Again he was told to hurry over the side, and the Captain went down into the cabin. He had no sooner got into the canoe than a discharge of muskets from the deck of the vessel took place, and he fell dead, pierced by four or five balls. From Whakatane, Captain Stewart went to Hickson's Bay, where he landed his second mate with goods to trade for flax.[14] At this place there had been previously a European named Taylor, who was trading for flax.[15]

A leap for life.

TOIHAU, THE FATHER OF NARARA on hearing of the death of his son, determined to have revenge, and hearing that the second mate of the New Zealander was landed at Hickson's Bay, proceeded thither, killed Taylor, and was about to take the life of the second mate, whom he had bound hand and foot with that intention, when he saw a vessel bearing down on the Bay, and a boat approaching the shore. Thinking that the second mate would be of service in decoying the boat's crew to land, he desired him to hail the boat, and induce the crew to come on shore; on which the second mate represented to him that if they saw him bound, they would fear to land, but if he were released, they would believe that no harm was intended. This proposition appearing feasible, he was relieved of his bonds, and placed on a rock which the boat could easily approach.

When it was within a short distance the second mate hailed the crew, told them what had occurred, the plot to capture and massacre them, and desired them to throw the steer-oar into the water. He said he could not swim, but he would leap into the water and endeavour to grasp the oar. They did what he desired; he leaped into the surf, and succeeded in getting hold of the steer-oar, and was picked up by the boat. The Maoris fired from the shore doing no injury, the sailors returned a volley, and pulled off in safety to the ship.

Thus Toihau had killed one European in revenge for the death of his son, but was not satisfied, having been heard to say that the life of Taylor was not sufficient payment, as he was only a taurikarika,[16] while his son Narara was a chief, and he expressed his determination to have the head of Tapsell, who was a chief like his son, and with that he would be satisfied.

Toihau's trap

ABOUT THIS TIME a chief of Matata named Kopenga offered to purchase flax,[17] and applied to Mr Tapsell for goods to trade with. Mr Tapsell then applied to the natives for a crew to pull him down to Matata, but was refused the people reminding him of Toihau's threat to take his head. On which he told them if they did not provide him with a crew he would walk thither, when they furnished him with about forty men, all well armed.

Kopenga's place was a considerable distance up the river at Matata, taking the best part of the day to pull up, so that it was towards evening before Mr

Tapsell arrived, and in consequence stayed there that night. In the morning he inspected the house, weighed the flax, and was satisfied that there was a prospect of trade to be done. About the middle of the day the natives prepared a feast for the visitors, and a pig was being cooked in the oven, when all at once, an undefined misgiving came over Mr Tapsell's mind and he determined to start homewards without waiting for the food which was prepared. The crew objected, wishing to wait for the dinner which had been cooked, but he insisted on setting off without delay. Accordingly they pulled down the river, and when about the mouth, met two men who enquired whither they were going. The crew returned answer that the pakeha was mad, as he had insisted on leaving Kopenga's place without waiting for his food. The men stated that if the canoe went out to sea it would infallibly be capsized, as bad weather was coming on. Mr Tapsell all the while had been watching the clouds, and observed that they were setting in from the Eastward. The crew called his attention to what the two men had been saying, but he still insisted that they should proceed, and when they were out at sea a nice easterly breeze set in, and they made their way in safety to Maketu.

He afterwards learned that Toihau had gone up the river with two canoes full of armed men, on purpose to intercept him and his party, and they certainly would have succeeded in doing so, had the party remained to the dinner provided for them.

After this Mr Tapsell took down Mr White to Matata with a fresh supply of goods for the purposes of trade, and arriving there proceeded down the river to Whakatane where Rangitikina was fortifying himself in a strong pa for fear of the Ngapuhi. Toihau was also there, at the time, to whom Mr Tapsell at once addressed, saying: "I understand you intend to take my head, and have come here to save you the trouble."

"Oh," replied he, "that was only talk."

A night at Matata

THIS WAS ALL THAT PASSED, and Mr Tapsell then proceeded down the river to Whakatane where he left Mr White with his trade, after which he returned seaward to Matata, where off that place experiencing a severe gale, which, together with the ebb tide made it a matter of extreme difficulty to get inside the river, even with the united exertion of the crew, who jumped out and towed the canoe with ropes against the tide. The party were completely drenched with the spray and rain which fell in torrents, but fortunately there were some unoccupied huts in which they sought shelter, lighting fires within. The one occupied by Mr Tapsell took fire accidentally, and for a while his party thought he was burned inside, but by and by he emerged unhurt.

After a short stay, when the gale had moderated they embarked for Maketu which they reached in safety.

The house at Maketu

IN ADDITION TO THE STORE and house at the foot of the cliff, Mr Tapsell had now a house on the top which he used as a dwelling, of very superior construction, fitted up and around with cedar lockers, with carved work all over; the spaces between the upright timber, being tastefully seeded in different colours. Besides this, there was a building for storing flax, a hundred and twenty feet long and forty broad, and in addition, a battery of twelve guns commanding the harbor and entrance.

Makutu men[18]

BATTLES WITH THE NGAETERANGI were now very frequent, scarcely a week passing over without one occurring, in one of which, Tipitipi, a noted chief, of the Arawa, was killed. Being a man of great distinction he was placed on a scaffold erected for the purpose at the foot of the cliff, and a number of prophets and Makutu men commenced their incantations.

These men, in most, if not all cases, imposters, possessed a strange hold on the credulity of the others, who refused to perceive the clumsy and transparent deceptions practised by them. When the spirit of prophesy came upon them, or, as they termed it, when the atua was in them — which was very often, the rest of the people would sit in a circle round them and listen reverently to their oracular sayings, now and then interrupting them with questions, which they answered in a tone of voice different to their natural one, The voice of the atua as uttered by them was a sort of whine, and the words, though generally senseless gibberish often artfully arranged like the sayings of the Delphic oracle, and made to cut both ways. But in many cases it resembled the impositions of professed mesmerists amongst ourselves, who permit strangers to converse with clairvoyant subjects. It would sometimes run in the following fashion;

Eager enquirer. "Where have you been to?"

Prophet. "I have been into the pa of the enemy at Tumu."

E.Q. "and what did you see there?"

The Prophet's next move would be a play of imagination, in which he would tax his invention and keep as near probabilities as possible. Presently he would say:– "I am going?" to which the enquirer, perhaps a confederate, would respond by asking whither, and the prophet answer, Tauranga or elsewhere, as the case might be, and so the consultation would drag its stupid length along.

On one occasion a Makutu woman under a prophetic impulse was talking to herself all day long and part of the night. A number of people with their dogs were clustered round the door of her whare listening in the darkness to her inspired gibberish. Suddenly, she claimed "Drive away those dogs, what are they doing here?" Her behest was obeyed, the dogs driven away, and her admirers left in amazement at her wonderful power of vision.

A Miracle

THE BODY OF TIPITIPI, being placed on the scaffold before mentioned, became the object of sundry mysterious rites performed by a goodly number of Makutu men, who went through many antics and gesticulations, praying every now and then after their fashion, and occasionally exclaiming "He'll turn soon, "He'll turn soon." They had prophesied that if the corpse should turn towards Tumu, victory would be on the side of the people at Maketu, while if it turned the other way, the fate of war would be against them. At last, by some sleight of hand, or by knocking away some previously arranged support, which Mr Tapsell was not near enough to see, the corpse turned partly round towards Tumu, and the admiring crowd shouted aloud with exultation at the wonderful miracle.

It happened that the Maketu people were victorious in the next engagement, and so the prophets' infallibility was established.

The widow's sacrifice

THE SUICIDE OF THE WIDOW of a chief was a prevailing custom at that time, and one of the victims of the war then going on was an influential chief of the Ngapuhi who had been shot in the head from the wound of which the brains continued to run away for the two days he survived. When he died, his wife who had been watching him all the time, stole away to a neighbour whare and procured a stout fishing line. It was known for what purpose she had obtained it, and Mr Tapsell tried to prevent her accomplishing her end, but was frustrated by those around, and she hung herself on one of a clump of trees still remaining near the mouth of the river at Maketu. After some time had elapsed Mr Tapsell went to see if she had completed her self destruction, and found her depending from a branch which had given way, on her knees, and with a smile on her face. Tapsell took from his pocket a small piece of black ribbon, which he tied round her wrist, and left her. One of Mr Tapsell's boat's crew of a merry and jocular disposition and having the reputation of not knowing fear, had often expressed a wish to become possessed of a soldier's coat, of which Mr Tapsell had several. This day the latter, desirous of testing the man's courage, informed him of the ribbon round the woman's wrist and promised him a soldier's coat if he would go in the dead of night and bring it away. A very great repugnance to stir out at night is a feature of Maori superstition. The man departed, and speedily returned, bringing back the ribbon. He confessed that he grew frightened as he got near the trees, and crawled on his hands and knees, averting his face and taking off the ribbon without looking. As he had fairly earned his reward he received the promised coat. Not one Maori in a thousand would at that time have performed the same feat.

Dr Tapsell

DURING THE FREQUENT BATTLES occurring at the period Tapsell's skill in medicine and surgery was frequently called into requisition. Some of the wounds were of a very curious kind. In one man a bullet had entered one ear and passed out at the other. Mr Tapsell did all that possibly could be done in such a case. He stopped the apertures with cotton dipped in Riga Balsam,[19] and the man was conveyed to Rotorua.

Some months after the same man returned to Maketu perfectly well. The ball had evaded the brain. Tareha, a Ngapuhi, had his hand nearly blown off by the bursting of a gun. This was dressed daily till he recovered.

On one occasion Mr Tapsell was cutting a ball out of a wounded man when the ball bounced out and fell on the ground. A relation of the patient standing by, picked up the ball, put it into his mouth, and chewed it savagely till it was reduced to powder.

A mission of peace

IT WAS JUST THEN that Mr Williams arrived for the Bay of Islands, and being desirous of putting a stop to the fighting that was going on, requested Mr Tapsell to make overtures of peace to the enemy at Tumu, which he consented to do. He was surprised and grieved to find that his wife, a woman of Waikato, intended to accompany him, nor could all his arguments dissuade her from her purpose. At length he said, "If any thing should happen, your blood be upon your own head." He hoisted the ensign and desired Mr Williams to observe through the telescope if any ambush were prepared for him, and in that case to haul it down and then set out on his journey. But when the people in the pah saw him approaching they all cried out, "Haere mai, haere mai,"[20] and waved their blankets in token of welcome, and when he got inside the pah, one of the leading chiefs seized Tapsell's wife round the neck, touched noses with her, and cried mournfully, ordering the best musket in the store to be given her as a present. Mr Tapsell's mission was not altogether successful. He was told that his people the Arawa were exceedingly treacherous and deceitful,[21] and only wanted an opportunity to commit murders to which Mr Tapsell replied that he thought not, but was answered warningly by the others, that he did not know his people. Nevertheless they assured him that they would not be the first to fire. When Mr Tapsell returned with these tidings, the principal part of the Ngapuhi went to Rotorua on a visit, and about a week after, a canoe from the Southward loaded with provisions for Tumu made its appearance off Maketu heads, where the wind fell away and it was becalmed. It contained only three men. No sooner did the natives on shore perceive the situation of the craft and its doomed passengers than they launched their canoes in spite of the endeavours and urgent remonstrances of Mr Tapsell, speedily overtook the stranger, murdered the unfortunate crew, and brought their bodies ashore where they went "the way" of all human 'flesh' in the good old Maori days.

NOTES

1. A harness cask is a tub or barrel that contains salted provisions.
2. The word atua is used to refer to one of the Māori gods or spirits, but also to a Christian conception of one god. In spite of Wharepoaka's lifelong friendship with the missionary Samuel Marsden, he was never baptised and his attitude towards Christianity remained somewhat ambivalent.
3. King George III is a mistake for George IV here. Hongi Hika and Waikato visited England in 1820 with Thomas Kendall. While there they helped the Cambridge Professor Samuel Lee (1783–1852) to produce a workable Māori orthography, grammar and dictionary. The two chiefs were popular in London society and introduced to George IV. The king gave the two gifts including muskets and Hongi also received a suit of armour.
4. Tautari ('Tautara') was a Ngāti Pūkeko chief from around Whakatāne, eastern Bay of Plenty. He lived with his wife's family at Lake Rotoehu and was a leader of Ngāti Pikiao. Matatā is located about 25 km northwest of Whakatāne.

Waikato, Hongi Hika and Thomas Kendall. Waikato (left) and Hongi (centre) are wearing kiwi feather cloaks (kahu kiwi) and both are carrying a greenstone club (mere pounamu). Hongi is also holding a thrusting weapon (taiaha). Kendall (right) is holding a copy of the Bible. The oil painting was painted by James Barry (fl. 1818–46) in England in 1820.

G-618: Alexander Turnbull Library, National Library of New Zealand · Te Puna Mātauranga o Aotearoa, Wellington

5. Rangitekina ('Rangitikina') was a chief of Ngāti Awa whose chief pā was at Matatā.
6. George White arrived in the Bay of Plenty in the 1820s and was one of the first settlers there. He was married to Ringa Ono, a daughter of Rangitekina, and became Tapsell's flax trader at Matatā.
7. The Sydney brig *Haweis* ('Hose') was under Captain John James at the time it was captured.
8. 'Cape' is Te Kēpa, son of the chief Toihau. On Te Kēpa's brother Ngārara and his death and its consequences, see Stephenson Percy Smith, *Maori Wars of the Nineteenth Century* (Christchurch: Whitcombe and Tombs, 1910), pp. 416–22.
9. The *Prince of Denmark* was a schooner (126 tons, built in 1798 in Scotland) under Captain John Clark (cf. p. 93). Whale Island, Moutohorā (from Motu-tohorā, 'Whale Island'), is an island measuring just 1.43 km² in the Bay of Plenty, about 9 km north of Whakatāne.
10. A different account of the capture and ransoming of a member of the *Haweis* crew can be found in C.W. Vennell, *The Brown Frontier; New Zealand Historical Stories and Studies, 1806–1877* (Wellington: A.H. & A.W. Reed, 1967), p. 84; Bentley, *Pakeha Maori*, p. 72.
11. Captain John Stewart (cf. p. 106).
12. The archaic phrase 'came off' means that he came away from a place in which he had been.
13. The name Kokopet should possibly be Kokope, Kokopeti or Kokopū ('trout').
14. Hickson's Bay is probably a mistake for Hicks Bay (Wharekahika, Gisborne).
15. Possibly the Taylor referred to in Joseph Angus McKay, *Historic Poverty Bay and the East Coast, North Island, New Zealand* (Gisborne: McKay · Poverty Bay-East Coast Centennial Council, 1949), p. 115.
16. Taurekareka ('taurikarika') is the Māori word for slave.
17. Te Kupenga ('Kopenga') was a chief.
18. Mākutu is the Māori word for black magic or sorcery.
19. Riga Balsam (Latvian: *Rīgas balzams*) is an alcoholic beverage infused with herbs that is often used in traditional medicine.
20. Haere mai means welcome.
21 This is the most explicit indication that Tapsell was considered a member of a Māori iwi, although the following statement ('he did not know his people') suggests that he was considered a novice or somewhat ignorant of the ways of his iwi.

129

9

Battle at Maketu

AFTER THE OUTRAGE mentioned in the last chapter, the fighting began again as badly as ever, engagements being frequent and numbers being killed on both sides, each party taking the slain bodies of the enemy to feast on. So frequent were the battles, that scarcely a week passed over without a banquet of human flesh. The custom was for the enemy to come from Tumu and give the challenge to those residing at Maketu, advancing within short musket range so near that the balls used to whistle about Mr Tapsell as he walked round his battery.[1]

There were holes dug in the top of the hill where the women and children usually took shelter when the firing commenced, and here they entreated Mr Tapsell to seek cover assuring him that otherwise he would be shot, but he always declined, and never was wounded.

The battery

THE CHALLENGE ALWAYS CAME from the Ngaiterangi, the Maketu natives remaining quiet until challenged, when the chiefs would call out to their men to get ready and go across to meet the enemy, on such occasions, Mr Tapsell took his station on the battery and watched proceedings through the telescope, his guns all loaded with five hundred balls each, besides large shot. One gun was placed at the foot of the hill facing the swamp and left bank of the river, by which the place could be approached and which side the battery did not command, and this was similarly loaded to the others. On inspecting this gun one day, Mr Tapsell to his mortification found that all the balls had been drawn.[2] He took the people to task for this misconduct, informing them that he had placed the gun there for their protection, and they had disabled it; to which they replied, "Well, but you could only have fired once with it, and see how many times we could fire with the balls."

The battery was useful as a menace to the advancing foe, who would no doubt have invaded and taken Maketu but for fear of the big guns, although Mr Tapsell never fired upon with intention to injure them, as they were his people as well as the Ngapuhi and Arawa, and brought him their share of flax.

Ngaeterangi defeated

ONE OF THE LAST BATTLES which took place before the departure of the Ngapuhi for the Bay of Islands, had nearly resulted in the discomfiture of the allied forces of the Arawa and Ngapuhi, who had set out for Tumu, and were then engaged with the enemy, the firing being plainly audible at Maketu. All the men able to bear arms had gone on the expedition, and none but women and children were left behind, except Mr Tapsell, who from his battery watched the progress of events through his telescope. Early in the day, an old prophet came running in great haste from towards Waihi,[3] and called out to the women, "Bear a hand! Bear a hand! and put me across the river. This day is ours. I have had a dream." They put him across, and he disappeared in the distance. But later on in the day, Mr Tapsell perceived his people retreating towards Maketu, and exchanging occasional shots with the enemy as they came. The shorts were few and far between, and it became evident to Mr Tapsell that this was owing to the ammunition being exhausted. Some of the retreating party had already arrived at the bank of the river, and were preparing to cross, when Mr Tapsell desired a white man living with him to go into the magazine, open one of the cases of ammunition, and send women off with cartridge, without loss of time. This was done; half a dozen women were loaded with as many cartridges as they could carry, and sent off to meet the retiring force, amongst whom the ammunition was speedily distributed and the firing suddenly became rapid, and the enemy took to their heels and fled to Tumu. The now victorious Arawa and Ngapuhi followed them up closely, entering the pa with them killing great numbers, and taking possession. The Ngaeterangi bolted from the pa, and fled by the beach for Tauranga. Thus the people of Maketu were victorious as the old prophet had foretold, though they were indebted for their victory to Mr Tapsell's timely supply of ammunition.

The banquet.

WHEN THE PARTY returned in triumph with a great supply of bodies the invariable carnival ensued legs and arms were cut off, and bodies chopped up, and thrust into ovens for the banquet. If a chief were amongst the slain, his head was taken off and cured, first by scraping out the contents, then placing it for a certain time in the oven till the flesh became set, then oiling it, and putting it in the sun, after which it was deposited with other precious relics in one of the tapu'd houses.

After this battle the Ngapuhi returned to the Bay of Islands, Mr Tapsell making a present of his large canoe to his brother in law, Mr Wharepoaka.

A wife bewitched.

IN THE LAST CHAPTER allusion was made to the faith in witchcraft so general amongst the New Zealanders. An instance of which may be mentioned here.

Mr Tapsell's wife, after living with him on the best of terms, ran away one night, and when found after a long search, refused to return. Her uncle gave it as his opinion that she was bewitched, and applied to two or three different Makutu men to remove the spell, but they failed to do so, as they were "not strong enough". At last, an old woman came forward and declared her ability to take off the spell, and then desired the uncle to procure for her a potato from the plate of Mr Tapsell, to be taken without his knowledge, while he was eating. Accordingly the uncle seated himself beside Mr Tapsell while at meal, and when the attention of the latter was partially diverted, he was surprised and much displeased to perceive the uncle stealthily snatch a potato from his plate. He rose up in great anger, just in time to see the uncle make a sudden exit through the door. The old woman prayed over the potato, which she took to the fugitive wife, who eat it, and afterwards returned to her husband, in a cheerful frame of mind, and with a smile on her countenance, and it might almost be said, as in the story books, "lived long and happily for ever afterwards" but for a calamity which the sequel will show.

A witch's prophecy.

SOON AFTERWARDS, the same old woman applied to Mr Tapsell for a pair of blankets which she offered to pay him for, in flax by and by, but he, not feeling quite sure of the payment, declined to supply her. The old woman in anger, remarked, "I do not want his blankets for nothing, I can scrape flax as well as others to pay him for them. Never mind, I will make him very sorry. He and his wife shall have many children, and they shall part. Mr Tapsell, hearing of this, and not wishing to offend the prejudices of those amongst whom he lived, gave the old woman the blankets, which she subsequently paid for in flax.

The singular part of the story is that he and his wife had a numerous family, and did part at last, the latter being shot at Orakau, for which he "was very very sorry".[4]

Natives outwitted.

IT WAS AFTER THIS that Hikairo, a chief living on Mokoia Island, in Lake Rotorua,[5] invited Mr Tapsell to send a white man there to trade for flax representing the great advantages that would ensue, and the large quantity of flax that could be obtained to which Mr Tapsell agreed, sending a man named Farrow with a quantity of goods for that purpose, and with instructions to write every week and let him know how matters went on.[6] For some weeks At first the letters were very encouraging, stating that about eighty or ninety baskets of flax had been purchased, but after that, each letter that came stated that the natives had suddenly given up scraping flax, and had begun to look upon the goods sent there as their own, which they could take when they pleased. Upon which Mr Tapsell wrote a letter by a special messenger, an American negro, directing Farrow to pack up all the goods amongst the flax and bring them to Maketu,

It happened that a Mr Scott, also trading for flax at Tauranga, hearing of the commencement of a nice trade at Rotorua, sent up a man with goods to open a rival establishment, but he was too late, and did not succeed in doing any business.[7]

When Hikairo found that Tapsell had successfully smuggled all his goods away, he was very furious, and vowed vengeance against him, saying that he was a robber, and had removed his goods like a thief.

The pakeha a victim

MR SCOTT ALSO, was of opinion that he had done wrong, and declared his intention to demand his goods boldly, and take them away in the light of day.

Accordingly he went to Rotorua, accompanied by two men, and all armed with pistols, cutlasses and muskets.

When there, he asked the chief where his goods were. The chief informed him that they were in a house which he pointed out, but on looking within, no goods were to be seen. He returned to the chief, and told him that his goods were not there. "Oh," said the chief, "pointing out another house, "they are in that one". But this house when examined was found to be empty. He remonstrated with the chief for making a fool of him, and the chief replied, "You shall have your trade by and by," and sure enough, the goods were presently brought down, and placed in a tiwai or canoe wanting the top streak.[8]

Mr Scott stationed a man with a drawn cutlass in the canoe to guard the goods while he conversed with the chiefs on shore; but while this conversation was being carried on, a canoe full of natives stole alongside the tiwai, the unfortunate sentry was seized by the hair of the head, dragged into the water, his throat cut, and his body quartered. The sight of blood, as in the tiger, seemed to inflame all the evil passion of the Maoris and to whet their appetite for more, and they would have made short work of Mr Scott and his companion, but for the timely arrival of Haupapa and Tongaroa,[9] two very influential chiefs from Maketu who pulled them into a tapu'd house, and protected them till the passions of the murderers had subsided, when they were allowed to depart, which they were only too glad to do with their lives, and without the goods they had come to remove.

At this time a chief of Waikato, named Mudipara had requested Mr Tapsell to send him a white man to trade for flax,[10] which Mr Tapsell promised to do when he could procure one and the opportunity occurred by the arrival of a vessel consigned to him from Sydney, which had come by way of Cook's Straits, bringing as passenger a Mr Clementson who was induced to undertake the agency at Waikato.[11] He had come to New Zealand under the following remarkable circumstances.

An eventful voyage

HE HAD SAILED FROM ENGLAND to Sydney as chief mate in a brig commanded by a Captain Stewart, which sailed thence for New Zealand on a trading voyage for flax.[12] At one of the places where she touched, to the southward of Turanganui, a chief named Raupara, made application for a passage for himself and a party of his people to the Chatham Islands, promising to furnish a large quantity of flax.[13]

On arrival at the Chatham Islands Raupara and his men murdered the unoffending and defenceless inhabitants, bringing away in the brig the women and children as prisoners, and the bodies of the slain to feed upon.[14] On the vessel's return voyage to the main land, these bodies were actually cooked in the ship's coppers, the captain not interfering to prevent it.

The captain did not succeed in procuring so much flax as he expected, and returned to Hobart Town, where Clementson left her, and accepted command of the brig Bee, chartered by a man known by the name of Lincoln Bill, an old convict, who had a quantity of goods on board which there is every reason to believe had been improperly acquired, as, when the vessel was about to sail, constables were sent on board to detain him.[15] But Lincoln Bill made the constables drunk, got the vessel under weigh, and sailed with them for Peru; on the way, putting into Tauranga and Cook's Straits at the latter of which places, he presented a pistol at the head of Clementson and ordered him to go ashore. There, Clementson remained with a Mr Ferguson,[16] then trading for flax, until the arrival of the vessel consigned to Mr Tapsell, by which he came as passenger to Maketu and landed, Lincoln Bill was afterwards hung in Peru.

Journey to Waikato

THE CONSENT OF CLEMENTSON being obtained, Mr Tapsell, Mr White, and he, went to Mata Mata on the Waikato,[17] to gain knowledge of the prospects of a trade there, travelling overland by way of Rotorua, taking several natives as guides, and to carry provisions for the road. For a part of the way the journey was very severe, over a succession of steep mountains, the sides of which were like precipices, and through the forest of Patatere, which was so dense, and obstructed with undergrowth and supplejack that their passage through it was toilsome beyond measure.[18]

Mata Mata at that time was an exceedingly beautiful place, and provisions of all kinds very abundant.

A great feast was prepared on the arrival of the party from Maketu. Pigs were killed and roasted, baskets of eels prepared, and stacks of potatoes sufficient for a hundred men; in addition to which a large number of live pigs were sent for the party to kill for themselves. To their abundant provision the Maoris of the party did sample justice, getting up in the middle of the night to renew their repast, and feeding to repletion.

The negotiations with Mudipara were satisfactory, and Mr Clementson was left behind, the rest of the party returning to Maketu.

During Mr Tapsell's absence, a chief of Tauranga collected a number of men, about two hundred, and was about to proceed to Maketu and plunder the store, the opportunity being favorable, as most of the people were scattered at some distance, employed in scraping flax. He would have put his design in execution but for the interference of Tupaia who prevented him from going.

Voyage in the Whale boat.

MR TAPSELL'S CUTTER not answering her purpose, he sent her to Sydney to be sold, and, being desirous of settling with the Bay of Islands people for flax received, started in a whaleboat with a crew of five, and, if the weather had been fair — a sufficient supply of provisions. But when off Motiti, or Flat Island, a strong gale set in with thick, hazy weather, so that it was impossible to see for any distance ahead. The Maori crew became frightened, lay down in the bottom of the boat, and refused to stir, making sure that they were all about to be drowned. To add to the disaster, the step of the mast gave way,[19] and the sail came down. This added to the terror of the crew, who still refused to move, and Mr Tapsell had, unassisted, to rig a new step for the mast by means of a pocket knife. While the boat was not under canvas she shipped a sea which spoiled all the biscuit and provisions of the Maoris, rendering them unfit for food. When the Maoris saw that Mr Tapsell had succeeded in again hoisting the sail, they remonstrated, saying that they would all be drowned, but Mr Tapsell ridiculed their fears, and made for Mayor Island. There they found a tremendous surf breaking on the beach so that the boat could not land, and the fears of the natives were renewed, but Mr Tapsell took them under the lee of the land where the sea was quite smooth, and where they beached to boat, hauling her up, turning her over, and lighting a fire. A good glass of brandy of which there was a keg in the boat reanimated the drenched crew, who were loud in their expressions of approval, exclaiming in tones of delight, "Pakeha! Pakeha!"

Some natives of Mayor Island, who had seen the boat approaching, now paid them a visit having walked across the island for that purpose. In those days every one was afraid of his neighbour, and Mr Tapsell when he saw them coming, told his crew that he would only give them a small quantity of grog, but would make the strangers drunk, which he did, and before they had slept off the fumes of the brandy, launched the boat, and was under weigh out to sea.

Arrival at the Bay

THE WIND STILL CONTINUED to blow a gale, and when off the Little Barrier, Mr Tapsell thought it advisable to run in for shelter, finding a large cave, in which they took up their quarters, for about three weeks.[20] Their provisions being wet with sea water, they would have fared very badly, but for finding great numbers of pigeons, which they had no difficulty in shooting. At length the weather became more calm, they ventured on their way, and arrived in the Bay of Islands in the night time. Mr Tapsell desired his crew not to let the people in the Bay know of his arrival till morning, but a woman chancing to become acquainted with the face came in and recognized him. The long voyage had exhausted the contents of his brandy keg, and, being weary and parched with thirst, he asked the woman for a drink of water, on which she went away and presently returned with a pannikin of gin,[21] which Mr Tapsell considered the most welcome beverage he ever had. In the morning, when the news of his arrival had spread abroad, all the people came down to see him and had a great cry in memory of his departed wife. He remained there for three weeks, and chartered a vessel to go to Tauranga and load up with flax. Before the vessel sailed, Wharepoaka presented him with about twenty acres of land at Rangiu, which had become tapu in consequence of his sister having committed suicide upon it.

As soon as the cargo was on board in Tauranga the captain and he walked by the beach to Maketu.

A case of leprosy

A FAVORITE BOY of Mr Tapsell's, of very clever parts, who had learned to speak English with remarkable facility, and whom Mr Tapsell had left in suffering from a lingering disease, which from the symptoms, appears to have been leprosy, was overjoyed at his return, exclaiming that this was all he was waiting for, as but for the hope of his coming he would have been dead long ago. Mr Tapsell gave him a small quantity of laudanum and brandy to ease his sufferings and left him. In the morning he was dead. He was buried in the battery between two guns, and a salute fired out of respect for his relatives, who were influential chiefs.

NOTES

1. Tapsell had surrounded his home with 12 cannons.
2. When Tapsell discovers that the cannon balls have been 'drawn', it means that they have been pulled out and removed.

3. Waihi is situated in Waikato at the foot of the Coromandel Peninsula and on the western edge of the Bay of Plenty.

4. The Battle of Ōrākau pā (31 March 2 April 1864) was the culmination of the invasion of Waikato — the most important military campaign of the New Zealand Wars (1845–72). It was fought between the New Zealand government, British army and Māori allies on the one hand, and on the other, an alliance of iwi known as the Māori King Movement (Kīngitanga) that aimed to stem the spread of Pākehā power. The movement was defeated by colonial powers at Ōrākau and the Kīngitanga warriors withdrew into the forested areas of the western North Island, now known as King Country.

5. Wiremu Hikairo (1780/90–1851) was a chief of Ngāti Rangiwewehi of Te Arawa confederation of iwi and hapū.

6. James ('Hemi') Farrow (c.1800–80) was born in London and arrived in Tauranga in 1829 to acquire flax for Australian merchants in exchange for gunpowder and muskets. He married a local Māori girl and settled in Otūmoetai. He purchased half an acre of land at the western end of the pā from chiefs Tūpaea, Tangimoana and Te Omanu on 10 January 1838 — this is the first authenticated land purchase in the Bay for which a Crown Grant was later issued. When Tapsell arrived in Maketū, Farrow became his agent in Tauranga. He remarried in 1861 and retired in Auckland where he died on 3 November 1880. The *New Zealand Gazette* and *Wellington Spectator*, 21 January 1843, includes an article on how Farrow's schooner was stolen and used in an attack on Mayor Island.

7. David Scott was one of the earliest flax traders in Tauranga.

8. A tīwai is a canoe without attached sides, a hull or a dugout. The description 'wanting the top streak' means lacking the top boards (rauawa) or sides of the canoe.

9. Tangaroa ('Tongaroa') was a powerful chief from Maketū pā.

10. Chief Murupara ('Mudipara') became an enemy of Tapsell (see p. 152).

11. The story of Clementson's journey to New Zealand is related in Robert McNab, *The Old Whaling Days: A History of Southern New Zealand from 1830 to 1840* (Christchurch: Whitcombe and Tombs, 1913), pp. 22–37.

12. John Stewart of Southtown, Suffolk, was both captain and half-owner of the brig *Elizabeth* (236 tons).

13. Presumably Turanganui refers here to the Turanganui River that rises in the Aorangi Range in the Wairarapa before joining the Ruamahanga River and flowing into Palliser Bay. Te Rauparaha ('Raupara', 1760s–1849) was a chief of Ngāti Toa and played an important part in the Musket Wars. In Tapsell's account, the Chatham Islands is a mistake for Banks Peninsula and Akaroa. Te Rauparaha's attack on Akaroa in 1830 is described in McNab, *The Old Whaling Days*, pp. 22–37; John White, *The Ancient History of the Maori, his Mythology and Traditions: Tai Nui*, Vol. 6 (London: Sampson Low and Co., 1890), pp. 129–35.

14. Either Tapsell or Little has confused the 1830 massacre of Ngāi Tahu and their leader Tamaiharanui (Te Maiharanui or Tama-i-Hara-Nui) with the massacre of the Moriori on the Chatham Islands by Taranaki Māori who had hijacked the brig *Lord Rodney* in 1835.

15. The *Bee* was a 135-ton brig that operated out of Sydney. Lincoln Bill was the nickname of William Cuthbert, a time-expired convict from Hobart Town. On this episode, see 'Rovers of the Brig "Bee": The Story of a Lawless Cruise in the Old Pacific', *The New Zealand Railways Magazine*, 13.3 (1938), pp. 17–20.

16. On Mr Ferguson, see chapter 7, note 3.

17. Matamata is a settlement in the Waikato region of the North Island. In the nineteenth century, it belonged to Ngāti Haua and was visited by Tapsell around 1830, making him the first European to visit the area.

18. Patatere probably refers to Te Kaokaoroa-o-Pātetere and more specifically to the area now covered by the Kaimai-Mamaku Forest Park along the border between the Bay of Plenty and Waikato. Supplejack (*Ripogonum scandens*), also known as kareao or pirita, is a climbing vine commonly found in the rainforests and swamps of New Zealand.

19. The mast step is the socket, often strengthened, into which the mast is placed and held in position.

20. Little Barrier Island (Te Hauturu-o-Toi) in the Hauraki Gulf, 80 km to the north of Auckland.

21. A pannikin is a metal or earthenware drinking vessel.

10

Mr. Chapman's arrival

IT WAS NOW THAT MR CHAPMAN ARRIVED at Maketu with a view of proceeding to Rotorua, there to establish a mission station.[1] He came from the Bay of Islands in the Mission vessel, and brought with him a quantity of packages, containing stores, furniture, clothing and other requisites for a residence in the interior. Before leaving Maketu for his new and distant home, he left his goods in charge of Mr Tapsell, who placed them in his store, of which he only kept the key. To his extreme distress and annoyance, one morning when he unlocked the door, he found that the place had been entered by an excavation under the wall, and plundered. Packages were broken open, their contents abstracted, and various kinds of goods scattered on the floor. Amongst the rest was a case of wine belonging to Mr Chapman, and a chest of drawers of Mrs Chapman, from which the clothing had been taken away. Tapsell was at first thunderstruck with the sight. He knew that no one kept the key but himself, and for some time he could not believe that the robbery had been the work of Maoris, while the conduct of the two white men living with him had never given him cause of suspicion. But the murder came out in an unexpected quarter, for Mrs Chapman on their arrival at Rotorua, had the mortification of seeing the Maori women there going about in dresses, silk and otherwise, her own personal property.[2]

Mr Tapsell defends his wife.

AT MAKETU SOME OF THE STOLEN GOODS were discovered in the possession of a man living in the pa who was more than once tasked with the theft by Mr Tapsell's wife, once under the verandah of the house, whither the thief had come to protest his innocence. An angry altercation ensued, Mr Tapsell standing quietly by, as he did not understand all that was said, until the man in a fury, seized hold of Mrs Tapsell's hair, when her husband thought it was time to interfere; so stepping forward, he gave the ruffian a well directed blow in the face, which his great physical strength enabled him to do with over-powering effect, and, to use his own words, sent the Maori away spouting blood!

A crowd of spectators who had witnessed the quarrel and its termination, now rushed to the fence which they began to tear down for sticks with which to beat out Mr Tapsell's brains. But he stood boldly in the verandah, and told them to come on, for he was ready to receive them. His resolute bearing cowed them, and they slunk away to their homes in different directions.

When the news reached Rotorua that the thief had been discovered, the uncle of Mr Tapsell's wife came down with a strong party and stripped the man and his relatives of every thing they possessed, canoes, pigs and other goods, which they divided amongst themselves.[3]

A perilous disturbance

MR TAPSELL HAD ON ONE OCCASION a very serious quarrel with a chief named Haupapa, whom, with his family, he had brought from the Bay of Islands. Haupapa had built for Mr Tapsell a house, the contract payment for which was to be a cask of powder, but on settling accounts one evening, Haupapa insisted that the agreement was for a cask of tobacco. Mr Tapsell replied that it was not. Haupapa repeated his assertion, declaring that it was tobacco he had agreed for, and tobacco he would have, to which Mr Tapsell as firmly answered, that he certainly should not. Haupapa then said that he would take it, and Mr Tapsell told him that it was more than he dared do. Upon which Haupapa gave him a push, and he returned the compliment. A remarkably fine bulldog belonging to Mr Tapsell, standing by, no sooner saw his master laid hands on by a stranger, than he seized the chief's leg in his powerful jaws, causing the blood to flow, which his followers perceiving, became fearfully excited, rushed, tomahawk in hand, into the store, stripped it before Tapsell's eyes of its contents, and carried them down to the beach, threatening to kill him in the morning.

At this time he was the only European in Maketu, the other two being then at Matata.

When night came on, he paced his room backwards and forwards, deliberating within himself on the course to pursue. His wife was seated in a corner of the room. Presently a rap came to the door, and in answer to the challenge from him, a request to be instantly admitted was preferred. On opening the door, the visitor proved to be the uncle of Tupaia with whom the Maketu people tho' not at war, were not on the very best of terms. The stranger informed Mr Tapsell that Tupaia had heard of the intention of Haupapa's people to kill him, and now sent a message to say that he had two hundred men ready, and if Tapsell would only say the word he would take them down to Maketu at once.

Mr Tapsell replied, "Tell Tupaia that I will fight my own battles, and that I do not need his help."

He then sent the messenger away with a present of some tobacco and a belt as a reward for his trouble in coming, the native as he left saying "Kanui te utu. Kanui te utu! Kill as many as you can."[4] Mr Tapsell's resolution was taken at last. He got out a cask of powder, of which he stove in the head, laying a train to the cask. Then he drew a large table across the door, upon which he placed a row of muskets and two blunderbusses, all of which were loaded, and then, as he said afterwards, he felt easy in his mind. He now desired his wife to go to the further end of the pa away from the building, but She however, instead of being asleep as he supposed, had been narrowly watching him all the time, and, in place of going away, seated herself out side the door, giving afterwards as her reason for so doing, that she knew the object of the preparations and, if the place were to be blown up, was determined that they should all go together. Mr Tapsell did not sleep that night, and looked anxiously for the first faint streaks of daylight to make their appearance, while hearing nothing, he looked carefully out, first at one window, and then at another, but could see no one. Thinking it possible that his adversaries might be concealed under the ledge of the window, and were keeping out of sight with a view of decoying him out, he cautiously raised one of the sashes, but no person was visible.

About broad daylight, a woman came to the door with a message from Haupapa to say that he was very sorry for what he had done, and that if Mr Tapsell would not take the 'trade' (as the goods were called) back, he would go away to Cook's Straits, as he would be ashamed to show his face again in Rotorua.

Mr Tapsell told her to desire Haupapa to bring all the goods back, and she had no sooner conveyed the message, than a crowd of people came running back with every thing they had taken away, and placed them back in the store.

Haupapa then came forward, and desired to shake hands with Mr Tapsell, to which the latter consented and the quarrel was made up. The latter took him into the room, and showed him the preparations made to receive him, on seeing which, the chief ran out, and said to his followers, "If we had come here, there was death for all of us."

Haupapa was afterwards one of Tapsell's best friends; very passionate, but his anger was soon over, and he was sorry after for what it sometimes impelled him to do.

The roasted dog

ON THE OCCASION of another battle with the Ngaeterangi, several were killed on both sides, and the Arawa captured a fine European setter dog belonging to Tupaia, the hair of which had been clipped in patterns resembling the tattoo on the human subject. This poor animal they commenced to roast alive as a token of their enmity to its master, and its piteous cries reaching the ears of Mr Tapsell, he ran out and reprimanded them severely for their cruelty, swearing at them in the Maori language. They took no apparent notice at the time but finished cooking the unfortunate dog, which they ate. But at night when Mr Tapsell was in bed, he was aroused by shouts outside his door, calling him to get up, as his house was on fire. Always suspicious of treachery, he seized a loaded blunderbuss and stood in the doorway looking out. The cause of the alarm was at once perceptible. The rascally natives had, out of revenge for the scolding he had given them, thrust a fire stick into the thatch of his cook house, expecting that on the alarm of fire he would rush out and leave his store unprotected, giving them an opportunity to plunder, but seeing that he was on his guard, the fire was speedily extinguished.

Tricks in trade

NO ONE THAT HAS NOT had dealings with Maoris can form any idea of the first troubles of Mr Tapsell in his trading operations with the natives. They would put stones in the baskets of flax to cause it to weigh heavier, and on one occasion a number of baskets were brought to him containing what to all external appearance was good dry flax, but the weight being much too great in proportion to the size of the baskets, on examination it was found that the under portion of the flax had been steeped greatly depreciated its value. When the deception was found out, the natives fled, leaving the flax behind them.

Again, it was Mr Tapsell's custom when weighing flax, to place the baskets that had been weighed, and the natives, when the attention was occupied, would quietly slip round, and transfer the weighed bags to the other end of the building by which device they were weighed over again, although in checking over the numbers, the cheat was afterwards discovered.

Then, perhaps, at a time when Mr Tapsell's stock of goods was run out, a native would bring him a pig, and on being asked its price, would answer "Homai, nomai," (nothing, a gift.)[5] But by and by when the vessel arrived with goods, the same native would come and say to him, "You don't remember me?" "You know that pig you got from me?"

"Yes, but you said you did not want anything for it."

"Well, you had nothing then, but now that you have got plenty, I want payment." and so on, continually.

The tables turned.

MR TAPSELL HAD ANOTHER DISTURBANCE with Haupapa, on an occasion when his man Farrow had come from Tauranga for a supply of goods to trade with. Mr Tapsell got out the goods, which were placed in the canoe and Farrow was ready to start, when Mr Tapsell invited him into the house to take some refreshment. They had no sooner gone inside, than Haupapa with a number of his men, who had been hiding in the bush, and jealous of any trade going to Tauranga, rushed from their place of concealment, emptied the canoe, and carried the goods into the bush. When Farrow went to the beach to get away, he found the canoe empty. On Mr Tapsell being informed, he at once sent for Haupapa, who came with a young chief named Pipi. Farrow was also present, and him Mr Tapsell desired to stand with his back against the inside of the door, and prevent any one leaving the room. Then taking down a loaded musket from the arm stand, he cocked it, and presenting it at the head of Haupapa, threatened to blow his brains out unless he called out for his people to bring back the goods. Haupapa, finding the tables turned against him, gave the necessary orders, and the goods were all restored, except an iron pot which a slave had secreted, but which was brought back next morning. This was the last serious quarrel with Haupapa.

143

An unatural mother.

AT THE TIME OF THE BIRTH of Mr Tapsell's first child, the mother of his wife brought the intelligence that the child was a girl.[6] It was then considered a misfortune if a woman gave birth to a girl, as girls were not considered of any value, while boys would grow into men, and be a protection to their friends. Mr Tapsell replied that it was very well, and he was glad to hear it. "Is it all right?" said she, enquiringly. Upon being assured that it was so, her countenance cleared up, and she departed quite cheerfully. The same old lady was then nursing a child of her own about two months old, and Mrs Tapsell being unable to suckle the newly born infant, it was given to her mother to nurse who considerately smothered her own child in order to enable her to do so. This same old lady, had on previous occasions killed two or three or her children, and indeed, attempted to destroy her daughter, Mrs Tapsell, while an infant, but the child was taken care of by neighbours and reared up.

This practice was very general in those days, and no disgrace was felt to attach to the perpetrator of the crimes. A mother on one occasion had endeavoured to stifle her child, and, before she had succeeded, hung it in a basket on a fence, intending when night came on to throw the body away. Some people while at their food, observing the kit to move, inspected its contents, and discovered the child still alive. It was taken away by them, and reared to womanhood.

Of the small value set upon girls as members of the community, the following is an example.

When a the daughter of a chief had her ears pierced for the first time, it was customary to kill a slave in honour of the occasion, and Mr Tapsell's wife at the time of undergoing the operation possessed a slave girl named Bungari, of whom she was very fond.[7] In accordance with usage, the chief, her father, gave orders to kill the slave girl and put her into the oven. But his daughter, anticipating this cruel fate for her favorite, took her between her knees, and covered her with her mat.

When the slave girl could not be found, the father, who it is most likely was not ignorant of her place of concealment, and his daughter's predilection, commanded as a substitute, that a pig should be baked instead; and so the girl was saved, grew to be a woman, lived for many years at Rotorua, became the mother of children and died not very long ago.

––––––––––

Ransom of two Europeans.

HAPANUI, A CHIEF OF WHAKATANE, arrived at Maketu, bringing with him white men, sailors who had run away from their ship, and whom Hapanui claimed as slaves.[8] These, ransomed, paying a musket for each. One of them, being a cooper, and a handy man, Mr Tapsell kept at Maketu, while the other was a person of good education, and him he entrusted with goods and sent back with Hapanui to trade for flax at Whakatane, Mr Tapsell providing him with a wife, in the person of Hapene, a slave girl taken during a fight at Tauranga, whom he ransomed from her master by payment of a cask of powder.[9]

NOTES

1. Thomas Chapman (1792–1876) and his wife Anne (1791–1855), both from Henley-on-Thames, arrived in Paihia as lay missionaries for the Church Missionary Society in September 1830. In 1835, they founded the mission station Te Koutu, Rotorua, but it closed due to warfare in under a year. In 1838, they established a new mission on Mokoia Island, Rotorua. They moved to Wharekahu, Maketū, in 1851. After Anne died in 1855, Thomas remarried and in 1861 settled in Auckland. His letters and journals are collected as three volumes in *Letters and Journals from Thomas Chapman to the Church Missionary Society*, qMS-0425, Alexander Turnbull Library. Chapman had first met Tapsell in spring 1831. In his journal (qMS-0425, p. 8), he wrote:

    > [...] we again journeyed on towards Mukato and arrived there before sunset, having walked that day about twenty one miles — At Muckato we were kindly received by a Mr. Tapsall, a resident there as a collector of Flax, not altogether unknown to the Mission, and married some years since by Mr. Marsden to a sister of Warepoka. He was exceedingly earnest in his invitation to his house and we took tea with him — his wife seemed quite English and comfortably provided every thing for us — she was formerly living with Mr. King, and her conduct and manners reflect much credit to our teachers — in the evening we repaired to our tent inviting our kind host and hostess with their natives to accompany us thither, to join in our evening prayers — this they willingly did, and our tent was full inside and surrounded without — these little refreshings like the shadow of a great rock in a weary land not only gave us peace but strengthened us also in our souls.

    In an entry for 11 September 1835 (p. 123), he wrote, 'Sunday — Held service in front of Mr. Tapsall's flax house to about a hundred.'

2. A letter from Chapman dated 26 March 1836 (qMS-0425, pp. 92–94) includes a description of the journey from Maketū to Rotorua and the theft of their property:

    > Sirs,
    > The Committee in New Zealand having appointed me to this station I embarked in company with Mrs. Chapman and Messrs. Pilley and Knight on board the Columbine on August 8th —35 — We arrived off Maketu and landed our Stores and Goods- this being the only way of conveying our things inland — I had (in company with Mr. Pilley) spent ten weeks among the Natives of Rotorua at the close of last Autumn, having taken this journey from Paihia (in my boat) in order to urge them to make such preparations for us to allow my going thither altogether in the winter, both in order to have the whole summer before us to get settled in and also on account of my trees — The native harvest was late last year and we were enabled to get very little done in consequence; but on our leaving, they faithfully promised that by our return the house should be fit for our reception — This they failed to fulfil, and on our arrival off Maketu they were too much 'ashamed' to come tho' very much urged, to my assistance in landing the foods &c. — I was therefore obliged to call in the assistance of a strange party and these in spite of every precaution I could use stole ten Axes, nine adzes and some other trifling articles — The following day our own party came down and in company with Mrs. Chapman set out for Rotorua the day after, with about sixty natives having five canoes and my boat — Messrs. Pilley and Knight had gone thither before — We were three days pulling up a winding river, then landed and carried the things over-land to a Lake called Hehu — there they were put in other canoes landed on the other side and again carried overland to Lake Iti, and from thence in other canoes to Rotorua; Lakes Iti and Rotorua being joined by a narrow river of about a mile in length — from the end of Lake Iti to the end of Lake 'Rua (roto being lake) is about sixteen miles — We were

altogether ten days in performing this journey — it being just mid-winter we suffered some little inconvenience from cold — The formation of this new Station in this remote (so to speak) part of the island has been a work of much toil, anxiety and care — Our anxiety was most painfully increased by our being kept three months in doubt respecting the safety of a young leading Chief named Waretutu of whom mention has previously been made; he being the person who has three times visited Paihia to solicit Missionaries for this station — and on our leaving Paihia where he had been some months waiting for us, the vessel was so full that he could not be received with this party of eight but the Tauranga boat was entrusted to him and in this they came down — He was just four months on passage — The whole party were altogether given up for lost — the native lamentations had been regularly gone thro' for them and reports were continually reaching us from other parts, that <u>reports had reached there</u> that we had been stripped and fled — certainly had all this happened to us it had been put 'straight' according to native ideas — During this period some goods of our were left in the flax house of a Mr. Tapsall of Maketu — the natives of this place dug under the door sill and entered and broke open a chest of drawers of mine and a chest of Mr. Knight's and robbed us of property to the amount of about twenty pounds — they were afterwards found out and boldly alledged that Waretutu was their relation and that they had done it to obtain a payment for his death — It was soon after this that he arrived — he obtained back two articles of Mr. Knight's but everything else of ours was made away with — They have promised restitution — Their corn will ripe in about ten days hence, and I shall then put their sincerity to the test — and as this party belong directly to this district I shall not easily be put aside.

Cf. his journal entry for 22 March 1836 (pp. 127–28):

This week has been one of great trouble obliged to leave property at Maketu in charge of Mr. Tapsall, placing it in his Flax house — some thieves dug under the sill and stole many things, mainly articles of dress from Mrs. Chapman's Chest of drawers, and contents of a case of wine — they are found out and our great men are wishing to 'get up' and to go and punish them, which many bring on fighting — recompense is out of the question in any other way — I endeavoured to impress on their minds the better way of getting back such articles as could be recovered and getting promises of payment of food for the rest — this did not seem quite to suit them, and as I would consent to no other plan there the matter rested for the present.

3. Hineitūrama's father's brother was Te Amohau (see p. 140).

4. Ka nui te utu is Māori for 'much revenge!'

5. Homai, noa is Māori for 'just a gift'.

6. Hineitūrama's mother (Te Koiki) and father (Te Koha-a-Ngatokowaru) had four children: Hineitūrama, Uremutu, Akuhata Kiharoa and Marino Te Waru.

7. 'Bungari' is Pangari.

8. 'Hapanui' is Apanui, a chief of Whakatāne.

9. Hapene is mentioned on p. 181.

11

The chief's threat

IT WAS THE CUSTOM with Mr Tapsell to give trade to a number of chiefs who supplied him with flax in payment, and when the payment for the first lot of goods was completed, to give them a fresh supply. It usually happened that several chiefs settled accounts in this way all at the same time, and on one occasion all the chiefs present had paid off their old debts and received more goods to trade with except Hapuru Huka, a chief of Rotorua, who notwithstanding, applied for more goods.[1] Mr Tapsell refused the application, informing him that there were six muskets for which he had not paid, and that all the others had squared up honourably. Huka departed, saying:-

"I will stop this flax scraping."

Mr Tapsell, and all the other chiefs laughed at the threat, but it was no idle one as the sequel proved.

Hunga a chief of Waikato paid a visit to his daughter then staying with a relation at Rotorua, and on leaving amongst others, took farewell of Huka.[2] This miscreant had arranged with his son that when he should touch noses with Hunga, the son should strike him on the head with his tomahawk, which instructions were obeyed by the dutiful son, at the appointed time, and the chief was killed. The Rotorua people were very much incensed at this act of deliberate treachery, which they knew would provoke a war with the powerful Waikato tribes and they inflicted punishment by plundering of all he possessed. When the outrage came to the knowledge of Mr Tapsell, he went without delay to Tauranga, where the Waikato and Ngaeterangi chiefs were assembled. He expressed his great sorrow for what had occurred, dwelt upon his neutrality, the peaceful nature of his occupation, and his indifference to their intertribal feuds, entreating them to fight the battle where the murder was committed, and, not to come to Maketu, which he had purchased for the purposes of trade, at the same time giving them four double barrelled guns as a kind of bonus to secure their goodwill. They expressed themselves satisfied, and all consented to his proposition to fight the battle at Rotorua, and he went away relieved of apprehension. But after he was gone, the Ngaeterangi people prevailed on the other chief to change their intention, saying, "Let us go to Maketu first; there are some good pickings there, and very few people," and accordingly preparations were made for a descent on that locality.

Consequences.

WHEN CLEMENTSON, Mr Tapsell's agent at Waikato, became acquainted with the serious turn that affairs had taken, he desired to inform Mr Tapsell of his impending danger, and with this purpose, sent a white man who lived with him off by night with the news. But in the morning, the messenger was missed, and about forty natives armed with tomahawks started in pursuit, overtaking him on the road. He was brought back, but succeeded in starting again only to be again captured, and brought back with the warning that the next time he would be killed.

Farrow Tapsell's agent at Tauranga also wished to convey a warning to Maketu, but was strictly watched, and prevented from accomplishing his design. Under the circumstances he consulted Mr Brown, the missionary — now, the Venerable Archdeacon — who called a committee of the Waikato and Ngaeterangi, chiefs, and obtained from them a promise not to touch Mr Tapsell's property.[3] About sixteen hundred warriors were collected for the expedition, which at length set out for its' destination. They kept Farrow as a prisoner as far as Tumu, where they crossed the river, intending to approach Maketu from the land side, where they would not be perceived, and then told him that he was at liberty to go to his master. Farrow ran along the beach at the top of his speed, and was observed by Mr Tapsell through his telescope.

"A running messenger bears bad tidings," said he, and ordered a canoe to be put across the river to meet him and bring him over.

He conveyed the unwelcome intelligence that sixteen hundred fighting men were on their way to take Maketu, and would be there in a few minutes. He also related the result of Mr Brown's intercession with the chiefs and their promise not to molest his property.

"Can they be depended on?" said Mr Tapsell.

"Oh! I think so," replied Farrow.

Haupapa

THEY WERE IN THE ACT OF taking refreshment, when the report of muskets was heard in the direction of Wharekahu, where the house of the resident Magistrate now stands, and, on looking out, firing could be seen coming from that quarter which was answered by the people below the hill where Mr Tapsell's house stood. He and Farrow ran out with a view of endeavouring to stay hostilities if possible, but found themselves in the gully between a cross fire from both parties, while the bullets were whizzing above their heads. Farrow ran for shelter to those Ngaeterangi, whom he called his own people, and Mr Tapsell retired again to his house, on the way, urging the very few Arawas left in Maketu, who were engaged in a vain effort at defence, to fly to Waihi, and make their escape to Rotorua. Some did so with success. Many others remained, and in so unequal a contest were all shot down. Amongst the rest whom Mr Tapsell entreated to secure their safety by flight was Haupapa, but he stamped his foot, and answered; "No, I will die beside you."

Battle, murder, and sudden death.

TAPSELL, HE, AND HIS WIFE stood within the fence surrounding the dwelling of the former, and looked down on the enemy as they marched along the foot of the hill. Haupapa's wife stood by his side with a loaded musket, while he held a double barrelled gun.

As the enemy passed, he fired, and shot a chief. Presently, he fired again, and shot another, but a shot from the enemy came through the fence, struck him in the breast, and he fell. Mr Tapsell carried him into the house, and laid him under the bed, hoping that amidst the confusion he would not be perceived. But there were too many eyes wandering over the scene. The fighting was carried on along the beach, the enemy following, and the Arawa retiring, and firing as they retired; all were killed who stayed to fight, except women and children, who were taken for slaves. The first who was shot was Nainai, a chief of note, whose head the enemy cut off on the gunwale of his own canoe.[4] Pipi, a fine young chief, fled along the beach as far as the cluster of trees, which still remain, where he was overtaken, his head cut off and his body divided in two. His nephew, who could have escaped, when he saw his uncle killed, came back to share the same fate, which was instantly awarded him, his head being removed, and is body divided like the other. The carnage being over, all were busy eating the bodies and curing the heads of the slain.

This they were in a hurry to perform, for they feared that the people at Rotorua would hear the news and come down upon them. Many rose at night to eat the bodies of their victims. It should have been said that amongst those who escaped were a party who came from Kapiti of the near relatives of Tupaia engaged in scraping flax at Waihi to whom he sent a messenger overnight warning them to fly to Rotorua, which they did.

The morning after.

THIS WAS NO NIGHT FOR SLEEP, and it was passed by Mr Tapsell in pacing the room backwards and forwards. If he had been disposed to sleep, his bed was not the most inviting, for underneath was a chief dying of his wounds with his sorrowing wife by his side.

In the early morning he was going through the yard when he was stopped by an armed Maori standing sentry at the gate, who said, "Tapsell, go back, go to your own place, you are wanted there."

He had scarcely left the building when an old woman climbed over the fence, and went into the room where Mrs Tapsell was seated, over whom the old woman threw her mat, to indicate that she claimed her as a slave, but the wife of Mudipara coming in at that moment, addressed her in the following terms; "What are you doing here, there are plenty of slaves down below. If you want her for a slave, you must kill Tapsell first." Mr Tapsell returning at that moment, the old woman fled precipitately. Shortly after this he went down to the beach where the enemy were busy curing the heads of chiefs who had been killed.

Ransom of captives.

AS HE PASSED ALONG, his leg was seized by a woman who proved to be the wife of Pipi, the young chief killed at the green bushes who was crying bitterly. Mr Tapsell knowing that slavery was the fate of all women, taken in battle, asked this one who was now her master, on which she pointed out a Waikato chief, from whom Mr Tapsell enquired if he would part with her. The chief consented, and accepted a cask of powder as a ransom. Five other women he also ransomed at the same price. They were then, with the consent of Te Waharoa and the others handed over to a Waikato chief, to be by him conveyed as far as

Waihi, there to be allowed to depart in safety for Rotorua. So much of his duty he performed with fidelity, but before leaving them, he appropriated to himself all the ornaments such as Maori women wear, in the shape of greenstones and shark's teeth. Te Waharoa insisted on a ransom of the store, and then of the boat, and the conquerors were tolerably quiet so long as any powder remained, but when it was all gone, they threw off the mask.

Pillage of the Store.

MR TAPSELL, ON COMING TO HIS STORE, found one end broken in, and some flax removed. He addressed Te Waharoa in angry terms, reproaching him with breach of faith, in as much as he had promised to hold his property inviolated. Waharoa waved his hand deprecatingly.

"Don't be angry," said he, "By and by, it will be all right."

Flight of Mrs Tapsell's.

ON MR TAPSELL'S RETURN to the house, he was urgently entreated by Tupaia to leave the place and provide for his own safety. "Come away, come away, or you will be killed. You do not know what may happen."

"Get my wife and child away," replied Tapsell, "and leave me here. I will look after myself."

Tupaia, finding his entreaties vain, led away Tapsell's wife with her child down the hill to the beach, where they were met by a woman named Karu, who had a musket in one hand and a tomahawk in the other.

"Give me this woman," said she.

"If you are a greater chief than I am, you can take her," was Tupaia's answer, as he passed on towards the canoe in which he placed Mr Tapsell's wife and child, himself accompanying them to Tumu, where he left them in safety.

Left alone with the foe.

MEANWHILE, the woman who had met Tupaia on the way to the beach, hastened into Tapsell's house, where she seated herself opposite to him at a table, glaring at him with eyes that almost flashed fire with stifled resentment, but, finding that her angry glances made no impression on the fearless pakeha, she took her departure. Then several hundred infuriated savages, reeking from their fiendish orgies, surrounded the house and clamoured for the body of Haupapa. As he was not yet dead, Mr Tapsell refused to give him up, and they threatened furiously to take his head, on which he stepped out in front of the door, grasping a sword in one hand, and a loaded musket in the other.

"You want my head," said the intrepid man. "Here I am, come and take it."

But they all drew back, muttering amongst themselves, and Mudipara coming up at that moment, sent them away.

Haupapa dies.

WHEN HE HAD RETURNED to the room and was again seated at the table, some one touched Tapsell gently from behind. He looked round, and saw Haupapa's wife. "He is dead," said she, meaning her husband "run your sword through my body."

"I cannot do that," replied Tapsell, "it is against our laws."

"Well, then, cut his head off," continued she.

Just as she said the words, Mudipara, the Waikato chief, entered the room. "I'll do that," said he, "Give me a knife."

Tapsell pointed to a large carving knife lying on the table, which Mudipara seized, speedily severed the head from the body, and hurried from the house as if he had been pursued, to exhibit his trophy.

------

and is eaten raw

NOW THAT HAUPAPA WAS DEAD, Tapsell informed the assembled chiefs that they might have the body, on which it was dragged from under the bed, and a general scramble ensued by the crowd, eager to cut off a piece of his flesh, and swallow it raw. In their frantic endeavours to obtain a morsel from the inanimate carcase, clambering over one another's shoulders, and stretching out their arms to snatch pieces away, they resembled a pack of hungry wolves gnawing at a dead horse.

When the head was cut off, blood ran in streams into the lockers surrounding the room which were full of melons. These were seized and eaten greedily by the cannibals, the blood in which they were soaked appearing to give great relish to the repast.

———————

Mr Tapsell flies

ALL THIS TIME, Tupaia, who had returned from Tumu, was urging Mr Tapsell to seize that moment for escape, to which he at last consented, and Tupaia sent his wife with him as a protection. When they crossed the river, Mr Tapsell walked at his usual pace without hurrying, and Tupaia's wife impatiently called to him. "Walk quicker, you foolish man, you will be killed yet." But he answered, I shall walk no faster, leave me alone, I will look after myself. When they had got some distance along the beach they met the two missionaries Messrs Wilson and Wade.[5]

"Where are you going to?" asked Tapsell

We are going to see if we cannot stop this dreadful work," was the reply.

"You ought to have come before, if you intended to do any good," said Mr Tapsell, "You can see my store all in flames, and I myself am stripped to the clothes I stand in."

They Wilson departed, but when they had got to Maketu, and seen the pandemonium which reigned there; the wanton destruction of property, the confusion and uproar; cooking of bodies, and curing of heads, they were struck with terror, and hastily returned, overtaking Mr Tapsell on the way.

Mr Tapsell, his wife and child stayed that night in the pa at Tumu, and the next morning the conquerors returned bearing the spoils of victory in the shape of his goods and chattels. They passed on towards Tauranga without stopping, observing to Tupaia, "You have got the best prize," meaning, Mr Tapsell. Amongst the rest was Mudipara's wife to whom Tapsell had been very kind, — carrying a box containing his valuables and best clothing. At one time he had thought that she purposed saving this for him, for when the confusion was at its height she had thrown herself across the chest, as if to protect it from the general pillage, but now as she passed with it on her shoulder, she looked at him with great disdain.

Amongst the barbarities perpetrated on this occasion by the victors was the digging up of the body of Mr Tapsell's boy who had died of leprosy, which they devoured. They also disinterred a child of Mr Tapsell's which had been buried about two months in the garden attached to his house. The tomb being surrounded with a neat railing, and the ground decorated with flowers, attracted the attention of the savages, who, on digging, were rewarded by finding a handsome cedar coffin, which they expected to contain a treasure, and carried away along with other prizes. But, on the march, to satisfy their curiosity, they opened the package, and, discovering the nature of its contents, tossed the little corpse into the surf.

The conquerors, before leaving Maketu, dismantled Mr Tapsell's battery, spiked the guns, and threw them into the river.

Mr Tapsell's loss by the sacking of Maketu in goods trade buildings and a hundred and twenty tons of flax in store, was estimated in Sydney at more than four thousand pounds.

Leaves Tumu.

AFTER THEY HAD PASSED, Mr Tapsell told Tupaia that it was no use remaining there, as he had no longer any trade to give him. He therefore expressed his wish to proceed in the boat to Matata, where was one of his trading stations in charge of Mr White. Tupaia observed that no crew could be got, the people were all afraid to go. To which Mr Tapsell replied, that he would to himself with the aid of the two white men that had been living with him. Tupaia declared his intention to go, also and, with his wife went into the boat.

From Matata to Rotorua.

ON THEIR ARRIVAL at Matata, Mr Tapsell requested Rangitikina to provide him with a canoe and a good crew to proceed to Kopenga, to which Rangitikina at once gave his consent, Tupaia covering his head with his mat. At Kopenga, Mr Tapsell's wife, who was near her confinement, became unable to walk, and a party of men were procured, who carried her in a litter all the way. Two nights they slept in the bush, without other covering than the clothes they wore

---

......ing reception

WHEN THE PARTY GOT WITHIN a mile or two of Ohinemutu,[6] the people there commenced firing volleys, which they continued till the party reached the place, in front of which the women met them with mats, which they spread out for them to sit down upon, and then surrounded them in crowds, crying with a loud and bitter lamentation, and gashing themselves with knives, shells and flints, till the mats were saturated with blood, and could be wrung out with the hand. When the reception — which lasted nearly all day — was over, Mr Tapsell went to the island of Mokoia to see his mother in law. Hekairo, the chief with whom he had traded, sent him a hundred baskets of potatoes, and two pigs, with injunctions to be careful of it, as food was likely to be scarce.

Retaliatory Expedition.

EVERY DAY MR TAPSELL was endeavouring to prevail upon the people to muster all their forces, and march for the coast, to retake Tumu. At length he succeeded, and the people collected from Tarawera and other settlements and started on the expedition, Mr Tapsell accompanying them. At each halt on the road, a committee was held, and one morning Amohau, uncle of Mr Tapsell's wife,[7] told him that he must not go along with them, in order to come on the enemy unawares, and would have in addition, several rivers to swim. Mr Tapsell replied that he was able to go where they did, and if they were required to swim, he could swim too. But finding that they raised fresh obstacles, and evidently did not wish to have him with them, he told them that, he knew they would take the pa, as he had had a dream to that effect, and his only object was to be able to lay hands on his own property, on which they assured him that all his goods should be held sacred and returned to him. Mr Tapsell then consented to go back after giving strict injunctions to spare Tupaia's life, as he had been good to him. This injunction he frequently repeated, and received their emphatic assurance faithfully to obey it. He then returned to Mokoia, and the party went on their way.

Retribution.

THE PARTICULARS OF THE FIGHT at Tumu were afterwards obtained from the European, Taylor, who was taken there.[8]

The attacking party arrived early in the morning, and one of their number was shot at the commencement of the proceedings. Many were killed on both sides, and a party of about thirty of the Tarawera people killed while cutting an entrance through the palisading surrounding the pa, one of the chiefs calling out, "Never mind who falls, let us get in." Women inside, dragged the bodies through holes made for the purpose, and cut off the heads, which they held aloft tauntingly, saying to the beseigers, "This is the way we will serve you." By this means they stung them into frenzy, and the attack was continued with great fury. At length, Tareha, a great chief, was shot by a ball from outside, and one of the women crying out, "Tareha is killed," the defenders became panic stricken and fled from the pa like a flock of sheep. They were pursued along the beach by the victorious Arawa, and most of them killed. Tupaia was nearly shot, a bullet grazing his forehead. His uncle urged him to fly instead of remaining to share his fate, which he did and with some difficulty escaped, the uncle being killed. When they entered the whare of Taylor, he, supposing Mr Tapsell to be with them — said, "Where is Tapsell, that is doing all this murdering work? Is he ashamed to show his face?" It will be remembered that Mr Tapsell had left the party on the road, and returned to Mokoia. It was about three weeks before the expeditionary party passed Mokoia on their way to Ohinemutu. They had recaptured a good portion of Mr Tapsell's goods, but returned nothing to him except a pocket book, which had contained with other papers an order for two hundred and fifty pounds upon Captain Patterson — Steward of the English Navy. When returned to him, every other paper was there but the order, which had been abstracted.

The old woman, Karu, who had desired to take Mr Tapsell's wife for a slave, was shot in the pa at Tumu. Another one, also the wife of a chief, being taken prisoner at the same time, was, with a friendly motive, brought to Rotorua for the wife of Mr Tapsell to kill, as utu for the insult she had received, but the latter refusing to avail herself of the offer, the wife of Haupapa, who, it will be remembered, died under Mr Tapsell's bed, cheerfully undertook the duty, and despatched her.[9]

NOTES

1. 'Hapuru Huka' is the (minor) Te Arawa chief Haere Huka who killed Te Hunga on 25 December 1835 and was involved in the destruction of Maketū in 1836.

2. On Christmas Day 1835, Haere Huka went to the Ngāti Rangiwewehi village at Parahaki close to Rotorua, where Te Hunga of Ngāti Hauā was visiting his daughter.

3. Alfred Nesbit Brown (1803–84), born in Colchester, arrived in Paihia in 1829 with his wife Charlotte. He was appointed to the mission station in Matamata in 1836 and was later appointed archdeacon of Tauranga (1843). Charlotte died in 1855 and Alfred remarried. He finally settled on land bought from the Te Papa Mission Station where he spent his final years.

4. Te Nainai was a notable chief of Ngāti Pūkenga, an iwi centred in Tauranga.

5. William Richard Wade (1803–91), printer, married to Sarah, arrived in New Zealand in 1834 and worked alongside William Colenso in Paihia. John Alexander Wilson (1809–87), lay preacher, married to Anne, arrived in New Zealand in 1833 and worked alongside James Preece in Pūriri. In 1835, the two became the first missionaries based at Te Papa Mission Station in Tauranga. They were involved in peace-making activities, but had little success. In 1836, they abandoned the Station fearing for the safety of their families.

6. Ōhinemutu is the Rotorua region's original Ngāti Whakaue settlement. Before Europeans it was the main centre for the Rotorua lake region; today it is a suburb of Rotorua lying on the lakeside shore.

7. Hineitūrama's father's brother Te Amohau (cf. p. 137).

8. In the *Otago Witness*, 6 November 1869, Captain Budd describes how, in 1832, his ship was over-run by Māori off East Cape and he was held hostage. Later, when the tribe which held him was preparing for a skirmish with another tribe from Whakatāne, Captain Budd took the opportunity to escape. He went nearby to where the Whakatāne Māori were and asked them for assistance. They took him and sold him to Mr Taylor in Whakatāne and from there he went to Tauranga and took a ship to Sydney. By this time it was 1834. In *A Trader in Cannibal Land*, James Cowan mentions Taylor being held captive and later telling him of the skirmish at the Te Tūmū pā (9 May 1836), which Tapsell was prevented from fighting in by his in-laws.

   Tapsell paid a ransom (goods to an equivalent of £20 each) for Taylor's wife, three children and his wife's sister who were all captured at Te Tūmū. After his relatives were returned, Taylor took them to the Urewera country where his wife's relatives lived. However, the Taylors soon became destitute and returned to Whakatāne and Tapsell. In the end, Taylor's wife left him with two of their children and returned to Te Urewera alone. Taylor became a beachcomber and died shortly afterwards. His wife came back to Whakatāne to claim one of the children and Tapsell adopted the other.

9. The killing of Murupara's wife by Te Haupapa's wife, Kata, as utu for the loss of her husband in no small way fuelled the later Te Mataipuku attack by Te Waharoa and Murupara on Ōhinemutu. See Paul Tapsell, *Pukaki: A Comet Returns* (Libro International, 2000), p. 56.

12

Ransom of slaves

THE VICTORIOUS ARAWA returned by canoes passing close to Mokoia, Mr Taylor, his wife and children amongst them. Mr Tapsell hailed the fleet, and Taylor answering, called out that his wife and children were slaves. Mr Tapsell promised to follow him very shortly, which he did. A woman seeing him approach, said, "I know what this pakeha is coming for. He wants our slaves, but I will not give mine to him for they are my own property." Mr Tapsell sought out Amahau, his wife's uncle from whom he made request for the wife, wife's sister, and children of Taylor who were given to him on payment of a ransom. After stopping three weeks on Mokoia, Taylor then went to the Uriwera country,[1] where his wife's relatives lived, and did not again make his appearance for some time after.

Ohinemutu attacked

ABOUT A MONTH after this, a strong party came from the Waikato, and pitched their camp a short distance from Ohinemutu, and some time was spent on both sides in preparing for the coming conflict. At length, all being ready, an attack was made by the Waikatos, which was witnessed from Mokoia by Messrs. Chapman and Tapsell, who could distinctly hear the firing, and, through a telescope, observe a good deal of what was going on.[2] Still, many of the details of the fight escaped their notice, and it may suffice to say that a good many were killed on both sides, and the enemy compelled at last to retire. After the commencement of hostilities, it was found that Mr Chapman's dwelling house was likely to afford shelter to the enemy, and it was in consequence burned down, Mr Chapman losing many valuables.

Goes to Sydney.

MR TAPSELL REMAINED on Mokoia about five months after these occurrences receiving frequent letters from Mr White at Matata, cautioning him against returning to the coast just then, as many of his enemies were about, who threatened to take his life. At last he became tired of his sojourn at Mokoia and told the people at Rotorua that he had determined to go to Matata with a view of taking a passage for Sydney to obtain more trade and that they must drag his boat for him overland to Kopenga River.[3] They accordingly furnished him with two hundred men for this purpose The task was accomplished with great labour in three of four days. The descent of one hill occupied seven hours. At length the Kopenga was reached and Mr White found waiting to receive them. The boat was launched, the natives fired a parting salute, and Mr Tapsell, with his wife and two children, descended the river. He remained with Mr White for a couple of months before a vessel arrived, and then he took his passage for Sydney. His first business there was to settle accounts with his merchants, who were heavy losers by the calamity which had deprived him of every thing he possessed. Meanwhile, he accepted the invitation of an acquaintance to lodge at his house. This individual, who had formerly been a whaling Captain, was now in difficulties, and obtained Mr Tapsell's promise to remain to protect and assist his wife and family while he himself should secretly take his departure for the Bay of Islands. This he effected without public knowledge of his creditors.

159

His accounts were at length settled with the merchants, who made over to him all the debts due on the coast, but were not willing to renew a trade so hazardous, in consequence of which, Mr Tapsell made an arrangement with a Mr Petersen for a fresh trade in flax with the natives,[4] a schooner called the Harlequin was loaded with goods for that purpose,[5] and Mr Tapsell, his wife and children, together with the family of the acquaintance with whom he had lodged, sailed for New Zealand. He landed his passengers at the Bay of Islands and came on to Tauranga.

Affairs on the East Coast.

HERE HE FOUND that his agent Mr Farrow, together with Mr Clementson, his Waikato agent, believing that he did not intend to return, had gone in a whale boat to Matata, for the purpose of consulting with Mr White and arranging to trade on their own account. News arriving the following day that they had been drowned in the surf at Matata, he went ashore, and took a quantity of flax and pork out of Farrow's store which he put on board the Harlequin, sailing thence for Whakatane, where he landed all his trade and took possession of a house he had had built for a man named Jackson who had previously acted as his agent there.[6]

Shortly after his arrival, Taylor, whose wife had been ransomed at Rotorua, came in from Uriwera in a very miserable condition, with no clothing but a blanket. Mr Tapsell gave him quarters and food clothed him, and employed him occasionally to superintend the pressing of the flax. All the manual labor was performed by natives. After being at Whakatane for some time, he sent for his wife and children, who, when they arrived, were well clothed by Mr Tapsell, and admitted to a share of the plentiful provision going.

At Whakatane Mr Tapsell again commenced trading for flax, and found the natives disposed to render him every assistance he required, and so extremely honest, that he never but once, lost any articles of value.

A bad speculation.

160 ABOUT THIS TIME Mr Mair of the Bay of Islands, equipped a boats' crew of whalers, and sent them to Whale Island with provisions and whaling gear to establish a fishery at that place.[7] These men, being well provided with the necessaries of life, and indifferent to the interest of their employer, idled their time away instead of looking out for whales, lay in bed till the sun was approaching noon, instead of rising before the first peep of dawn as bay whalers ought to do, and allowed the season to pass away without the capture of a single fish. When Mr Mair found that the fishery was a failure, he came down in a schooner, anchored off the island, and sent a boat to Whakatane for Mr Tapsell, to try and make a bargain with him for the whaling gear. The boat was seen approaching with three men, and Mr Tapsell ran down to the heads to prevent them from attempting to land, as in consequence of a gale the day before, a heavy surf was breaking. But the men did not observe the signals and continued to pull for shore until within the surf, when the boat capsized, and two men, a Maori and an Englishman, were drowned. The other, a man named Lord, who was steering, had on him a cloak which the wind blew over his head as the boat turned over and over, he grasping the thwart in his hands.[8] There is no doubt that this covering prevented him suffocating with salt water, which would otherwise have been the case. A native youth named Cape, mentioned in a previous chapter, rushed into the surf, and succeeded in bringing him lifeless to shore. There the Maoris lighted a fire, and remained

with him till he was quite recovered. The bodies of the other two men were not found.

A dummy.

MR TAPSELL OFFERED A REWARD for the recovery of the corpse of the Englishman, and sometime after, two natives came forward and told that when on their journey thither from Matata, and stopping to eat a meal, their attention had been attracted to what looked like the hair of a man buried in the sand, on scraping which away, they had discovered the entire body. The hair and head were, they said, entire with the exception of the eyes, which were gone. The body was also open, but otherwise, they said, the remains were as perfect as so long an exposure would permit.

All this was very feasible. The attack of birds and fishes would account for all the injuries described. Accordingly Mr Tapsell gave the men a blanket in which to wrap the corpse, and told them to bring it there for interment. In a short space of time they brought a figure tied up in the blanket, and Mr Tapsell, with a man named Middlemas, then living with him, made preparations to deposit it in the ground.[9] The natives had previously been very reluctant for any one but themselves to dig the grave.

"Do you not think," said Middlemas, "that it would be advisable to say a prayer over him first?"

"Yes," replied Mr Tapsell, "I have my prayers all in my head. They are short, and to the purpose. I have buried many people in my time, but I never yet buried one without looking in his face first that I might know whom I am burying. So, cut him adrift, and let us see him."

The natives, upon hearing this, became very uneasy, and delayed obeying under all sorts of pretences, until Mr Tapsell, becoming impatient, called for a knife. Middlemas had none, nor had he. For want of a better implement, Middlemas began to saw the flax with which it was tied with a sharp stone.

The two natives then ran away.

Suddenly, Middlemas exclaimed, "I'm d—d if I think it's a man at all." It was not. The head, when uncovered, proved to be a large pumice stone, with flax on the top to resemble hair. Two sticks did duty for arms, while two stouter ones answered the purpose of legs. The crowd of natives standing round appeared petrified with astonishment, while Hapanui, the chief, was all in a tremble as if anticipating Mr Tapsell's displeasure.

The two rascals who had attempted the cheat were no where to be seen, and did not turn up for at least two months afterward.

Clementson drowned.

SOON AFTER Mr Tapsell arrived at Whakatane he received a visit from Farrow, who with Clementson and another had been reported to be drowned. He came along with Mr George White, and gave the following particulars of his escape:–

He, his wife, and Clementson, with a young man named Jenkins, had set out in a whale boat from Tauranga for Matata with a view of meeting Mr White there, and when off the latter place, were overtaken in a gale of wind.[10] It would have been easy for them to run under the lee of Whale Island, where they could have had smooth water, and there, have waited till the storm subsided, but their young companion, being inexperienced, and very confident, was strongly desirous that they should at once land at Matata, which he was of opinion they could easily do. Yielding to this opinion, they pulled for the main land, on approaching which, they found a very heavy surf breaking on the bar. Appearances were so threatening, that when near the entrance of the river, they laid on their oars to deliberate on the best course to pursue. They consulted so long that before they were aware, the boat drifted into the breakers, and was capsized. Jenkins, not being able to swim, went down like a shot. Clementson was a good swimmer, but so encumbered with heavy boots, and buttoned up to the throat in a pea jacket, that after a few strokes, he sank also, not to rise again. Farrow, though also a good swimmer, would have given in from fatigue, but for his wife, who stripped, and swam by his side, encouraging him continually with the assurance that the people were coming down to the beach; till he reached the shore in safety.

Trade with the Uriwera.

AFTER REMAINING SOME TIME at Whakatane, Taylor one day spoke to Mr Tapsell, representing that he was under obligations to him for his kindness in clothing and supporting him and his family, and that he felt uncomfortable because he was not able to render any service in return. He said he believed he could obtain pork very cheaply in the Uriwera Country if Mr Tapsell would give him 'trade'. He was confident that, for two or three figs of tobacco he could procure a fine pig.

Mr Tapsell consented, informing him that he would be satisfied if a good pig could be bought for two or three pounds of tobacco. The length of time he would be absent was the next question. Mr Tapsell supposed a month, but Taylor was sure that less time would be required. He was furnished with a quantity of goods, and departed with his wife and children.

It was eleven months before he came back again alone as wretched as before, clad only in a blanket. When asked for the pigs he was sent to procure, he said they were coming by and by. But they never came.

It appeared that Uriwera people were very anxious to obtain goods, though they did not bring the pigs at the time, but promised them by and by, and, his wife assuring Taylor of the honesty of various individuals, he parted with all his 'trade' for which he never received any payment. Mr Tapsell again clothed him and he stayed at Whakatane as before. His wife having deserted him at Uriwera for a Maori living there, he sent a message desiring her to come to him, but she returned a refusal. The chief of the Uriwera on being informed of the circumstances sent her away, and she returned to Whakatane with her children. They were almost devoid of garments of any kind when they arrived, and Mr Tapsell again clad them as before. The woman remained some time, but presently became restless, and expressed a wish to visit her friends again for a short time, promising to return in two or three weeks. She went away, but did not return, and the chief, considering the case a hopeless one, would not again interfere, but suffered her to take up her abode with the Maori for whom she had deserted Taylor. On learning which, Taylor endeavoured to procure a wife from among the women at Whakatane, but none of them would have anything to say to him, as it was reported that he had been seen carrying potatoes on his back, which no chief was ever known to do. A chief might carry any sort of a burden that did not consist of food, but such a one was tapud, and consequently forbidden. Taylor, therefore was only a taurikarika, and unworthy the notice of a wahine of reputation.

So strongly had Taylor become imbued with Maori superstitions, that he now believed himself to be bewitched, of which Mr Tapsell at this time had very good proof for.

163

A pakeha bewitched

ONE DAY, the wife of the latter pointed to a man passing by the fence surrounding the house, who, she said, was one of the two natives who had attempted the imposture with a fictitious corpse; on which Mr Tapsell ran out, and the man ran away, Mr Tapsell pursuing. This man in question was a tohunga, and was believed to possess a knowledge of 'makutu', and Mr Tapsell, being very angry, called out "Puko kuhua" which, in Maori, is a very heavy curse against the head of the person sworn at,[11] the head of a chief being always tapud; so much so, that if an article of food, or an iron pot were hung from the roof, or over the door of a whare, no chief would enter. The hair of a chief's head was especially tapu-tapu, and when cut, was always carefully stowed away in the thatch of the roof; for if any one having a spite against the person from whom it had been taken, should become possessed of any portion of it, and take it to the makutu man, he could accomplish the destruction of the original proprietor.

As Mr Tapsell was chasing the native, Taylor rose to join in the pursuit, but, hearing the dreadful oaths just referred to, he seized a couple of kumeras from the table, which he threw before him as he ran. This being observed, he was afterwards asked his motive for so doing, to which he replied that he did it to take the spell off his children; on which Mr Tapsell remonstrated warmly with him, assuring him that witchcraft could have no effect on his children. It was only foolish men who believed in it that could be influenced by it.

It was not long after, that Mr Tapsell came unexpectedly into a room where he found Taylor reading his Bible.

"You have got a good book there," said Mr Tapsell.

"I am only looking to satisfy my curiosity," replied Taylor.

"Nevertheless, it is good book," repeated Mr Tapsell.

Taylor was that night in his usual good health, and early the following morning had called to a boy employed at the place. An hour or two later, Mr Tapsell sent into his room the boy, who quickly returned, saying he thought Taylor was dead. This announcement quite unnerved Mr Tapsell and some moments elapsed before he ventured into the room. It was quite true. Taylor was dead, lying on his back with a child on each arm.

Mr Tapsell buried him, and took charge of the children until some time afterwards, when the mother came from Uriwera and begged for the eldest one, which she took away with her. Mr Tapsell adopted the youngest as his daughter.

At that time the people of Whakatane were very good to Europeans. Thieving or begging were not known amongst them, and it was customary to leave tools and other articles lying about without any fear of their being stolen. But if strangers arrived, Hapanui, the chief, would say, "You had better take your things in, some strangers have come, and I cannot answer for them."

A detective prophet.

BUT ON ONE OCCASION, a pair of trousers belonging to Mr Tapsell were missed from a fence, and Hapanui informed of the circumstance. He was very much disturbed with the intelligence, and sent off immediately to a prophet living at some distance. When it became known that the makutu man was coming, the thief became alarmed, and the trousers were flung into the cook house of Mr Tapsell, who, on discovering them, brought them to Hapanui.

"Oh, you should not have touched them," said he "You should have let them remain where they were."

Presently, the prophet came, and immediately exclaimed, "You have found what you lost, but you should not have touched it, and I could then have told you the name of the thief."

On another occasion, the same prophet was consulted by a woman about a string of beads which she had lost, and which she prized very highly. The prophet named a certain young boy (now living) as the thief, and informed the woman that she would find the beads hung up behind the door in the house of the boy's mother. The woman found the beads in the place indicated, and told the mother of the boy's theft, she however was very indignant, and asserted that the prophet had spoken falsely. On this being reported to him, he was extremely angry, and exclaimed, "What, does she call me a liar?" Then I will makutu him."

Sure enough, the boy took so ill, that the alarmed father waited on the prophet, and entreated him, for the sake of relationship, to withdraw the spell, at the same time presenting him with a cask of powder. The makutu man ordered the boy to be sent to him, kept him for about a month, and restored him in health to his parents.

Mr Tapsell bewitched.

SHORTLY AFTER THIS, it became known that the Makutu man had bewitched Mr Tapsell in retaliation for the terrible curse he had uttered against his head, and one evening as the latter was seated at table in conversation with Middlemas, Toihau entered and whispering commenced between him and the women folk there present. Mr Tapsell at length perceived that he was the subject of their discourse, and enquired the nature of it, but they replied, "Nothing, it's nothing." but as the mysterious communications did not cease, he became angry, and insisted on knowing the meaning of it, when it came out that Toihau had come to take off the spell from Tapsell's children, but as for himself, that was impossible. He must die. At this Mr Tapsell and his companion laughed very heartily. The women were appalled at the callousness of his behaviour.

"Did you ever see such a mad fellow?" said one, "He laughs and smokes as if nothing were the matter, and he knows that he must die tonight." At which he laughed the more.

In the morning, he was not dead and called their attention to the circumstance.

"Wait a bit," said they, "you will see."

A month passed away, and he again reminded them of the spell, asking what they thought.

"Yes," replied they, "He is not strong enough for you."

"No, he is not," answered Mr Tapsell, "and there is not a man in New Zealand strong enough to bewitch me, for my God will protect me."

This occurrence inspired the natives with great respect for the strength of a character which could withstand the incantations of their "medicine-men", as they are termed by the North American Indians.

Makutu.

THE URIWERA TRIBE have always been considered the wildest and most savage race in New Zealand, and at one time were regarded with terror because they were believed to be preeminently endowed with the power of witchcraft.

Even Hapanui, the intelligent and friendly chief at Whakatane, was so much under the influence of this apprehension, that on one occasion when about to receive a visit from a powerful Uriwera chief, brought his gun to Mr Tapsell, requesting him to take care of it, for if his expected visitor were to see it, he would take a fancy to it, and he would be obliged to give it to him or he would be makutu'd by him.

The principal chief of the Uriwera had many wives whom he had procured by the aid of witchcraft. If he saw a woman who took his fancy, he would hold out his hand, and she dared not refuse to go to him, for if she had done so he would makutu her, and she would inevitably die. It was said that many women whom he had makutu'd had come to an untimely end.

Bishop Pompallier.

BISHOP POMPALLIER ARRIVED about this time at Whakatane in a schooner of his own called the Santa Maria, with the object of visiting Opotiki, Rotorua and other places.[12] In the course of conversation he asked Mr Tapsell if his children had been christened, to which Mr Tapsell replied that he had christened them himself; that he had applied to the missionaries but they had refused.

To this the Bishop answered that the missionaries had not known their duty. Said he: "Your christening of them was equally, as good in the sight of God as if I had done it myself, nevertheless, if you like, I will christen them first, and marry you afterwards."

Tapsell replied, "That is what I want." The Bishop enquired where he would wish to have it done.

"In the middle of the yard," said Mr Tapsell, "where every one can see it."

And so the interesting ceremonies were performed by the amiable Prelate, under the canopy of heaven, with the uncultivated landscape for an altar piece, and a crowd of wondering savages for a congregation.

Almost immediately after this all the population of Whakatane became Roman Catholic.

167

Runaway Slaves.

AT THIS TIME, a slave woman belonging to a native named Martin Luther ran away to Ohiwa,[13] where she was caught and brought back to Whakatane and when in front of Mr Tapsell's fence Martin Luther and another were about to kill her with their tomahawks when Mr Tapsell ran out, and throwing his arm over her head to shield her from the blow led her into the house, where he gave her protection till the fury of her master had subsided, when Martin Luther came and asked to have her given up to him. To this Mr Tapsell consented on condition that her life should be spared and she should be kindly treated. Martin Luther promised to do this, and was allowed to take her away, nor did he fail faithfully to keep his promise.

Subsequently, an inferior chief of Whakatane ran away with a slave girl belonging to Hapanui, and went to Maketu, where Hikairo, who was a relative of his, resided, and where Mr Tapsell then happened to be for the purpose of bringing away his wife and daughter, then on a visit to their relatives there.

Mr Tapsell on his return to Whakatane brought the two fugitives with him in a canoe. They were approaching the landing place where a man could be seen awaiting their arrival. He was naked, all but a band round his waist, in his hand was a greenstone mere, which he brandished in a frantic manner, he clenched his teeth with savage spite, his eyes rolled with diabolical exultation, and his whole frame quivered with excitement. It was Hapanui. As the party leaped ashore, he sprang towards the two runaways, and would have cloven their skulls but for the interposition of Mr Tapsell who thrust himself between them to cover their retreat into his house.

While this was effected he stood in the doorway guarding the entrance in front of which Hapanui danced about waving his mere, and talking till he was hoarse. By and by, Pono and another relative came up and took the mere out of his hand, after which his anger gradually subsided, and, as if suddenly seized with consideration for the inconvenience to which he was subjecting Mr Tapsell, told him that he need not be afraid now, as his passion was over, and he would not do the people any harm. Accordingly, they were permitted to depart. But the compensation had yet come, the utu had to be paid. On the day following, the man was stripped of every article of property he possessed, and heavy contributions were levied upon all the relatives of both individuals, the happy couple were acknowledged as man and wife, and left to begin house keeping on the slender resources which they had received from nature.

NOTES

1. Te Urewera ('Uriwera country') is a sparsely populated area of dense forest and rugged hills situated in the Huiarau, Ikawhenua and Maungapōhatu ranges in the Hawke's Bay and Bay of Plenty regions of the North Island. It is the historical home of Ngāi Tūhoe and was largely untouched by British colonists until the twentieth century, effectively remaining under Māori control until then.

2. A letter from Chapman dated 26 March 1836 (qMS-0425, p. 96) includes the following:
    > [...] accounts were brought of every kind that could terrify, and hearing that a strange war-party from Waikato were also in the neighbourhood I judged it prudent to remove the principal part of our Goods and Stores to the island in the middle of the lake — Just as we were in this state, and on the day I had also removed Mrs. Chapman to a little hut (hastily built) on the island; Mr. Phillip King arrived with an invitation from Mr. Wade to Mrs. Chapman inviting her most kindly to his house — Waharoa having left Tauranga the day previous (whither he had been to obtain a supply of arms and ammunition) in order to proceed hither at once — and Mr. Wade being aware of his intentions thus kindly hastened to save Mrs. Chapman form the expected horror of a residence so near to the seat of War, our settlement being only ten minutes' walk from the great Pa Inamutu — Mrs. C. left under charge of Mr. King the following day and arrived safely on the evening of the next day at Mr. Wade's — and certainly under such circumstances my mind was much relieved.

    And in another letter dated 14 May 1836 (qMS-0425, p. 99):
    > I had purposed writing at length — but from journies and the confusion we have been in, have been altogether prevented — War has broke out all around us — but for our persons we have no fear — all has originated in the one murder described in this letter — the two Pa's (Maketu and the Tumu) the former belonging to Rotorua, the latter to Tauranga, have been taken and men, women and children of both massacred and eaten.

3. 'Kopenga River' is the Kapenga River.

4. Frederick Peterson of Spring Street, Sydney.

5. The *Harlequin* was a 71-ton schooner that operated out of Sydney. Its departure with the Tapsells was noted in the Australian newspapers: 'Departures [...] June 4. — The Schooner *Harlequin*, Anderson Master, for New Zealand. Passengers — Mr. and Mrs. Tapsell, Mr. Banks, and two children, and Mr. Hitchcock', *The Australian*, 6 June 1837, p. 2.

6. This may possibly be William Jackson, who traded out of Onehunga to Kāwhia Harbour for Frederick Peterson.

7. Gilbert Mair (1799–1857), a sailor and trader, was originally from Peterhead, Scotland, and settled in the Bay of Islands in 1824. He built a trading station at Te Wahapu Point near Kororāreka in 1830 and later moved to Whangarei. He traded principally in kauri timber and gum and engaged in whaling. He is the father of William Gilbert Mair, the celebrated soldier. See also Johannes C. Andersen and George Conrad Petersen, *The Mair Family* (Wellington: A.H. & A.W. Reed, 1956), where Tapsell's account of Mair's whaling venture is quoted on pp. 55–56.

8. The 'thwart' is the seat across a boat on which the rower sits.

9. John Middlemas (1810–99), settler born in Alnwick, England, died in Whitianga, Coromandel.

10. In his letter written 2 August 1837 to Reverend John A. Wilson, James Kemp mentions the accident saying: 'Clementson was drowned at Matata also that young man "Jenkins" who was living with him. They were in Mr Tapsell's boat I believe going into Matata. There were 3 Europeans in the boat, Mr C[lementson], Mr Jenkins and James Farrow who was saved by the natives.' See John Alexander Wilson, Letters 1835–87 (Ref: MS 98/76, Auckland War Memorial Museum Library, Auckland, New Zealand).

11. Upoko kōhua ('puko kuhua') is Māori for 'boil your head!' According to typed notes in James Cowan's papers (MS-Papers-0039-39), Tapsell never learnt to speak te reo Māori properly:

    Curiously, although he had native wives, (not more than one at a time!) and lived with Maori tribes for more than forty years, he did not become a fluent speaker of the Maori language. Indeed he scarcely troubled to learn the tongue at all. The masterful sailor compelled the Maoris to understand his vigorous English backed up with a strong pair of fists.

    However, Cowan's statement about Phillip Tapsell's linguistic abilities conflicts with the Tapsell family's own knowledge about their tipuna. See p. 9.

12. The *Sancta Maria* (formerly the *Atlas*) was a schooner bought by Bishop Jean-Baptiste Pompallier and used in his voyages around New Zealand. Ōpōtiki, Bay of Plenty (or more specifically the kāinga at Pā Kōwhai) has a French Catholic mission and was visited by Bishop Pompallier in 1840. During his stay in Whakatāne he celebrated mass and baptised a baby girl.

13. Martin Luther was also known by the Māori version of the same name, Mātene Rūta. Ōhiwa lies halfway between Ōpōtiki and Whakatāne where the Nukuhou River reaches the Bay of Plenty.

13

An adventurer

ABOUT THIS TIME Mr Tapsell received a visit from a Dr Newman, who, with his servant or companion were ostensibly making a tour through New Zealand. Dr Newman was an extremely prepossessing man, who dressed well, and whose polished demeanour was calculated to throw a stranger entirely off his guard. He represented to Mr Tapsell that he had a number of large packages of goods coming forward to him at Whakatane which he desired Mr Tapsell to get made into smaller ones for the convenience of carriage through the country. This Mr Tapsell promised to do, the stranger established himself on a most friendly footing, and in the glow of generous hospitality mutual confidences began to be exchanged.

Mr Tapsell informed his guest that he had prepared a petition to the Queen to be rewarded for services he had rendered to the British Government by the rescue of the Wellington in years gone by. His distinguished guest, after reflecting a moment, gave his opinion that he had a very strong claim for reward and expressed his willingness to give the petition into the hands of the honourable Captain whom he was sure to meet in the House of Commons on his return to England. Such an opportunity was not to be lost, and Mr Tapsell confided the valuable document to his care. Before leaving, Dr. Newman would have drawn some stores from Mr Tapsell, but the stock of the latter was at that moment rather low, and all he could spare was a quantity of tobacco, a ham and some bacon.

From Whakatane Dr. Newman proceeded to Rotorua where he became the guest of Mr Chapman, who was pleased with the religious tone of his conversation and whom he informed that he belonged to the presbyterian body. From Mr Chapman he procured goods to the value of about thirty-pounds, and then departed for Opotiki, where as a good Catholic he enjoyed the hospitality of the resident priest, from whom he obtained a number of articles. His next appearance was at Port Nicholson, where he put up at the best hotel and was treated as a visitor of distinction. During his stay at the hotel various articles of value began to disappear. Spoons were missing and the peace of the quiet household distracted by suspicion. The case was one of delicacy, for the house was only frequented by gentlemen, against whom it seemed impossible to make a charge. But Dr. Newman being taken ill, and requiring clean linen, unfortunately for himself, entrusted his keys to the sympathising landlady, who, on opening his box, was surprised to see her missing property. Dr Newman was apprehended, tried, convicted, and transported.

Huhi, the cannibal.[1]

A WAR AT THIS TIME broke out between the natives at Whakatane, and those living up the river, in consequence of a chief of the former, named Era causing the infidelity of the wife of Huhi belonging to the latter place.

The war was of short duration, lasting only a couple of days, an equal number being killed on both sides. Amongst the killed was an old chief of Whakatane, whose blood was greedily drunk by Huhi, the monster cutting off a piece of his flesh and eating it raw. The grief of the son of this old chief on learning the death of his father was affecting to witness. He stood weeping as if his heart would break till sunset, and refused to taste food.

This same Huhi was afterwards concerned in the murder of Mr Falloon and is at present undergoing his sentence for that crime.[2]

171

A dangerous host.

MR TAPSELL AT WHAKATANE besides his purchases of flax, carried on a considerable trade in pigs and maize, at one time having a large quantity of the latter article stored for shipment, when a brig commanded by a Captain Hart arrived off Opotiki,[3] where Captain Hart went ashore to endeavour to purchase maize. Not being successful, he travelled by land to Ohiwa, where a Mr Nicholson resided,[4] who informed him of Mr Tapsell's stock, and they came together to Whakatane.

The brig followed them up the coast, and stood off and on abreast of Whakatane, but a gale of wind set in, lasting two or three days. After it had moderated, Mr Tapsell took the Captain and Mr Nicholson off in his boat, and was welcomed on board with great cordiality by the Captain, who invited them both below, and caused wine to be set before them. Something in the manner of Captain Hart warned Mr Tapsell to be moderate in his potation a caution which the subsequent behaviour of his entertainer fully justified.

Captain Hart began to speak of business, requesting to purchase the maize from Mr Tapsell, and offering a price for it. This Mr Tapsell declined, remarking that it was not to be sold.

"I'll fight you then," suddenly observed Captain Hart.

"Well, you are Captain on board your own vessel, but you do not frighten me," coolly answered Tapsell.

"D—d if I don't shoot you," was the singular reply, and, calling the steward, he ordered him to bring his pistols. They were brought, and the Captain proceeded to load them with ball.

All this time, Mr Tapsell was narrowly watching the movements of his host, and he thought that it would be desirable to draw a little closer, to him which he did, till the captain was within easy reach of his arm.

Captain Hart cocked his pistol and presented it at the head, of Tapsell who almost at the same moment struck his arm upwards, and the pistol exploded, the ball passing through the deck, and very nearly shooting the man at the wheel.

"Now, Captain Hart," said Mr Tapsell, rising to go, I think we have been shipmates quite long enough. It is time we should part." With these words he went on deck. The Captain quickly followed him.

"Come, Tapsell," said he, "you are not going to leave me that way. Mr —— (naming the mate) get up a case of wine and put it into Mr Tapsell's boat."

The order was obeyed, the wine put into the boat, and they parted never to meet again.

The Shipwreck.

IT WAS SOON AFTER THIS that the schooner Falconer of about two hundred tons came to Whakatane consigned to Mr Tapsell, with a quantity of goods on board.[5] After discharging the cargo, Mr Tapsell brought her to Maketu to take on board the flax that was there, and anchored her, outside the bar at the entrance to the harbour. He had also on board his two children, a boy of about eight, and Catherine a girl of ten years of age, for the purpose of sending them to school at Sydney in compliance with a request from his merchant,

Mr Petersen, who had written him a letter to that effect.[6] There was then a light wind off the shore, but a very heavy swell setting in from the Northward. He purposed taking the flax on board the following morning, and those who had berths retired to rest, while those who had not, amongst whom was Mr Tapsell, lay on lockers in the cabin.

About midnight, suddenly, without a moment's warning, a hurricane, the fury of which can hardly be conceived, struck the vessel, and made her tremble in every part. This was accompanied almost simultaneously with a fearful sea such as few have ever witnessed, both wind and sea gradually increasing in violence, till it would be impossible to describe their terrible intensity. Though an order were given at the top of the voice to a man standing close by, it could not be heard; all other sounds were drowned in the frightful roar of the elements. The sea between Flat Island and the main was one sheet of immense breakers, in which no ship that was ever built could have lived. A tide higher than any ever known before or since swept over the sand-hills dividing the Maketu river from the sea, and flooded the plain, rising half way up the elevated ground on which the pa of the inhabitants were situated till, with the exception of the summits peeping above the water, nothing was visible, but a boiling sea, and flying foam.

The night was clear, and the moon shone, and Mr Tapsell went up the rigging to endeavour to ascertain whereabouts the vessel was. While he held on to the shrouds[7] with his hands the wind blew his body and legs out like a flag, and it was with difficulty he regained his footing. Some idea of the height to which the tide rose may be formed where it is said that a seventy-four gun frigate might then have crossed the bar at Maketu.

The vessel having one anchor out, was kept head to wind, though it soon became evident that she was drifting. The sea beating against the small bay at the entrance to Maketu, underwent a recoil, and as the Falconer was dragging her anchor, carried her further up the coast.

By and by the enormous seas, which augmenting with the continuance of the tornado, began to break over the schooner, and the captain consulted Mr Tapsell on the course to be pursued. The latter advised that all hands should be called aft, and the hatches battened down. The men were called into the cabin, instructions issued and carried into execution. As the Captain was going on deck, he remarked that he thought it advisable to let go a second anchor.

"No! no! whatever you do, don't do that," called Tapsell, for he made sure that if the anchor should hold, the vessel must inevitably founder in deep water and all hands be hopelessly lost while, if the anchorage ground gave way she must be driven on the sandy beach, where there would be some faint prospect of life being saved. Nevertheless, the anchor was let go, and the chain whizzed through the hawse hole[8] with the velocity of an arrow from a bow till it came to the full stretch at the windlass,[9] where it parted. Some hours passed in this fearful condition: all knowing that sooner or later the vessel must strike the shore. Mr Tapsell's sufferings being painfully increased by apprehension for the safety of his two children. It could not have been very long before daylight when a gentle grating sensation made all on board sensible that she first touched the ground. Presently a gigantic roller lifted her up and carried her further in shore, and, on its recoil, left her nearly high and dry on the beach. It was desiring the state of affairs that the black cook made his appearance in the cabin with his bag slung over his shoulder, and a stick in his hand as if prepared to walk comfortably ashore.

"My cookhouse has gone," said he.

The gravity of the situation could hardly prevent a smile on the countenance of those present.

"Never mind," said Mr Tapsell, "something more will go yet."

The hour of peril was now come. Anticipating the striking of the vessel, it was Mr Tapsell's earnest hope that she might 'cast in', with her masts inclined towards the shore, for then, there might be a chance of some life being saved; whereas if she had 'cast out', with her masts inclined towards the sea, — as he afterwards observed, — she would have proved a coffin for them all.

She cast in. The captain and crew now jumped over the side and got ashore almost without wetting their feet. Mr Tapsell remained behind, in painful uncertainty about his children. For a long time he was undecided whether to take them with him when he attempted to reach the shore, or whether to adventure first himself, and afterwards return for them. He looked on them as they lay to all appearance asleep, although they were awake, and feigned sleep to hide their terror, and his indecision increased. At last he committed himself to prayer, cast his perplexity before One whom the winds and seas obeyed, and who could hear him amidst the thunder of the roaring surf and the piteous howling of the distracted wind; after which he rose with his resolution taken, to venture alone.

He jumped into a foot or so of water, no more than the wash of a receding wave, and the next moment a stupendous breaker like a mountain came curling behind him in an angry flood. Being a good swimmer, he did not lose his presence of mind, and commenced to tread water with a view of keeping clear of the keel of the vessel, which was every now and then lifting up and falling again with the intermitting waves, but all his efforts were unsuccessful in enabling him to contend against the suction of each sea as it retired, until at last, his lungs began to be choked with water, his strength and consciousness forsook him, and he lay beaten about in the surf like a log.

But for the moonlight he would never have been perceived by those on shore, and the first who saw him, was the Lascar, who at once yelled out.

"Bear a hand! Bear a hand! All of us, and bring Tapsell ashore."

They rushed into the water, and by their united endeavours, succeeded in drawing him, apparently lifeless, to land.

His first act on recovering consciousness was to enquire for his children, who still remained on the Schooner, and one of the sailors volunteered to go on board for them. This man was inveterately fond of grog, and was stimulated by a desire to obtain a supply of the fluid he so highly prized. Fortunately for the safety of the children as well as for his own while he looked around the cabin, a heavy sea smashed in the skylight, broke all the bottles, and warned him that what he had to do, he must do quickly, or it would be too late. He seized the girl in his arms and reached the shore in safety. He returned again for the boy, whom he also delivered to the anxious father.

The shipwrecked party then walked away from the water to an elevated sand hill distant from the stranded vessel about thirty of forty yards, and were congratulating themselves on their escape, one at least, overpowered with reverent gratitude for the rescue from a watery grave of his affrighted children whom he clasped convulsively to his breast, when a wave, exceeding all former ones in magnitude, came rolling up towards the doomed craft, with a white and seething crest, hissing as it approached, till it curled, toppled over, and buried the schooner in an avalanche of waters, broke her into a hundred pieces, and washed the fragments over the sandhill into the river on the other side. Nor was its force even then entirely expended, for the wash of so great a volume of water with the momentum it had acquired out thro' the isthmus of land dividing the river from the sea, connecting them both, and undermining the sandhill on which the shipwrecked party stood so many to cause it to crumble, in, and plunge them once more in the angry flood.

It was now about daybreak and the tide having ebbed, the first moving objects that the disconsolate crew could discern in the distance were several hundred natives, all stark naked, tomahawk in hand, racing eagerly towards them to plunder the wreck. Such is the law of the natives of New Zealand. Should a canoe upset, a vessel be cast ashore, or a house be burnt to the ground, all the fragments become public property, and the legitimate objects of a general scramble. It is not very long ago since a similar practice was in existence and even tolerated on the coast of England, where the 'wreckers' have been known to commit murder in order to possess themselves of the good of some poor castaway.

As the gleeful Maoris drew near their prey, the captain apprehensively

175

enquired if Tapsell thought they intended to murder the survivors to which Mr Tapsell assured him that of that there was no danger. Soon they arrived, and an excited scramble ensued, each one securing what he could, or thought of most value. Even the boxes of clothing belonging to the young children were not spared, but became the property of some beldame or other who probably had no children to wear them, or if she had, whose offspring would infinitely have preferred to caper about in the tightly fitting suit which nature had given them than be encumbered with the folds or hampered with the restraints of European clothing, and in all likelihood would the next moment after being invested, tear the garments off and cast them from them.

One of the native wreckers unintentionally did Mr Tapsell a real service. Mr Tapsell having been nearly drowned, had sat shivering with cold ever since his escape from the wreck, when a native named Tongaroa came forward with a bottle which had been washed into the river. It contained brandy. Mr Tapsell removed the cork and took a hearty draught of the generous liquor, and felt such invigoration ensue therefrom as those only can appreciate who have been like him drowned and come to life again, and afterwards sat drenched and shivering on a lee shore in the teeth of a piercing gale of wind.

The natives afterwards brought canoes and conveyed the shipwrecked mariners down to Maketu. [...] their lives, amongst whom were Mrs Tapsell and the remainder of her family, who were rescued by neighbours from a situation of great peril, their dwelling, as well as the pa occupied by the natives, being many feet under water. Opotiki had also experienced the fury of the hurricane and the extraordinary tidal disturbance, being for a time overwhelmed with the encroaching sea. The terror inspired by so unlooked for a catastrophe was universal, one European at Opotiki under the impression that the earth was about to be visited by a second deluge, exclaimed hastily,

"O Lord, remember thy promise."

The Captain and crew of the Falconer having lost their all in the wreck were supplied by Mr Tapsell with clothing and blankets from his stores at Whakatane and remained with him there till the arrival of another vessel from Sydney in which they embarked and Mr Tapsell shipped the few goods he had saved from the wreck, and what produce remained at Whakatane.

Another misfortune

IT IS AN OLD PROVERB that disasters never come singly, and the next advices Mr Tapsell received from Sydney brought the intelligence of the failure of Mr

Petersen, his merchant there, who had at the time a considerable balance of Mr Tapsell's in his hands. Thus, one calamity pressed on the hub of another, and Mr Tapsell found himself after many years of extraordinary reverses, again deprived of resources and left, at an advanced age, to begin the world afresh.

Nevertheless the same fortitude which had carried him through difficulties under which an ordinary mind would have sunk, preserved him from yielding to despair.

NOTES

1. The chief Te Uwhi Te Haraki ('Huhi, the cannibal') was found guilty of being an accessory to the murder of James Fulloon on board the *Kate* (see p. 171). He was sentenced to death (5 April 1866), commuted to penal servitude for life and later pardoned (26 November 1867).
2. James Francis Fulloon (1840–65) was the son of an Anglo-French immigrant and a Māori chief's daughter. He worked as a junior clerk in the Land Purchase Department in Auckland and later as an interpreter, often travelling to various trouble spots in the North Island. In 1865 he was appointed the captain of a militia and sent to Whakatāne to recruit Ngāti Awa to help fight against Hauhau in the Bay of Plenty. However, his ship never made it — the crew were killed and the ship set alight in the Whakatāne River by Pai Mārire supporters. Te Uwhi Te Haraki ('Huhi') was one of the attackers (see *Wellington Independent*, 13 February 1866, p. 6).
3. There was more than one captain called Hart sailing to and around New Zealand at the time.
4. Albert John Nicholas ('Nikorehe') established a trading post on Uretara Island, Ōhiwa, by 1839. He bought the island from Te Kēpa, son of Toihau.
5. For another crewmember's recollections of the *Falcon's* end, see Part 3, 'Contemporary accounts of Phillip Tapsell's life'. Written at Kororāreka on 5 December 1842 by William M. Umbers, second mate of the *Falcon*, the account differs from Tapsell's narrative in several respects. See also Alister Matheson, 'The Storm that Wrecked the *Falcon*, 1 March 1840: Eyewitness Accounts', *Historical Review: Bay of Plenty Journal of History*, 48 (2000), pp. 8–24. On the name of the schooner, see 'Bay of Plenty Shipwrecks: Corrections and Additions', *Historical Review: Bay of Plenty Journal of History*, 47.2 (1999), pp. 77–81 (77–79), s.v. 'Falcon, 1840'.
6. These are Phillip and Hineitūrama's children Retireti (born 1836) and Kataraina (born 1834).
7. The 'shrouds' are a set of ropes leading from the head of a mast and forming part of the standing rigging of a ship.
8. The hawse hole is the small hole in the hull through which cables and ropes ('hawsers') used for mooring the ship may be passed. Cf. chapter 5, note 7.
9. The windlass is the winch used to raise the anchor.

14

Effects of the storm

IT WAS ABOUT A WEEK after the events described in the last chapter that Mr Tapsell with his children and the shipwrecked crew of the Falconer were able to proceed Southward to Whakatane, and fully that time before the commotion of the waters had sufficiently subsided to permit of the passage being made with safety, and on arrival at the latter place it was found that the effect of the storm had been felt all along the coast in a manner such as never had been experienced before. At Whakatane the sea had risen and flooded the settlement so that many of the inhabitants had difficulty in escaping with [...]

During his numerous whaling voyages he had acquired a knowledge of various descriptions of handicraft connected with ships, such as, boat building, carpenter's work, sail making, and indeed, as many whalers do, could turn his hand to almost anything, so at this time, he commenced building a schooner for the Maoris, which they paid for in flax, and afterwards, rose on a large boat of his own, which he converted into a schooner, and in which he made several trading trips to the Bay of Islands, all of which were unsuccessful, and he ultimately sold her to the Maoris.

A legacy

IT WAS ON THE OCCASION of one of his trips to the Bay of Islands that Mr Berksham the boatmaster there[1] handed him a letter from the Danish Consul, apprising him of the death of his father at Copenhagen, fourteen years before, and that a considerable sum of money had been left to him at the decease of his parent. The letter instructed him to forward a certificate to the effect that he was still in existence, in order that he might claim the bequest.

Accordingly, he proceeded to Auckland, and by the legal advice of Mr Bartley, procured the necessary certificate which, together with a power of attorney, was sent to Copenhagen. The next letter which he received acquainted him that the business was not quite settled, and by a subsequent one, he learned that his legacy had been given to a near relation, but that if the decision of the Court should be unfavorable, the Master in Chancery would have to pay all expenses. He heard no more on the subject.

More disaster

HE THEN CARRIED ON A TRADE with the natives at Whakatane and those further up the river, until a war broke out between them which lasted nearly two years, with considerable loss on both sides. After it had been in progress for some time, the Whakatane people desired to obtain possession of his house for a fortification, and he sold it to them for six horses, which at that time, being scarce, were worth £20 each. He then moved up the river, and took up his abode there, purchasing from time to time, wheat and maize, and had accumulated a considerable quantity, which he was desirous of shipping, but the Whakatane people from jealousy, refused to let it pass through their district, and it remained in store till completely destroyed by weevils.

During the progress of the late Waikato war, Mrs Tapsell left Whakatane on a visit to her daughter Mrs Hooper, wife of Dr Hooper, then at Orakau with the troops.[2] Mrs Hooper died the day before she arrived, and Dr Hooper removing with his family, Mrs Tapsell went into the pa to see her relatives, some of whom were within, defending the fort against the soldiers, by whom it was surrounded, and there received her death wound by a rifle ball during the engagement.[3]

The stirring events of Mr Tapsell's life may be said to cease with the disastrous shipwreck of the Falconer at Tumu. The incidents of his stay at Whakatane were not marked by any extraordinary interruption, the good behavior, and humane dispositions of the natives rendering his stay there comparatively peaceful. Not much more remains to be told.

Complicated misfortunes towards the close of a more than ordinary life time, found him with failing energies and elasticity of mind impaired deriving consolation from the dutiful affection of his children, supported by the encouragement of religion and the consciousness of having through life been actuated by rectitude of purpose.

179

Later years

HIS RESOURCES were now completely at an end, for a time he remained at Whakatane unemployed, until his son, residing at Maketu, brought down a schooner and took him away.[4] He remained at Maketu a few months, and afterwards, went to stay at the farm of his son in law, Mr Simpkins, at Onehunga, where he remained nine months.[5] From thence he went to Tairua and remained there for a period of two years,[6] employed in trading and boat building, after which he resided on Whale Island, where Mr Simpkins had a station, until it was given up, when, hearing of the expected arrival of H.R.H. the Duke of Edinburgh in New Zealand,[7] he at ninety years of age, walked to Maketu a distance of forty miles, with the purpose of getting a petition to the Prince prepared, enumerating the services he had rendered to the English Government and people, by the rescue of the convict brig, and the ransom at his own cost of many British subjects, and praying for some consideration. The unexpected return to England by the Prince in consequence of an atrocious attempt on his life at Sydney,[8] prevented the presentation of the document in person, and it was sent to Governor Sir George Bowen with a request that it might be forwarded to the Prince.[9] A reply was received from Sir G. Bowen stating that the request would be compiled with, and no more has since been heard of the application.

During his periods of prosperity Mr Tapsell never prosecuted any application for reward for what must undoubtedly have been at the time a most important service rendered to the English Government by the recapture of so great a number of convicted criminals who would otherwise have been let loose on society, but when he became crushed by misfortune it occurred to him that, notwithstanding the lapse of years, an appeal to the sympathies of the Government for some small provision for his remaining days might not be altogether overlooked.

Ransoms

HE WAS ALSO OF OPINION that his at the time disinterested ransom of many captives, some of whom were British subjects, might fairly be taken into account.

The persons ransomed were the following:–

Three — One Englishman, and two Americans, (names not remembered) purchased from the Ngapuhis in the Bay of Islands for an equivalent in value of £20 each.

Three — an Englishman, (Abraham), a Lascar, and an American negro,[10] out of a crew, five of whom were murdered and eaten in Cook's Straits, twenty pounds each.

Two — Englishmen, Jackson and a cooper, purchased from Hapanui at Whakatane, twenty pounds each.

Six — women of the Arawa tribe, slaves to the Ngapuhi, some of whom are now living. Twenty pounds each.

Six — Taylor, (English), wife's sister, wife and three half caste children, some of whom are living, and have families. Twenty pounds each.

One — Son of Rewa, a great Chief of the Ngapuhi, purchased from the Waikato and Ngaiterangi for twenty pounds.

One — Hapene, a native woman of Tauranga ransomed from the Arawa for twenty pounds.

One — daughter of Rangitikina the principal chief at Matata. The values ransomed from the Ngapuhi for eighteen pounds are set down in specified sums, instead of repeating the goods given to which they were equivalent.

At this period referred to, money was never used as a current medium, muskets and certain goods representing an established rate, supplying its place. A musket would purchase eight hundred weight of flax, which in England then sold for seventy five pounds a ton. It would therefore be equal to thirty pounds and, allowing a reasonable deduction, may fairly be set down as twenty pounds.

It will then be seen that twenty three individuals were ransomed at an average value of twenty pounds or an aggregate of four hundred and sixty pounds, paid by Mr Tapsell for the liberty, and in most of the cases, for the lives of persons in whom he was in no way interested except from motives of humanity.

With regard to the latter individual ransomed, it may be mentioned that Mr Tapsell, being desirous of obtaining the island of Matata,[11] offered to purchase it from Rangitikina, who, rather reluctantly, and only out of gratitude for the ransom of his daughter, was induced to sell it, and accepted a quantity of goods agreed upon, in exchange, giving Mr Tapsell a written document as a title.

About the year 1867 the sons of Mr Tapsell preferred their claim to Whale Island, White Island,[12] and the island of Matata, all of which were acquired by purchase. The title to Whale and White Islands was admitted, and Crown Grants for them issued, but the title to the island of Matata was refused.

Two married daughters and three sons comprised the family of Mr Tapsell now living.[13] Retreat, the eldest son, tall, and handsome, of aristocratic bearing, and amiable disposition, holds the office of Sergeant of Police and customs officer at Maketu. Phillip, of scarcely less stature, stalwart and muscular, is a corporal in the Arawa contingent, and Ians, slender active and intelligent, a sergeant in the Native division of the Armed Constabulary actively engaged on the West Coast.[14] They have all "done the State some service". The two latter fought with distinction at Whakatane and Matata after the repulse of the Hauhaus from Maketu, and were present in the expeditions from Tauranga in January 1867.[15] Ians was instrumental in capturing the notorious Peter Grant, who deserted to the Hauhaus from the Waikato Militia.[16] All are parents of families, and sixteen children call Mr Tapsell grandfather, so that the old Dane, after serving the country he adopted has contributed to the number of loyal British subjects several representatives of whom he has no cause to be ashamed.

Conclusion.

THE INCIDENTS OF THIS BIOGRAPHY have almost the air of romance. It is like opening an old volume of history to obtain from a living source the personal adventures of one whose recollections extend into the past century. One who can remember the Mutiny of the Bounty[17] — Norfolk Island before it was a penal settlement, — who was in New Zealand sixty two years ago, — was one who helped to avenge the massacre of the Boyd, — touched at St. Helena when Bonaparte was a prisoner there, — was present at the Battle of Copenhagen, and who, though living for forty years amongst the cannibals of these islands amidst revolting scenes of bloodshed and savage perfidy, has preserved his simplicity of character, and now remains, a pious, contented, old man; the experience of such a one is of no ordinary kind. Of the persons with whom he came in contact in the active portion of his life, very few remain. Tupaia and Hapanui still survive, but one by one, his contemporaries in the stirring scenes he has witnessed are passing away. To the present generation he is almost a stranger, and the story of his career like a tradition. Occasionally an old, old chief will pay him a visit, and weep with emotion at the recollections which the interview awakens. "It is the ghost of the past," he will say. The sight of the venerable pakeha brings back to his mind warriors of renown whom he has outlived, and recalls events tho' actors in which have long since disappeared.

The story of Mr Tapsell's life is almost done. This remarkable man, who has passed through vicissitudes and adventures such as fall to the lot of few, who has endured misfortune with heroism, suffering with fortitude, and confronted danger with courage when pusillanimity or indecision would have ensured destruction, whose transparency of character, and singleness of purpose won him fast friends amongst civilized, and inspired respect and admiration amongst savage people, is now, as King Lear says, "a poor, old man". Nearly a hundred winters have whitened his hair, age has slightly bent his once erect and sinewy frame; wounds received in battle have left traces in trembling hands that can no longer clasp knife or fork, and, after having possessed thousands and enjoyed prosperity at various periods of his life, he is now, as far as worldly goods are concerned, ending life as he began. Not entirely so, however. He cannot reproach himself with the stain of treachery or dishonour. He may have survived the generation he has served, but he has acquired the comforts of religion, which, if his services here should never be acknowledged, will hereafter secure him a recompense and an exceeding great reward.

NOTES

1. Possibly a mistake for Thomas Beckham, magistrate and postmaster at Kororāreka.
2. 'Mrs Hooper' is Ewa, born 1839. In 1855, she married Robert Richardson Hooper (1828–86).
3. In an account of the Battle of Ōrākau pā written some 30 years after the event (and here quoted from Andersen and Petersen, *The Mair Family*, pp. 120–22), Major William Gilbert Mair (see chapter 12, note 7) describes the death of Hineitūrama:

    In a corner I found a woman kneeling by the half buried body of a man. Her clothes were girded up ready for flight, and she had evidently stopped to take a last look at her dead husband [Rōpata], from whose face she had scraped away sand. My aim at this time was to get hold of someone who could give some information, for we did not even know who the people were who had been fighting us so desperately for three long days. I was just stooping to speak to her when, hearing a yell, I turned and found myself face to face with five or six maddened soldiers with their bayonets at the charge. I tried to beat them back with my carbine, and did knock one of them into the ditch, but while some of them threatened me with their bayonets, others got past me. I heard no cry from the woman, but when I turned to look at her again she was down and the blood was spouting from her bare breast. [...] The woman whom I tried to save in the ditch was Hineiturama, formerly the wife of Tapsell, the famous East Coast trader. She, with Te Paerata, his son Hone Tere, son-in-law Wereta (my friend!), Piripi te Heuheu, and others, making thirty in all, were buried in the ditch at the south-east corner of the pa.

4. 'His son' here refers to Retireti.
5. Kataraina married George Simpkins in 1853. Onehunga is a town (now suburb) about 8 km south of the centre of Auckland on the Manukau Harbour. It was developed by Europeans as a commercial port and received ships from Australia and South Africa. It was also the main route for shipping to the south.
6. Tairua is a town on the east coast of the Coromandel Peninsula. During early European settlement, it became a centre for the timber industry and gold mining.
7. Alfred (1844–1900), the second son and fourth child of Victoria I, was known as the Duke of Edinburgh from 1866 until he succeeded his uncle as the reigning Duke of Saxe-Coburg and Gotha in the German Empire.
8. On 12 March 1868, there was an assassination attempt in Sydney when Henry O'Farrell shot Prince Alfred, in the back and wounded him.
9. George Ferguson Bowen (1821–99) was a colonial administrator who had various postings throughout the world. Between 1867 and 1873 he was Governor of New Zealand.

10. This 'American negro' is identified as Powers in Bentley, *Pakeha Maori*, pp. 72, 224.

11. The 'island' of Matatā was the area of land lying between the lagoon and the sea that existed before the Tarawera River was cut through to the sea. Mention of Tapsell's proof of ownership is noteworthy here: see following note.

12. The Tapsells' connection with White Island/Whakaari and Matamata is described in W.T. Parham, *Island Volcano: White Island, or Whakaari, New Zealand* (Auckland: Collins, 1973), pp. 40–41:

    He successfully established his ownership of both White and Whale Islands, but failed to secure a third property at Matamata. These claims were heard in 1868 when he was 89, and no doubt because of his great age title to White Island was granted on 27 June to his son Retireti and his daughter Katharine (Katerina), who was married to George Simpkins, a trader at Whakatane. The latter also owned a trading station on Whale Island where Tapsell lived at one period after serious reverses. The number of family connections among those associated with the island's fairly short history is rather unusual. [...] Retreat Tapsell and his sister did not retain possession for very long, since in the year following the Crown grant they transferred their joint interest to George Simpkins. Once again the capital needed to develop the property was too great for a trader in such a small provincial centre as Whakatane. Five years later, on 28 February 1874, he sold the place to Mr Justice (John Alexander) Wilson and William Kelly.

13. Tapsell had three daughters who all married: Kataraina (married George Simpkins in 1838), Ewa (1839–64, married Robert Richardson Hooper in 1855) and Tote (1842–70, married Tamati Hutchinson year unknown). The reminiscences were noted down at some point before Tote married, so he is here referring to Kataraina and Ewa.

14. Perepe (Phillip) was born in 1838 and Ïeni/Jens ('Ians'), named after Tapsell's father, was born in 1841.

15. The Hauhau (Pai Mārire) movement was a religion founded by the prophet Te Ua Haumēne (1820s–1866) in Taranaki. It flourished in the North Island between 1863 and 1874. Pai Mārire became a violent resistance movement against the New Zealand government's military operations against North Island Māori. Europeans tended to call all Māori fighting the government's attempts to exert British sovereignty and gain more land for Pākehā settlement 'Hauhaus' regardless of whether they followed Pai Mārire or not.

16. Peter Grant (1845–1924) deserted the Waikato Regiment in December 1865. He adopted the Pai Mārire religion and joined the Hauhaus, supplying them with horses and rifles. He was captured by Ïeni (Hans) Tapsell in February 1867 (see *Daily Southern Cross*, 1 March 1867, p. 7). Grant was court-martialled and received 50 lashes and two years' imprisonment with hard labour (see *Hawke's Bay Times*, 1 April 1967, p. 2). His obituary in the *Bay of Plenty Times* (4 February 1924, p. 2) gives his life story with no mention of his desertion.

17. The mutiny on HMS *Bounty* occurred in the South Pacific on 28 April 1789. Led by Fletcher Christian the mutineers took control of the ship from its captain, William Bligh.

...e may be said

...disastrous thin...

...the "Falconer" at...

...his stay at whi...

...arked by any...

...ption, the good...

...nal disposition...

...the rendering...

Not much...

...all feel.

PART 3

TAPSELL'S LIFE AND AFTERLIFE IN WRITING

The Tapsell manuscript

Composition

TOWARD THE END OF HIS LIFE, 'the old Dane' dictated his reminiscences to Edward Little who was a member of the Armed Constabulary and clerk at the magistrate's court in Maketū.[1] The historian James Cowan dates the manuscript to 1869 and although this year may well be correct for this particular version of the narrative, we know that Tapsell had in fact narrated his life story, or parts of it, to Little by late autumn of 1868. The clerk had sent the episode about the recapture of the *Wellington* for publication in Australia where it appeared in several newspapers in August/September of that year.[2] Although the chronology (and more rarely, the location) of events is occasionally confused, Tapsell was clearly a gifted storyteller and able to describe his experiences in surprising detail and — most likely after Little had done some editorial polishing — in a lively and captivating manner. The author and editor clearly had their intended audience in mind and they did not shy away from exaggeration or a little invention if it made the story more interesting (and sellable).

The text as we have it today is written in Little's small, tidy hand on the back of rather fragile blue, occasionally white, court paper, which has been torn into smaller pieces measuring just 10 cm × 16 cm. In all, 287 pieces of paper were arranged into chapters, each of which was carefully tied with string at the top left-hand corner. There are numerous corrections made *in scribendo*, in other words, changes made by Little while writing the text. These primarily comprise crossings-out with a new word written alongside. However, some changes are more substantial with rewordings of entire phrases added above the line using an insertion mark and the original words crossed out. These changes, written in ink, were probably made when Little was preparing and reworking the manuscript for publication in the *Daily Southern Cross*.[3]

These alterations raise the question, to what extent does the manuscript

The Tapsell manuscript.

Page 1 of the Tapsell
manuscript.

faithfully represent Tapsell's own words? Should the text be considered a composition by Tapsell or by Little? There is no real way of untangling the individual men's involvement in the work, which is best considered a co-authored piece: Tapsell supplied the story and the details, Little took care of the wording and structure. We can imagine Little asking Tapsell for names, dates, clarifications and specifics of certain events and episodes. A handwritten letter by Tapsell from 1845, now housed at the Alexander Turnbull Library, shows that even if his spelling was wanting, Tapsell's level of English was good, which is hardly surprising after decades of sailing on British ships and living in New Zealand.[4] He would certainly have been able to dictate his life story in clear, if not entirely idiomatic, English.

Pages 153 and 154 of the Tapsell manuscript.

qMS-1977: Alexander Turnbull Library, National Library of New Zealand · Te Puna Mātauranga o Aotearoa, Wellington

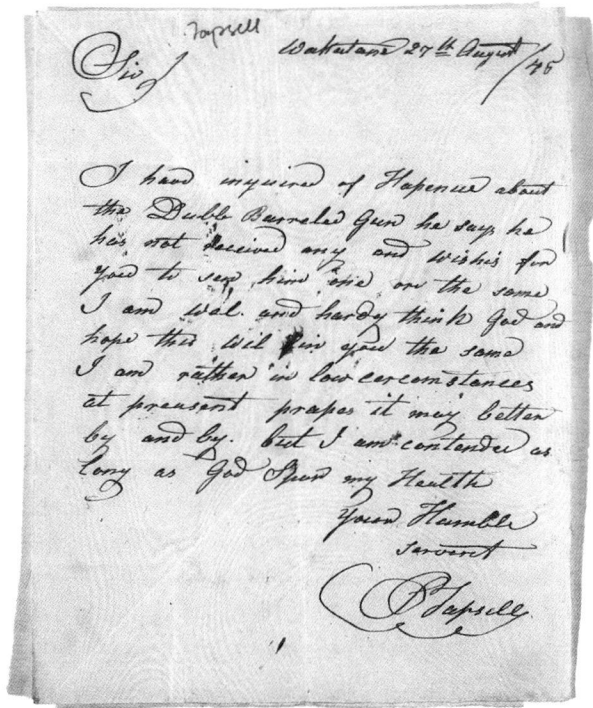

Wakatane 27 August/45
Sir,
I have inquired of Hapenue about the
Duble Barreled Gun he says he has not
received any and wishes for you to send
him one or the same I am wel and hardy
thank God and hope this wil fin you the
same I am rather in low cercumstances
at prensent prapes it may better by and
by. but I am contended as long as God
Spar my Health
Your Humble Servant
P Tapsell

It is noteworthy, however, that the reminiscences are written in the third person and the subject of the work is usually referred to as 'Mr Tapsell' (not 'I') and the story is told using 'his own words' (not 'my own words').[5] This is the principal difference between the Tapsell manuscript and the narrative published in the Australian newspapers in 1868. In the Australian version, the story of the recapture of the *Wellington* is told in the first person 'in the actual words of Mr. Tapsell [...] which are so simple and graphic that alteration would only have spoilt them'.[6] If we compare the wording in the manuscript with that in the newspaper, we see that there are substantial differences. The actual events and, peculiarly, the direct speech, are almost identical, but clearly the two versions cannot both be an accurate word-for-word record of one and the same dictation. The Tapsell manuscript — if not also the Australian version — is a reworked and cleverly crafted version of a dictation. On the reverse of page 131 of the manuscript there are crossed-out notes on the contents in the form of a list, which is possibly evidence of Little's work on ordering the pieces of paper or structuring the narrative.

When we consider the manuscript we can see that in spite of occasional lapses events are for the most part chronologically well-ordered and the level of detail is astounding. This suggests that Little's hand in the work was substantial. In places the serialised articles in the *Daily Southern Cross* are almost verbatim copies of the manuscript as we have it. It would be an incredible feat for Tapsell to have dictated this long story in a version that was this polished, correct and ready for publication in serialised format. It seems most likely that the manuscript is a reworking of now lost notes previously dictated by Tapsell, which Little has arranged into a suitable form for publishing, perhaps to raise funds for the elderly and financially pressed trader (as seems to be the motive behind the Australian newspaper article). Indeed, this is the reason behind the more fanciful elements in the reminiscences, whether Tapsell's own inventions or Little's, that made the Old Dane's life as exciting as possible for readers who were apparently hungry for bibliographical tales of adventure. Little's role as editor of the memoirs is of enormous importance in shaping the manuscript and the story of Tapsell's life as we have it today.

Provenance

AFTER PHILLIP TAPSELL RELATED his reminiscences and Little produced the manuscript, it came into the possession of the Tapsell family and remained there until 1913 when Retireti passed away. According to a letter written in 1943 by Enid Tapsell (the wife of Phillip Tapsell's grandson, Kouma),[7] the manuscript was subsequently taken to Whakatāne, without the rest of the family's knowledge, by Retireti's sister, Kataraina. When Kataraina died in 1917 the manuscript went to her daughter and son-in-law, Eliza Annie

Simpkins and John McAlister. Their son, also called John, passed it on to historian James Cowan (1870–1943) in 1920.[8]

> Police Station
> Newton 13/4/20
> Dear Sgt Cowan
> Sgt Waterman was telling me that your brother was imployed
> by the Gov collecting ancient New Zealand history Well I have a
> manuscript of the life of Philip Tapsell He was my great-grandfather
> & that is why I have it in my possession. He came out to N.Z about
> 110 years ago & was one of the first European settlers. He resided
> with the Maories in the Bay of Plenty & led an adventurous life.
> If it is possible to have it printed into book form I would like it done
> I would be pleased if you could let your [brother] know of it & if he
> thought it worth while to communicate with me.
> Yours truly
> John McAlister Sgt
> Newton Police

> Police Station
> Newton
> 20/4/20
> Dear Mr Cowan,
> I enclose the manuscript It is not in proper order but that is easily
> done. I have not read it through. Only a chapter here & there So
> cannot say whether any of it is missing or not. This is all of it as was
> given to me. If there is any further information you need I know
> of no one who could give it to you excepting perhaps one of his
> grandsons Mr Rewi Tapsell of Maketu.
> The paper clippings may be of some use.
> I remain yours truly
> John McAlister

Several years later, in 1926, Cowan started publishing articles in the *Auckland Star* based on the manuscript.[9] In one article he wrote about various episodes that were 'given in a MS account now before me'.[10] On reading the article in the *Auckland Star*, Enid Tapsell realised that Cowan was in possession of the family manuscript and contacted the historian to ask for its return. Cowan acceded and returned the manuscript to the Tapsells, at the same time asking them for permission to publish the manuscript in book form. As the family had already had a similar idea, they agreed to collaborate. However, on inspecting the returned manuscript the Tapsells were upset to discover that it had been very badly treated by Cowan. All of the bundles of paper had been untied and rearranged, some pages had been glued onto other pieces of paper, whole sections had been crossed out, 'corrections' had been superimposed over the original text, and additions and headings had been added. In short, the historical document had been vandalised and parts of it were ruined.[11]

In 1935, some eight years after returning the manuscript, Cowan published his book A Trader in Cannibal Land,[12] 'the memoir of a boldly dramatic figure in New Zealand's history', and the family once again felt betrayed.[13] The book did not represent an accurate account of Tapsell and Little's manuscript. Cowan had hacked it about in places, made his own changes to the text and excluded pages of narrative despite claiming in the introduction that, 'No fiction enters into the narrative. The temptation to expand the biography into an historical novel was hard to resist, but it was felt that the plain story was sufficiently vivid to arouse and hold the interest of the reader.'[14] In her notes on the Tapsell manuscript and Cowan's book, Ruth Burnard draws attention to one passage in particular:[15]

> To Te Puke by Rotorua bus, thence to Maketu by taxi. The Tapsell M[anu]s[cript] had, as Mrs [Enid] Tapsell told me, been sadly knocked about by Cowan. He has chopped it about in places, made his own alterations in grammatical construction and shamelessly crossed out pages and pages of narrative. One instance of this is nothing but dishonest. After recording in his book with that perfectly awful title — A Trader in Cannibal Land — that when Tapsell returned to NZ after his sojourn in Sydney he had found both Farrow and Clementson gone from Tauranga, a report coming later that they had been drowned at Matata, he completely ignored a passage later on in the MS to the effect that the rumour about Farrow was unfounded for he later turned up at Tapsell's Whakatane station. The passage to this effect in the MS he has just put a line through thus leaving in his book a statement which he knew to be untrue. A small thing no doubt but not calculated to inspire one with any faith in the man's methods of research. To one brought up to believe original MS sacrosanct the treatment meted out to the Tapsell semi-original MS is rather disgraceful. However in spite of its maltreatment one can read it as Tapsell dictated it and this has given me several useful points mentioned in neither Cowan nor Enid Tapsell[16] together with the satisfaction of actually seeing the stuff.

An example of omission by James Cowan. The passage about Farrow's visit to Tapsell's station in Whakatāne was deleted in the manuscript (pp. 238–39) by Cowan and subsequently omitted in *A Trader in Cannibal Land*.

qMS-1977: Alexander Turnbull Library, National Library of New Zealand · Te Puna Mātauranga o Aotearoa, Wellington

If we compare the beginning of the Tapsell manuscript with Cowan's version, we can see that the historian's editing goes beyond the correction of historical data into the realm of invention.

Manuscript, pp. 1–3	Cowan, *A Trader in Cannibal Land*, pp. 17–18
Hans Hömman Falk, better known in New Zealand as Phillip Tapsell, the subject of the following biographical sketch was born in Copenhagen somewhere about the year 1777, the eldest son of Jens Hansen Falk, an important public functionary in that city.	In the city of Copenhagen, in the year 1779, there was born to one Jans Hansen Falk (or Felk), an official of the Danish Government, a boy who was christened by the name Hans Homman.
At the early age of eight his mother dying, he was sent for by his grandparents living at Jutland to take up his abode with them, and for this purpose put on board a small coasting vessell sailing for that place.	When he was eight years old his mother died, and the grandparents, who lived in Jutland, sent to the father offering to take charge of the little boy and bring him up and attend to his education. To this Jans Falk agreed, and the son was put on board a cutter sailing for Jutland.
On the voyage thither, he met with an adventure which was only a precursor of an almost unintermitting series lasting through the greater part of a very long life. The sloop had not been long at sea, and one night while young Falk was slumbering peacefully in his berth, he was awoken by a sense of suffocation caused by dense fumes of smoke which filled the cabin. Scrambling with difficulty up the companion way, he reached the deck, and found the fore part of the vessel on fire, the bulwarks, rigging, and sails, all in flames, the taffrail being the only part they had not reached. The terror and dismay of young Falk may be imagined when he looked around for the crew and not a soul was to be seen. The boat was also gone. They had all taken flight and forgotten him! The rapid reflections of so young a voyager in such a crisis may be imagined, but cannot be described. There is little doubt that he wished himself at home again in Copenhagen, and safe under his father's roof. But the exigencies of his situation did not permit of delay. Two courses were open for him. Before him were the blazing planks and rigging, and a cruel death by fire. He looked over the side, and the cool water, glistening in the moonlight, seemed the easier end of the two. He made up his mind to the latter alternative, and was about to plunge into the sea, when his ear caught the sound of a voice hailing him.	This coasting voyage was the beginning of a life-long series of perilous adventures for Hans of Copenhagen. The cutter was nearing Jutland, when the boy, lying in his bunk in the midnight hours, was awakened by dense suffocating fumes of smoke which filled the cabin. Struggling with difficulty up the companionway, he reached the deck. The vessel was on fire. All the forepart was in flames; the bulwarks, rigging and sails were blazing. The terrified boy looked frantically around for the crew. Not one of the men was to be seen. The boat was gone, too. They had all pulled away and forgotten him. Before him were the blazing planks and rigging, and a cruel death by fire. He ran to the side. The cool water, glistening in the moonlight, seemed the easier end. He resigned his little heart to drowning, and he was just about to plunge into the sea when he hear a voice hailing him.

Cowan added information, motives, emotions and thoughts, all of which must have been based on supposition rather than written evidence.

Manuscript, p. 4	Cowan, *A Trader in Cannibal Land* (pp. 18–19)
[...] at the end of which they both died, and Hans was sent by his uncle back to Copenhagen, where he was put to school till his fourteenth year, when he was bound apprentice to the sea, and he served his time in the Miditerranean and East County trades.	Then the two old people died, and Hans was sent by an uncle back to Copenhagen. Once more with his father, his education continued, but at fourteen the lad had had enough of school. His short coasting voyages, the sights and sounds of sailoring, filled him with a longing to get aboard some far-roving craft and sail away to foreign parts. That wish his father gratified by binding him apprentice to a shipowner, and he served that hard but ever-enchanting mistress, the sea, for more than half his life time. Young Hans made his first deep-sea passage in a Danish brig trading to the Mediterranean. Voyage after voyage he sailed, each one teaching him more of sea-lore, of ships and their handling, of rigging and sails, and of men. By the time he was verging on his twenties he was a well-schooled seaman. As for navigation, he was mastering its theory and its practical application and could find the latitude and longitude and work out the ship's position and course on the chart.

Clearly, Cowan did not think that 'the plain story was sufficiently vivid'. It makes little sense to try to present a comprehensive account of the differences between the manuscript and Cowan's version here. Suffice to say that Cowan has deleted and added material and rewritten those parts of the manuscript that he has kept and episodes in the Tapsell manuscript testimony have been elaborated on and bridged using paragraphs of his own.

In Little's newspaper serialisation there are five episodes of varying lengths that are missing both from the manuscript as we have it today and from Cowan's *A Trader in Cannibal Land*. These are:

1. **Youthful errors.** Tapsell's stepmother catches him stealing money from his father to fund his card-playing habit.
2. **Fate of an unfaithful wife.** A woman is stripped naked, bludgeoned to death and eaten.
3. **Sells his voyage.** A Jew purchases Tapsell's goods for £550, but it turns out they were only worth £70, so the Jew loses £480 on the deal.
4. **Maori dogs.** Tapsell traps dogs on fish hooks and kills them. Domestic animals are described as degenerating 'by companionship with the savage. Even the dog ... becomes cowardly, slinking, and treacherous.'
5. **Jealousy of traders.** Other traders plot to kill Tapsell. Their means are 'less justifiable and scarcely less atrocious than those practised by the savages themselves'.

These episodes might have been missing from the manuscript when Cowan borrowed it — or he might have removed them. We simply do not know. If he did remove them, perhaps he felt that they detracted from his narrative or that the stories were too sensitive, cruel or in some way irrelevant for his purposes.

Of course, none of this makes Cowan's book a bad read in the tradition of 'pioneer stories of Old New Zealand', but the reader must bear in mind that the historian's claim that it is an accurate rendering of the manuscript and that no fiction enters into the narrative is simply not true.[17] It is a biography or interpretation of Tapsell's life that is substantially based on Little's manuscript but coloured by Cowan's own views, intentions and writing style. The blending of history and popular fiction is a key feature of many of Cowan's publications.[18]

Enid Tapsell gifted the manuscript (qMS-1977) to the Alexander Turnbull Library in December 1969 (Acc. nos 136,754, 136,754/A–C).[19] The original is very fragile and access is restricted, but photocopies (MSY-6864) are available to the public.

NOTES

1. The first clerk to the Resident Magistrate's Court at Maketū was J.J. Piercy, who served between 1864 and 1868/1869. The official records give no further information about later clerks, but in *A Trader in Cannibal Land* Cowan says that Little of the Armed Constabulary Force was 'Clerk of the R.M. Court at Maketu' (p. 7) in 1869 when he recorded Tapsell's reminiscences. See Alister Matheson, 'Law and Order in Maketu', *Bay of Plenty Journal of History*, 43.2 (1995), pp. 106–122 (114).

   This is the 'Edward Little' who later became an alcoholic and whose miserable death is related in the *Bay of Plenty Times*, 5 August 1874, p. 3:

   > Mr Edward Little, of Tauranga, was found dead in an out-house off the Wesleyan Chapel. Medical examination showed that death was caused by cold and cramp. When found the deceased was almost perfectly naked. He had apparently, either in a wandering state of mind, or while labouring under the effects of alcohol, stripped himself under the impression that he was going to bed, then laid himself down, and perished during the last severe frosty night.

   Cf. 'Miserable Death', *New Zealand Herald*, 1 August 1874, p. 5; 'Coroner's Inquest', *New Zealand Herald*, 3 August 1874, p. 3; 'Telegraphic News', *New Zealand Times*, 3 August 1874, p. 3: 'Edward Little [...] was well educated, but of dissolute habits'; 'Death in a Water-Closet', *Daily Southern Cross*, 3 August 1874, p. 3: in this account it is said that Little 'was connected with the press in Tauranga in the capacity of a reporter and correspondent' (cf. also his title in Part 3, 'Contemporary accounts of Phillip Tapsell's life', 'Edward Little, Esq., Tauranga [...] New Zealand Correspondent').

2. See Part 3, 'Contemporary accounts of Phillip Tapsell's life'.

3. Little serialised and published the manuscript in 1869 as 'Events in the Life of Phillip Tapsell, the Old Dane' in the *Daily Southern Cross*. The chapters appeared on 6, 9, 17, 26 February; 12 March; 1, 2, 5 April; 20 May; 24, 28, 29 July; 4 August; and 14, 15, 16, 17 September. His interest in publicising Tapsell's life story may have been due to the popularity of such 'New Zealand of yesteryear' serialisations of the time. However, it may also have been a concerted effort to raise funds for 'the old Dane'.

4. Sir Donald McLean's Papers, MS-Papers-0032-0598, Alexander Turnbull Library (also, Papers, MS-Copy-Micro-0535-093).

5. See, for example, pp. 139–40: 'he gave the ruffian a well directed blow in the face, which

his great physical strength enabled him to do with over-powering effect, and, *to use his own words*, sent the Maori away spouting blood!' (author emphasis). Of course, the fact that Little explicitly states that what follows are Tapsell's own words suggests that what came before were not — rather they were Little's own phrasing of the story.

6. See Part 3, 'Contemporary accounts of Phillip Tapsell's life'.

7. Letter from Enid Tapsell to Ruth Burnard of the Historical Branch of the Department of Internal Affairs (5 October 1943), MS-Papers-0230-008, Alexander Turnbull Library. The following account of the manuscript's provenance is largely based on that letter. Historian Ruth Miriam Burnard (née Guscott, later Ross, 1920–82) worked as a research assistant for the Historical Branch of the Department of Internal Affairs. She travelled the country checking archival sources and finding new material for the Department's research project on mapping settlement and pre-1840 trade. She visited Enid Tapsell in Maketū in March 1944.

8. Letter from John McAlister to Cowan (13 April 1920), Cowan Papers, MS-Papers-0039-32, Alexander Turnbull Library; cf. Cowan, *A Trader in Cannibal Land*, p. 7.

9. For example: 'Ransom. Cash Value of a Pakeha. Old-Time Transactions', *Auckland Star* (27 March 1926), p. 21, columns 2–4; 'Old Maketu Days. The Life of a Trader. How Tapsell bought his Flax', *Auckland Star* (29 June 1926), p. 8, columns 4–5; 'First Pakeha-Maori Marriage. A Footnote to History', *Auckland Star* (30 August 1932), p. 6, column 5.

10. James Cowan, 'Ransom. Cash Value of a Pakeha. Old-Time Transactions', *Auckland Star* (27 March 1926), p. 21, column 2.

11. For example, due to Cowan's crossing out it is now impossible to read the chapter heading on p. 213.

12. James Cowan, *A Trader in Cannibal Land* (Dunedin: A.H. & A.W. Reed, 1935).

13. It should be noted that John McAlister, who had originally given the manuscript to Cowan, had a different response (MS-Papers-0039-32, Alexander Turnbull Library):

    Parnell Police Station
    Auckland
    28/12/35
    Mr Cowan
    Dear Sir
    I have to acknowledge receipt of the book 'A Trader in Cannibal Land' and for which I have to thank you kindly. I am delighted with it and must say how well it is put together.
    Your brother Sgt Cowan of Pukekohe sent it on to me and I lost no time in reading it. The book came as a Xmas present.
    Again I thank you & wish you the compliments of the season.
    I remain yours truly
    John McAlister

14. Cowan, *A Trader in Cannibal Land*, p. 5. In addition to the Tapsell manuscript, Cowan's book also makes use of supplementary material taken down in 1873 by the magistrate Francis Edward Hamlin and of oral accounts provided by Gilbert Mair, Chief Kiharoa, Te Rangituakoha, Te Whanarere of Ngāti Pikiao, Te Araki Te Pohu of Ngāti Tu, and various other acquaintances. Furthermore, he says that he has corrected the historical data that are wrong in Little's manuscript. See Cowan, *A Trader in Cannibal Land*, pp. 7–8.

15. Wednesday, 22 March 1944 ('brief report of my recent tour', p. 22), MS-Papers-0230-008, Alexander Turnbull Library.

16. That is, Enid Tapsell's book: *Historic Maketu. Hui Hui Mai!* (Rotorua: *Rotorua Morning Post*, 1940).

17. On Cowan's historical works, see Chris Hilliard, 'James Cowan and the Frontiers of New Zealand History', *The New Zealand Journal of History*, 31.2 (1997), pp. 219–33.

18. Hilliard, 'James Cowan and the Frontiers of New Zealand History', p. 223: 'The overlap in style between yarning, anecdotal histories and some popular fiction is nicely emblematised by the way Wellington City Library and *PEN Gazette* classified separate Cowan collections of historical stories as "fiction", much to the author's chagrin.'

19. In a letter from Ruth Burnard to Enid Tapsell dated 9 September 1943 (MS-Papers-0230-008, Alexander Turnbull Library), she asks about the:

whereabouts of the MS dictated by Mr Phillip Tapsell in 1869, mentioned by you in your book *Historic Maketu*, and by the late Mr James Cowan in the preface of his *A Trader in Cannibal Land*. In the latter Mr Cowan said that it had been sent to him in 1920 by John McAlister of Auckland. Does this mean that it was lent to Cowan, or was it given to him?

Further, in a letter dated 1 February 1944, she wrote:

[...] last week I heard from a somewhat indirect source that the Tapsell family had decided to present the manuscript to the Dominion Museum. I therefore rang up Dr. Oliver, the Director, but he had heard nothing of the matter. Thinking my informant had perhaps mistaken the institution I rang the Turnbull Library, but drew a blank there also. So I am now wondering if the story is merely an idle rumour in which case I should continue with my arrangements to visit Maketu, or if you have the intention to present the MS to some institution in the near future, which would make the trip unnecessary. I would be very grateful if you would let me know at your earliest possible convenience the present whereabouts of the papers and if it will be necessary for me to inspect them at your home, or whether by this time they have been deposited somewhere else.

In her reply dated 10 February 1944, Enid Tapsell wrote:

[...] no quite definitely nothing has been done or suggested by us regarding disposal of Tapsell MS. Early in 1940 a suggestion was made to me by Mr Martin Nestor to deposit in Turnbull Library, & that is all.

The Tapsell story in Danish

TAPSELL'S STORY HAS APPEARED in print several times in his country of birth, Denmark. These works, which are two biographies (Nielsen, Dich), a children's book (Bluitgen, Gabel) and a chapter in a travel-writer's account (Falk-Rønne), span 70 years between 1940 and 2010. The two biographies are reworkings of Cowan's *A Trader in Cannibal Land* (1935), supplemented with photographs, anecdotes by the authors and background information on New Zealand history and geography. They share the same advantages and disadvantages as Cowan's book but overall they are respectful toward both Tapsell and tangata whenua of New Zealand. The traveller's account and the children's book are, however, a different story and therefore take up most space in this chapter. The first attempts to provide an insight into the impact of European colonisation on wildlife and Māori, while the other attempts to tell a ripping yarn for young readers. However, in both works there are examples of racism, exoticism, fabrication and disparagement concerning the achievements of Phillip Tapsell, of Te Whānau a Tāpihana and tangata whenua more generally.

Five years after the appearance of James Cowan's *A Trader in Cannibal Land*, the doctor and travel writer Aage Krarup Nielsen (1891–1972) published his *Hans Falk fra Maketu: En dansk Sydhavsfarers Liv og Eventyr* (Hans Falk from Maketū: The Life and Adventures of a Danish Sailor of the Southern Seas). Printed in Copenhagen in 1940 by Gyldendalske Boghandel and Nordisk Forlag, this 136-page book contains nearly 60 black and white plates, including reproductions of some of Gottfried Lindauer's Māori portraits, old paintings, photographs of Tapsell's descendants and tourist shots of Whakarewarewa, Rotowhio and Rotorua.

In the first 30 pages, Nielsen relates his sailing voyage to New Zealand as he travelled around the Pacific. During a visit to Rotorua he heard talk of a Dane who had settled in the area many years previously. His interest was piqued

202

and he began a journey of discovery, travelling to Maketū and meeting descendants of Tapsell who shown him various heirlooms, including the Tapsell manuscript. He also contacted James Cowan and acquainted himself with *A Trader in Cannibal Land*.

The following hundred pages or so are largely a translation and reworking of Cowan's book with interspersed digressions on different aspects of New Zealand history. The pages include the same omissions as Cowan's work. For example, Nielsen states that Farrow drowned off Matatā along with Clementson (p. 114; cf. Cowan, *A Trader in Cannibal Land*, p. 127; manuscript p. 232, here p. 159), but no mention is made that his drowning was a rumour and he was in fact very much alive, later visiting Tapsell in Whakatāne (manuscript p. 238 , here p. 162). The author also reproduces Cowan's additions. For example:

Danish books about Phillip Tapsell. There are three books in Danish about Phillip Tapsell, two for adults and one for children, as well as a single chapter in a travel book.

Author's photograph, 2017

Manuscript, p. 4	Nielsen, *Hans Falk fra Maketu*, p. 32	Cowan, *A Trader in Cannibal Land*, pp. 18–19
[...], when he was bound apprentice to the sea, and he served his time in the Miditerranean and East County trades.	The scary experience that Hans had had on his first sea voyage had not proved more frightening than he, like so many healthy lads at that age, had just one burning wish: to go to sea. In those days, Denmark owned a large fleet of big, grand sailing ships, and every time Hans saw one of the proud ships for the East Indies set off out of Copenhagen Harbour on its way to the marvellous lands of the East, he dreamt that he himself would one day sail on an adventure to distant shores. His father, who was aware that the only sensible thing to do was to let the boy have his way, got him hired as a cabin boy on board a Danish brig that was sailing in the Mediterranean. That day when the little fourteen-year-old cabin boy on board the Danish brig headed off on his first long journey, Hans Falk began his tumultuous and adventurous career as a sailor, which was to last over half of his lifetime.[1]	Then the two old people died, and Hans was sent by an uncle back to Copenhagen. Once more with his father, his education continued, but at fourteen the lad had had enough of school. His short coasting voyages, the sights and sounds of sailoring, filled him with a longing to get aboard some far-roving craft and sail away to foreign parts. That wish his father gratified by binding him apprentice to a shipowner, and he served that hard but ever-enchanting mistress, the sea, for more than half his life time. Young Hans made his first deep-sea passage in a Danish brig trading to the Mediterranean. Voyage after voyage he sailed, each one teaching him more of sea-lore, of ships and their handling, of rigging and sails, and of men. By the time he was verging on his twenties he was a well-schooled seaman. As for navigation, he was mastering its theory and its practical application and could find the latitude and longitude and work out the ship's position and course on the chart.

203

Correspondence between Nielsen and Cowan, now held in the Cowan family collection of papers (MS-Papers-11946-180, Alexander Turnbull Library), is of interest in elucidating the relationship between *Hans Falk fra Maketu* and *A Trader in Cannibal Land* (and Cowan's own sense of ownership over the Tapsell manuscript).

Copenhagen, Denmark, febr. 24th 1940.
[...]
Dear Sir,
I wonder if you still remember me from my visit in your home in Wellington in spring 1938. Beeing a danish author of travelling books and a newspaperman I was roaming in the South Sea and

happened to get a short stay in New Zealand on my way to Australia. A Friend of mine in Auckland showed me your book: 'A Trader in Kannibal Land' and told me that Captain Tapsell happened to be a Dane. I got hold in your book and was of course very interested in the strange story of my countryman; I went down to Wellington and saw you and — as you may remember — we discussed the possibility that I after my return to Denmark should try to get further informations about Philip Tapsells childhood and early youth in his native land, and then perhaps offer you a sum for the exclusions rights to addapt and rewrite your book.

However after my return to Europe I have had my hands full of work and not before now, when Europe is deeply involved in this sinister world conflict and my own travelling prospects therefore is badly cut down I have returned to the idea of working with the story of Philip Tapsells adventurous life.

I therefore take the opportunity to ask you if you will be willing to give me the exclusion rights to addapt and rewrite your book for a publication in articles short stories or a book with a supply of the material I have been able to collect for myself here in Denmark — for which rights I can offer you 15 — fifteen — english pounds — outright.

As nobody can tell what the near future brings I may not remain in Europe for a very long time and would therefore be very grateful if you would convey to me your kind reply at your earliest convenience — and if you accept my offer the amount will be forwarded to you as soon as I have your answer.

Courteously begging you to send a deferred telegram to my cable address: Gyldendal, Copenhagen just saying yes or no, I am with kind regards
Yours faithfully
Aage Krarup Nielsen,
M.D. B.A.

[...] Wellington, N.Z.
April 12, 1940.
[...]
Dear Sir,
On receipt of your letter of February 24 regarding my book 'A Trader in Cannibal Land: The Adventures of Captain Tapsell', I sent you a deferred cablegram (March 28) saying 'Yes' — in response to your

request to make exclusive use of the book. However, I had occasion to reconsider the matter, both on account of my own interests and those of my publishers — whom I had not consulted. (The copyright is mine). I therefore sent to you a second deferred cablegram, on April 12, as follows:

"Proposal cancelled. Do not send money. Await letter." Both cablegrams were sent to your full address — [...] Kobnhavn K., Copenhagen, as the New Zealand telegraph office would not accept cable addresses only. ("Gyldendal, Copenhagen" was that given in your letter).

Since the first cablegram was sent in response to your letter, Denmark has been taken over by Germany and is of course now technically an enemy country. This automatically prohibits business transactions between us and Denmark.

I do not know what you have gathered in Denmark about the subject of my book. It cannot be much; and the chief, or only source of anything you know about Captain Tapsell is no doubt my book. My publishers have a large stock of the book still on hand, and must sell these copies in this country and overseas before anything can be done about reprinting or otherwise dealing with the book.

It seems to me therefore that it would not be possible for me to sell you the exclusive rights as you propose (except for Danish translation). The MS. used in the book was given to me exclusively by the Tapsell descendant in Auckland. In addition to using and enlarging and editing the MS. I worked into the story a great deal of data given to me by the veteran's contemporaries, pakeha and Maori, all of whom are now dead. That can never be obtained again. I am the only one who possesses that knowledge, a history-gathering task spread over many years. It would greatly underrate the value of my exclusive knowledge were I to accept your offer. Also, I propose, when the time comes, to publish the book in a larger edition. In the interests, therefore, of the publisher and myself I find it impossible to accept your proposal, except for Danish language only.

You are, of course, at liberty to publish what you have gathered yourself, apart from my book, in New Zealand and in Denmark. I suggest therefore, you should confine yourself to that. Reasonable quotation from my writings is permissible, so long as the source is fully acknowledged, according to literary customs.

[Three] Four of the illustrations in my book — the frontispiece of a ship, the photographs of Captain Tapsell, Te Araki te Pohu, and

Patara te Ngungukai, are my property and exclusive, and must not be copied. The other pictures are not my original property, and you are at liberty to use them, of course.

In the present uncertain state of affairs, in publishing articles and books, as well as everything else, it is difficult to make conclusive arrangements. In the meantime, therefore, we must suspend all matter about the narrative of Tapsell and his times.

I should like to hear from you whether you received my cablegrams.

Yours with sincere good wishes,

J. Cowan

It would seem that Cowan's cablegram never arrived at Nielsen's home — or if it did, it was ignored.

Nielsen travelled extensively and was one of the first bestselling travel writers in twentieth-century Denmark. The genre of travel writing became especially popular after the Second World War, and a gamut of books by authors travelling the Seven Seas hit the shelves in bookshops across the country. Among the most prolific we find Hakon Mielche (1904–79), Arne Falk-Rønne (1920–92), Jens Bjerre (1921–2020) and Troels Kløvedal (1943–2018). Nielsen's book introduced Tapsell to the Danish public for the first time.

In *Sydhavets syv bølger* (The Seven Waves of the South Sea),[2] travel writer and photographer Arne Falk-Rønne relates his first encounter of Phillip Tapsell when reading Nielsen's *Hans Falk fra Maketu* during the summer holidays as a student, and how his visit to the Bay of Plenty changed his view of the man. In rather unflattering terms, he describes meeting some of Tapsell's descendants.

I could certainly have wished for a more romantic encounter with his descendants, but fate did not will it so. Old Winiata Tapsell, who is a fisherman and well into his eighties, is the grandchild of Tāpihana and has heard many stories about his famous grandfather.[3] He will tell me some of them if he is regaled with soft-serve ice cream from the ice-cream kiosk in Maketū. And there he is, so independent of time and place and sucking on one strutting ice cream after another and destroying the dreams from my student summers. Later we drive up to the Pākehā-Māori cemetery above the village. We soon find the grave, clear it of wild roses and read the inscription [...]: '*Here lies Hans Homman Falk* (mistakenly spelt *Felk*), *known as Philip*

*Tapsell, born in Denmark, who distinguished himself as a good officer on
the seas. Died at an age of 94 years, 6 August 1873.'*[4]

Winiata, now munching on his fifth ice cream, announces that
Tāpihana himself chose to be buried at this spot. He went so far
as to establish the cemetery himself. [...] In the same grave and in
several surrounding graves, his family is lying. The living Tapsells
have accompanied Winiata, John and me up to the cemetery and are
eagerly debating where they will one day lie.[5]

The author proceeds to describe Tapsell's years of sailing, dwelling on the
gruesome aspects of whaling and sealing as well as the *Boyd* massacre and
its aftermath. He records that, 'My new acquaintance with Hans Falk — I
must confess straight out — gives me a different and less pleasant picture of
my namesake than that I had when I was a student.'[6] Then follow three pages
on the history of convict transports and an account of the recapture of the
Wellington. Tapsell's brief marriage to Maria Ringa is also related.

In the Bay of Islands, he has met a female relative of the infamous
and famous Māori king *Hongi Hika*. Her name is *Maria Ringa*, and
she is said to be rather delightful to behold. He wants to marry her
but it has to happen in Pākehā fashion with a church blessing and so
on. The bizarre thing about these so-called *adventurers* from the last
[nineteenth] century is that there is a not-so-small petty bourgeois
inside most of them. They can happily murder with the one hand
and get all teary-eyed when saluting the flag with the other. They sob
about their dear mothers back home under elder bushes in the little
country by the sound, while they equanimously transport female
prostitutes and elderly fences [that is, petty criminals who receive
stolen goods] to the hell of Port Jackson. And when Hans Falk, who
probably had countless lovers from all kinds of races during his
lifetime, finally wishes to marry a Māori girl, then a man of the cloth
absolutely has to assist.[7]

207

Falk-Rønne discusses Tapsell's time at Maketū where the trader experienced
that 'cannibal chiefs became good Victorian citizens'.[8] He concludes with a
damning assessment of the trader's 40 years in the Bay of Plenty and more
than insinuates that Tapsell traded in mokomōkai (preserved heads). I quote
at length here to provide the reader with a taste of the manner in which Falk-
Rønne retells the Tapsell story.

Tāpihana comes to live in the Bay of Plenty for more than forty years; he marries again, this time with more luck. He has many sons and daughters. He no longer goes to sea, but sets himself up as a trader, one of the traders of death who sell guns to the Māori and make it possible for them to shoot freely at each other and murder each other, family after family. It is difficult for us to understand what great value a gun had for a Māori chieftain. But the trading goods can tell us something about this. In London a bright young boatsteerer can buy an old, used musket for between three and five shillings; among the Māoris in New Zealand he can get for the same musket a small forest of kauri trees or two young women or ten tattooed cut-off heads (which are a really big export item). Indeed, he need only show an interested Māori warrior the weapon, and the man will immediately go and get ten human heads in the old-fashioned way by using a war club and a wooden spear. A Pākehā with ten guns in his possession can open a store and get timber, flax (New Zealand hemp) and as mentioned human heads — each head can then be sold in England for a sum, which in turn can transform into eighty–ninety guns.

I am not claiming that Hans Falk traded in cut-off human heads. He says nothing about this in his reminiscences, but then why should he? It was not something that people spoke about, just like people also completely failed to let the missionaries know, how many barrels of rum had been handed to the Māori pās. With a gun in his hand and rum in his belly, the Māori was a completely different person, and in this state, the Māori people began a series of bloody wars, which with a few interruptions lasted for nearly half a century.

Time after time, I have asked Hans Falk's descendants: What was he like? What was old Hans Falk like?

But no-one has been able to give me the answer. They have only been able to say: 'He was like the others.'

Indeed, he was just like all the others, a child of his time. And now he lies buried under the blossom of the wild roses with a view across the bay, where the people of Te Arawa canoe came ashore more than six centuries ago.[9]

Falk-Rønne's account of Tapsell's life is not very well researched, for example he mentions just two wives, and he attacks the Dane for his whaling, sealing and gun-trading activities. He is disparaging of Tapsell's Māori contemporaries, who are presented as alcohol-fuelled and murderous, and his descendants, who are presented as simple and childish. In the same way as Falk-Rønne calls Tapsell a man of his time, the same can be said of Falk-Rønne, who despite his many years of travel and exploration perpetuates a Eurocentric, colonialist view of the world — at least in his encounter with the Tapsells.

In *Blandt hvaler og kannibaler: Hans Falk — en dansk eventyrer i New Zealand* (Among Whales and Cannibals: Hans Falk — A Danish Adventurer in New Zealand) published in 2006,[10] Preben Dich (b. 1933) does not explain how he first came across Phillip Tapsell. His book is another reworking of the Cowan publication but includes several discursions, for example on cannibalism (pp. 91–99), Ditlev Gotfred Monrad (the Danish bishop who settled in New Zealand, p. 108), islands in the Bay of Plenty (pp. 141–45) and Tapsell's descendants (pp. 146–52). However, descriptions of others' lives that are found in the manuscript, such as Clementson, are not mentioned by Dich. Indeed, the author has not used all of Cowan's book or Tapsell's manuscript and there are consequently several lacunae. The book contains numerous photographs, including of objects in private ownership, for example Tapsell's sea-chest and tobacco box, p. 13,[11] and Tapsell's homemade flag, p. 152, and the author's own photographs taken during a trip to Maketū. The promotional text on the back cover sets the tone for the book.

209

> The journalist Preben Dich has visited Hans Falk's descendants
> who are proud to have Danish blood in their veins. The book is a
> dramatic story of tribal fighting, murders and cannibalism — but
> also the tale of an extraordinary Dane who during his 84-year
> existence has made lasting marks in this distant country.[12]

The book is in the same spirit as Cowan and Nielsen and, particularly when compared to Falk-Rønne's text, presents a very positive image of the Dane.

The final work for consideration is *Hans Falk i menneskeædernes land* (Hans Falk in the Land of the Cannibals) by Kåre Bluitgen (b. 1959),[13] a well-known author and journalist in Denmark who writes for children, teenagers and adults. *Hans Falk* is his fifty-fifth book. According to the publisher's webpages, the book (50 pages long and designed as a primer) is aimed at children between eight and 12 years old 'with a taste for adventure and amazing stories from real life'.[14] The blurb reads:

> Hans Falk wanted to get out into the big world. As a young man, he
> went on whaling voyages in the Southern Ocean. For a time he was a
> pirate for the Danish king. Then he travelled right over to the other
> side of the Earth and lived a dangerous life among cannibals. Hans

Falk cheated death not once, but many times![15]

These episodes of cheating death are what create the structure and recurrent theme in the book: surviving the fire aboard the ship to Jutland, surviving the cruel Captain Jonathan Clarke, surviving an attack while a mercenary and so on. The chapter recording Tapsell's arrival in New Zealand is called 'cannibals' (*Menneskeædere*) and begins:

> Hans arrived in New Zealand. Here he encountered the Māori.
> They are the native people in New Zealand. Even though Hans had
> experienced many things, the Māori made him afraid. They wanted
> to sell him meat. Human flesh. Hans had landed among cannibals.[16]

At no point in his memoirs does Tapsell ever mention being afraid of Māori when he first met them, nor was he ever approached to buy human flesh. Kaitangata (cannibalism) was connected with warfare and utu: human flesh was not some delicacy or a dainty commodity to sell. The idea that Māori sold human flesh to Pākehā (or anyone else) is not only preposterous but also deeply offensive. Similarly, the readers are told that Māori tried to sell mokomōkai to the book's protagonist, even though this is not mentioned once in Tapsell's memoirs.

> The Māori also wanted to sell chopped-off heads to Hans. The heads
> came from the captives that they took during their many battles with
> each other. The Māori were beautifully tattooed in their faces. When
> the heads were dried, they could be sold in England. Genteel people
> there had them standing around as decoration. Hans did not want to
> be part of that sort of trade.[17]

The topos of Tapsell the civilised Dane living among the wild, primitive natives continues:

> The Māori ate their enemies. One day a tribe prepared their food
> right outside Hans' house. He could smell the roasted human flesh.
> Hans felt dreadful. But there was nothing he could do. He was in
> New Zealand. Not in Denmark.[18]

The presentation of interactions between Pākehā and Māori is particularly misleading and focuses entirely on conflict based on each side enslaving the other(!):

Shipwreck and bankruptcy
In 1829, Hans married another Māori woman. Many white men
had only contempt for the natives. They attacked the Māori and
stole their women. Many Māori were taken as slaves. The Māori
responded by killing the whites. Or they took them as prisoners and
also made them slaves. Hans was not like the other whites. He was
good at making peace. That's why he made friends among the Māori.
And not just in his wife's tribe.[19]

In addition to being violent, murderous, slave-owning kidnappers of women,
local Māori are portrayed as absurdly gullible:

Some of the European traders cheated the Māori. They said that rum
worked in the same way as potatoes: If you buried the empty bottles
in the ground, then full bottles would grow. And then they sold the
Māori empty bottles.[20]

The short book includes several further errors and invented events.[21] Although
it is unclear what sources the author used for the book, it seems likely that
he followed Preben Dich's Cowan-informed work, which had been published
four years previously.

In *Hans Falk*, 'civilised' Tapsell represents the virtues of modernity and
progress in a colonial setting. The Danish child-reader is encouraged to identify
with him. The 'others' appear as either ridiculous or monstrous. The protagonist
was able to make friends with some of the 'natives' through his ability to make
peace (a uniquely Danish trait?), but readers are not told much about the lives
and personalities of the 'natives'. Tapsell's three wives are unclear characters.
Karuhi is primarily mentioned in relation to her illness and death, an event
that is used to juxtapose Wharepoaka's screaming at the sky and Tapsell's quiet
reflection and sorrow.[22] Hineitūrama is credited with teaching him many
things he needed to know about New Zealand, such as tapu.[23] But the clearest
impression is one of club-swinging savages decapitating their enemies. Indeed,
decapitated Māori heads are found in the illustrations on the front cover, on
pages 28 and 37 and on the back cover. Of the ten illustrations featuring one
or more Māori, six portray acts of violence. The book's illustrations by award-
winning freelancer Lars Gabel (b. 1971) reflect a colonialist fantasy of primitive
natives and underscore the racist tone of the book. The illustrator is not overly
concerned with reproducing New Zealand in his illustrations, preferring to
conjure up an imaginary, exotic world of difference and 'otherness'. For example,
on the front cover alongside the decapitated head of a Māori male, a Māori man

clenching a human thighbone between his teeth, a Māori woman wearing a kākahu (cloak), a young Māori girl and two European men, one of whom is holding a musket, there are a sulphur-crested cockatoo[24] and a monkey.

Whereas the Danish biographies of Tapsell by Nielsen and Dich largely follow Cowan (and ultimately the Tapsell manuscript), the travel story and the children's book follow quite different lines. Falk-Rønne's publication is a damning account of Tapsell as a wildlife hunter and guntrader and hints at even darker trade and actions. His marriages are treated mockingly. Nothing is mentioned of his achievements, his role in biculturalism and amalgamating Māori and Pākehā, his attempts at making peace between warring parties at the height of hostilities, or even his importance as a non-British voice in the history of the European settlement of New Zealand. Missing entirely from Falk-Rønne's account is a sense of Tapsell's humanity: when he adopted children, ransomed prisoners and slaves, and met the convicts on the *Catherine*. Instead, the author makes the mistake of using sensibilities that characterise the time he wrote the book to judge and condemn Tapsell.

Falk-Rønne's take on the Tapsell story is a rather clunky but typical expression of 1960s Danish culture: post-religious, anti-bourgeois, anti-imperialist and pacifist. Yet his account of meeting Tapsell's descendants is dressed in the tired language of difference and of 'grown-up Europe' versus 'child-like Oceania'. Bluitgen's children's book draws strongly on the theme of Tapsell as a civilised light of the Old World in the cannibalistic darkness of the New World. 'Danish' qualities of bravery, peace-making and humanitarianism are contrasted with those of the 'savages'. It is quite a different form of prejudice about Māori and Tapsell's life, and verges on jingoism. Indeed, little seems to have changed since Jules Verne published *Among the Cannibals* (*In Search of the Castaways*, 1867–1868). The continued peddling of this worldview to children in Denmark is a particularly disturbing misuse of Tapsell's legacy.

NOTES

1. Nielsen, *Hans Falk fra Maketu*, p. 32:

    Den uhyggelige Oplevelse, Hans havde haft paa sin første Sørejse, havde ikke virket mere afskrækkende end, at han, som saa mange raske Drenge i den Alder, kun havde ét brændende Ønske: at komme til Søs.

    I hine Dage ejede Danmark en talrig Flaade af store, prægtige Sejlskibe, og hver Gang Hans saa en af de stolte Ostindiefarere stævne ud fra Københavns Havn paa Vej mod Østens vidunderlige Lande, drømte han om selv en Dag at sejle med ud paa Eventyr til fjerne Kyster. Hans Fader var, der var klar over, at det eneste fornuftige vilde være at lade Knægten faa sin Lyst styret, skaffede ham Hyre som Skibsdreng paa en dansk Brig, der sejlede paa Middelhavet.

    Den Dag den lille fjortenaarige Skibsdreng om Bord paa den danske Brig styrede ud paa sin første lange Rejse, begyndte Hans Falk den omtumlede og eventyrlige Sømandsfærd, der kom til at vare mere end Halvdelen af hans Liv.

2. Arne Falk-Rønne, *Sydhavets syv bølger* (Copenhagen: Lindhardt og Ringhof, 1969), pp. 283–98.
3. 'Old Winiata Tapsell' (1892–1974) was Retireti's grandson (and thus, Tapsell's great-grandson). At the outbreak of the First World War he joined the 1st Māori Contingent and fought for over four years in the trenches of Europe and Turkey. His bravery in helping the New Zealand Division capture the French town of Le Quesnoy was honoured in an exhibition in 2015 (*Bay of Plenty Times*, 10 November 2015). On his return to Maketū at the end of the war, Winiata was selected into the Māori All Blacks. Winiata's feats are a source of great pride for his family, but Falk-Rønne's depiction of this accomplished man is unkind and offensive.
4. The inscription actually reads: 'In memory of HANS HOMMAN FELK known as Philip Tapsell, a native of Denmark, who distinguished himself as a Naval Officer died at an age of 94 years on the 6th of August 1873.'
5. Falk-Rønne, *Sydhavets syv bølger*, p. 285:

   Jeg kunne godt have ønsket mig et mere romantisk møde med hans efterkommere, men skæbnen vil det ikke sådan. Den gamle Winiata Tapsell, som er fisker og godt oppe i firserne, er barnebarn af Tapihana og har hørt mange historier om sin berømte farfar. Han vil gerne fortælle mig nogle af dem, hvis han bliver beværtet med soft-ice fra iskiosken i Maketu. Og der står han så uafhængig af tid og sted og suger den ene strut-is i sig efter den anden og ødelægger en hel del af mine studentersommer-drømme. Senere kører vi op til pakeha-maori-kirkegården over landsbyen. Vi finder hurtigt gravstedet, rydder det for vilde roser og læser inskriptionen [...]: '*Her hviler Hans Homman Falk* (ved en fejltagelse bogstaveret *Felk*), *kendt som Philip Tapsell, født i Danmark, som udmærkede sig som en god officer på havet. Død i en alder af 94 år, 6. august 1873.*'

   Winiata, nu gumlende på sin femte soft-ice, meddeler, at Tapihana selv valgte at blive begravet på dette sted. Han har for så vidt også selv anlagt kirkegården. [...] I samme grav og i adskillige grave omkring ligger hans slægt. De levende Tapsell'er har fulgt med Winiata, John og mig op til kirkegården, og de debatterer ivrigt, hvor de engang selv skal ligge.
6. Falk-Rønne, *Sydhavets syv bølger*, p. 285: 'Mit nye bekendtskab med Hans Falk giver mig — det må jeg desværre bekende ligeud — et andet og mindre sympatisk billede af min navnebror, end det, jeg tog til mig som ung student.'
7. Falk-Rønne, *Sydhavets syv bølger*, p. 296:

   I Bay-of-Islands har han mødt en kvindelig slægtning af den berygtede og berømte maorikonge *Hongi Hika*. Hendes navn er *Maria Ringa*, og hun skal have været ganske dejlig at beskue. Han vil gerne gifte sig med hende, men det skal ske på pakeha-facon med kirkelig velsignelse og så videre. Det er det besynderlige ved disse såkaldte *eventyrere* fra forrige århundrede, at der stikker ikke så lidt af en småborger i mange af dem. De kan myrde løs med den ene hånd og få tårer i øjnene, når de gør honnør for flaget, med den anden. De hulker over deres gamle mor derhjemme under hyldebusken i det lille land ved det blanke sund, mens de med sindsro fragter prostituerede kvinder og ældre hælersker til Port Jacksons helvede. Og da Hans Falk, som sikkert har haft utallige elskerinder af alle slags racer i sit liv, endelig ønsker at gifte sig med en maoripige, skal der absolut medvirke en gejstlig person.
8. Falk-Rønne, *Sydhavets syv bølger*, p. 285 'at kannibalhøvdinger blev til gode viktorianske borgere'.
9. Falk-Rønne, *Sydhavets syv bølger*, pp. 297–98:

   Mere end 40 år kommer Tapihana til at leve i Bay-of-Plenty; han gifter sig på ny, denne gang med større held. Han får mange sønner og døtre. Han står ikke mere til søs, men etablerer sig som handelsmand, som en af de traders-of-death (*dødens handelsmænd*), der sælger geværer til maorierne og gør det muligt for dem at skyde løs på hinanden og myrde hinanden, slægt efter slægt. Vi har vanskeligt ved at forstå, hvor stor værdi et gevær havde for en maorihøvding. Men handelsvaren kan fortælle os lidt om det. I London kan en vågen ung boatsteerer købe en gammel, brugt flintebøsse for mellem 3 og 5 shillings; for den samme bøsse kan han blandt maorierne i Ny Zealand få en lille skov af kauri-træer eller to unge kvinder eller ti tatoverede afskårne menneskehoveder (som er en ret stor eksportartikel). Ja, han behøver kun at vise den interesserede maorikriger våbnet, og manden går straks ud for at skaffe ti menneskehoveder på gammeldags maner ved hjælp af krigskøllen og træspydet. En pakeha med ti geværer i sin besiddelse kan åbne et varehus og skaffe sig tømmer, flax (ny zealandsk hør) og som sagt menneskehoveder, som pr. stk. i

213

England kan sælges for en sum, som igen kan blive til mellem 80 og 90 geværer.

Jeg påstår ikke, at Hans Falk har handlet med afskårne menneskehoveder. Han fortæller ikke noget herom i sine erindringer, men hvorfor skulle han også det? Det var ikke noget, man talte om, ligesom man også helt undlod at lade missionærerne vide, hvor mange tønder rom, som blev afhændet til maori-*pa*'erne. Med et gevær i hånden og rom i maven var maorien et helt andet menneske, og i denne tilstand begyndte maorifolket en række blodige krige, som med små afbrydelser varede i næsten et halvt århundrede.

Igen og igen har jeg spurgt Hans Falks efterkommere: hvordan var han? Hvordan var gamle Hans Falk?

Men ingen har kunnet give mig svaret. De har kun kunnet sige: 'han var som de andre.'

Ja, han var vel som de andre, et barn af sin tid. Og nu ligger han begravet under vilde rosers flor med udsigt over bugten, hvor Te Arawa-kanoens folk gik i land for mere end seks århundreder siden.

10. The publication reappeared as an e-book in 2019 (Copenhagen: Lindhard og Ringhof) with a Shuttershock image of a model dressed and made-up as a Māori warrior on the front page.

11. The author borrowed the photograph from Quentin Tapsell (pers. com.). Cf. Cowan, *A Trader in Cannibal Land*, p. 8: 'The late Mrs. C. Garlick of Taneatua, showed me a treasured family relic, Tapsell's sea-chest or ditty-box, inlaid with ivory-like whalebone, after the manner of the old-time whalers' scrimshaw artcraft.' In 2004, the chest and box were in the possession of Tote Hutchinson's great-great-granddaughter Maureen Chalmers, but I have been unable to uncover their present location.

12. Dich, *Blandt hvaler og kannibaler*, back cover:

Journalist Preben Dich har besøgt Hans Falks efterkommere, som er stolte af at have dansk blod i årene. Bogen er en dramatisk historie om stammefejder, myrderier og kannibalisme- men også beretningen om en bemærkelsesværdig dansker, som gennem sin 84-årige tilværelse har sat sig varige spor i det fjerne land.

13. Kåre Bluitgen, *Hans Falk: i menneskeædernes land* (Hans Falk: In the Land of the Cannibals), illustrated by Lars Gabel (Copenhagen: ABC, 2010).

14. http://www.abc-forlag.dk/produkt/opdagelsesrejsende-hans-falk/: 'med hang til eventyr og fantastiske historier fra det virkelige liv'.

15. Bluitgen, *Hans Falk*, back cover:

Hans Falk ville ud i den store verden. Som ung tog han på hvalfangst i Sydhavet. En tid blev han sørøver for den danske konge. Derefter rejste han helt om på den anden side af Jorden og levede et farligt liv blandt menneskeædere. Ikke én, men mange gange snød Hans Falk døden!

16. Bluitgen, *Hans Falk*, p. 20:

Menneskeædere: Hans kom til New Zealand. Her mødte han maorierne. Det er det indfødte folk på New Zealand. Selv om Hans havde været ude for mange ting, gjorde maorierne ham bange. De ville sælge ham kød. Menneskekød. Hans var havnet blandt kannibaler.

17. Bluitgen, *Hans Falk*, p. 27:

Maorierne ville også gerne sælge afhuggede hoveder til Hans. Hovederne kom fra fanger, som de tog i deres mange kampe med hinanden. Maorierne var flot tatoveret i ansigtet. Når hovederne blev tørret, kunne de sælges i England. Der havde fine folk dem stående til pynt. Den form for handel ville Hans ikke være med til.

18. Bluitgen, *Hans Falk*, p. 29:

Maorierne spiste deres fjender. En dag tilberedte en stamme maden lige uden for Hans' hus. Han kunne lugte det stegte menneskød. Hans havde det forfærdeligt. Men der var intet, han kunne gøre. Han var i New Zealand. Ikke i Danmark.

19. Bluitgen, *Hans Falk*, p. 23:

Forlis og fallit: I 1829 blev Hans gift med en anden maori kvinde. Der var mange hvide mænd, der kun havde foragt til overs for de indfødte. De overfaldt maorierne og stjal deres kvinder. Mange maorier blev taget som slaver. Maorierne svarede igen ved at dræbe de hvide. Eller de tog dem til fange og gjorde også dem til slaver. Hans var ikke som de andre hvide. Han var god til at stifte fred. Derfor fik han venner blandt maorierne. Og ikke kun i sin kones stamme.

20. Bluitgen, *Hans Falk*, p. 38:

Nogle af de europæiske købmænd snød maorierne. De sagde, at det var med rom som med kartofler: Hvis man gravede de tomme flasker ned i jorden, groede der fulde flasker op. Og så solgte de maorierne tomme flasker.

21. For example, the female convicts on the *Catherine* are described as coming from England (p. 17), and Tapsell is buried wrapped in sailcloth rather than placed in a coffin (p. 47; cf. Cowan, *A Trader in Cannibal Land*, p. 8). Furthermore, although Tapsell is described as having christened his children himself, no mention is made of the Catholic Bishop Pompallier christening them in Whakatāne and criticising the refusal by Protestant missionaries to do the same (cf. manuscript pp. 249–50 , here p. 167): 'The Christian priests had said no to marrying Hans and Hineitūrama. Nor was there anyone who would baptise their children. Hans had to do this himself. (De kristne præster havde sagt nej til at vie Hans og Hine-i-turama. Og der var heller ingen, der ville døbe deres børn. Det måtte Hans gøre selv.)', p. 42.

22. Bluitgen, *Hans Falk*, p. 30.

23. Bluitgen, *Hans Falk*, p. 32.

24. Sulphur-crested cockatoos, native to parts of Australia and New Guinea, were introduced to New Zealand but were not reported in the wild until the early twentieth century (in the Waitākere Ranges in West Auckland).

Contemporary accounts of Phillip Tapsell's life

The marriage of Phillip Tapsell and Karuhi

Sunday, April 4th.–

[...]

A Mr. Tapsell, who had been long in the whale-fishing on the coast of New Zealand and lately a master of a whaling vessel belonging to Port Jackson, applied to me after Divine service was over to marry the sister of the head chief. I had known this young woman for the last fourteen years. She is a very fine young woman as a native, clean in her person, well-dressed in European clothes, and of a very amiable disposition. She came along with Mr. Tapsell. Tapsell is returning to Port Jackson. I told them I would marry them in New South Wales, but they both, as well as her friends, wish the marriage to take place before he sails and then she will accompany him. If he leaves her she says she will go into the interior and live retired by herself. I shall speak to the Revs. Messrs. Williams on the subject. The young woman is pretty well acquainted with the English language and has long resided amongst the missionaries, who speak well of her. I see no objection against marrying them myself.

[...]

Tuesday, April 20th.–

When I was at Rangihoua a Mr. Philip Tapsell wished to marry a native young woman, as already mentioned. She was the daughter of the head chief there. She had long been in the families of the missionaries at that station. They all spoke very highly of her conduct. I had known her for about fourteen years. As she understood the English language and our customs I promised to marry them to-day, but the heavy rains prevented them from coming in time as they had ten miles to come by water. I shall expect to marry them to-morrow. Tapsell has lately commanded a whaler belonging to Port Jackson and has been on the coast of New Zealand many years. As she is a very well-behaved young woman and a person of rank, I saw no impropriety in marrying them. Mr. Tapsell told me if they could not get married here they would go to Port Jackson and get married there. As she is now married, the missionaries' wives may show her some attention which they could not have done had she continued to live with Tapsell in an unmarried state, which was contrary to both their wishes.

Some persons may condemn the act of marrying them as she is a native heathen, but I have no doubt from my long knowledge of her character but that she will as a wife act with the greatest propriety, and give no cause of offence to the civilized world; I felt no objection in my own mind against their marriage.

Wednesday, April 21st.–

This morning I went to the chapel to perform the marriage ceremony. Upwards of thirty natives had come from Rangihoua to the marriage. Most of the natives of Kerikeri attended, and several of the missionaries and their children. Warepouka, the principal chief, who is her brother, attended to give her away, and her sister [Tungaroa] was bridesmaid. The young woman repeated the ceremony very correctly in the English language, which she perfectly understood. She conducted herself with the greatest propriety. The company came in a war-canoe, and brought their provisions with them — a pig alive, which was killed, and plenty of potatoes. In the evening they returned home much gratified with the marriage. I stated to the clergy, Messrs. Henry and William Williams and to Mr. Brown, that Mr. Tapsell had applied to me to marry him to the young woman, and wished to know if they saw any objection to it, but they appeared to have none. I then proposed to marry them at the chapel at Kerikeri as I should be there, unless any of them wished to marry them at Paihea, when it was agreed that they should go to Kerikeri, which they did and were married this day.

The young woman was neatly dressed in European clothing. They were of her own making. She is stated by the missionaries' wives to be a good seamstress as well as domestic servant. The more Christian customs and manners prevail in New Zealand the more improvement the natives will make in the arts of civilization, and I consider lawful marriage to be of the first importance.

The Letters and Journals of Samuel Marsden, 1764–1838, Senior Chaplain in the Colony of New South Wales and Superintendent of the Mission of the Church Missionary Society in New Zealand[1]

217

The recapture of the *Wellington*

"Let justice be done, though the heavens pass away," is a motto to which every Englishman should proudly, and we would say, fastidiously adhere. This will apply to the case of the Sisters, and the re-capture of the brig Wellington at the Bay of Islands. All along we have been imparting praise to Captain Duke, whereas now we find, upon testimony the most respectable and indubitable, that we were doing a flagrant act of injustice to that Gentleman, because we have been invariably awarding him, the said Captain Duke, that consideration which exclusively appertains to his chief officer, the brave Mr. Tapsell, and also the gallant crew of the Sisters! So far from Captains Duke, and Clink (of the Harriet) wishing to interfere with the pirates, they came to and expressed a contrary determination. "Who is to recompence me," said Captain Clark, of the Harriet, "for the probable loss of my ship?" "And who will repair our fractured limbs, or reward us," replied the Harriet's men, "if we trouble ourselves with such affairs?" These remarks had a great influence on the cautious mind of the sober-thinking Captain Duke, who was willing to extricate his fellow-subjects from the awful condition in which they were placed, but who at the same time trembled for the consequences — at least, they were such as he apprehended. We understand the chief mate and the crew of the Sisters reprobated the idea of allowing their countrymen to be carried away by the pirates from under their very nose, and regretted the hesitancy and caution of the Captain. The British feelings that pervaded the hearts of the Sisters' gallant tars was not to be repressed. No sooner had Mr. Tapsell, who has been a sailor and warrior from the womb — calculated on the disgrace that would eternally attach itself to his name, and to the character of the men under his command as chief officer, than he resolved on the liberation of the parties on board the Wellington, as well as her re-capture, in which he was nobly joined by the other officers and crew of his vessel. The Harriet, was inflexible — her Captain and crew were willing to yield the honours to the Sisters — whilst Captain Duke himself was ignorant, of the plans formed on board his own vessel for the accomplishment of an act of heroism and justice that Mr. Tapsell and his fellow tars will carry with them to their native country, and which will cover them with honour in the silent tomb. When Captain Duke was absent from the ship, in company with the skipper of the Harriet, and it afterwards turned out they were on board the Wellington, Mr. Tapsell (having previously taken two guns from the hold) clapped a pair of springs on the cable, so as to enable him to lay his vessel broadside on the pirate. Walton saw this manoeuvre. He complained to Captain Duke — the Captain pleaded ignorance of any hostile intention, and ignorant he was at the time — Walton, however, declared he would detain him a prisoner — but, upon asserting, on his word and honour, that he would not fire on the brig, the pirates suffered him to return to his own ship. As soon as he got on board, some rather strong language passed between Captain Duke and the magnanimous Tapsell, in reference to the springs on the cable. Tapsell said it was necessary for the purposes of defence. The Captain replied, by that act, his life had been placed in jeopardy, and that he had pledged his honour against, interference with the pirates. But the chief mate and the crew, not having plighted their faith to so lawless a banditti, were differently inspired from their cautious Commander, and avowed their readiness to sacrifice their lives rather than surrender their character as Englishmen, in allowing such a host of incorrigible fellows to escape. Captain Duke was grieved with the conduct of his mate and crew — but they were inexorable, and were prepared to leave the ship rather than abandon the hope of re-capturing the brig, and extricating innocent men from destruction: Capt. Duke, therefore, laudably gave the command to "FIRE!" The result of this noble determination is fully known and Mr. Tapsell, and the crew of the Sisters, merit the distinguished regards of His Majesty's Government. We should be sorry to deteriorate the services that Captain Duke has rendered the State by happening to command the Sisters, and being placed in authority over such heroes as his chief officer and crew — but, with all the information of which we have become possessed from a variety of respectable sources, the preponderating merit of the enterprise, and the success which attended it, belong to Mr. Tapsell, and the crew of the Sisters. The merit of Captain Duke is *accidental* — the merit, of his chief officer and crew is *positive*, and characteristic of the brave Sons of Albion. Report even goes so far as to assert, that, but for Mr. Tapsell's personal exertions subsequent to the re-capture, the pirates might have been successful in eluding the condign punishment which justly awaits them, and for which the unfortunate but determined men should prepare themselves — for mercy, to most, of them, on this side the grave, is beyond all hope. They should therefore prepare to meet their GOD!

219

We should like to hear that report fully contradicted which is in circulation, namely, that prisoners, on their way to our penal settlements, have an opportunity of supplying themselves liberally with spirits from commanders, and others on board the various vessels occasionally employed in these Services. We are not prepared to establish this report, but it is worthy of being enquired into, so that such an evil — one so tremendously destructive in its consequences — may successfully be crushed by the Government. We don't say this will apply to the Wellington, but we fervently trust that Captain Harwood will authorise us, under his own hand, to announce, that the prisoners on board the Wellington were not in the habit of buying rum at 7s. the bottle. No doubt Captain Harwood will allow us to do him this act of common justice. Indeed it speaks no great things for those ships in New Zealand, who, after they knew they were pirates, could trade with the brig Wellington — but, perhaps, this is only a vague report.

The Sydney Gazette and New South Wales Advertiser, 19 February 1827[2]

THE SHIP SISTERS.

Captain Duke (the skipper of the abov[e mentioned] whaler) would be a clever fellow if he only knew *Howe*. But we are afraid he will discover, before many days roll over, that he is acting rather a silly part, after manifesting such courage in taking "so desperate a gang" of pirates. The *Duke* has assumed to himself the authority of knocking the chief officer — the independent and brave Tapsell — from off duty, and making him a prisoner at large. This is done, too, though the other officers, who may be good fellows, as well as the whole crew, are satisfied that Mr. Tapsell has done nothing, at least that we can glean, to merit such degradation. Mr. Tapsell has been called on to deny the statements made in the Sydney Gazette; and the *Duke*, supposing that Mr. Tapsell furnished us with the information, has been the more urgent with him on that account. In this respect, however, the *Duke* is out of his reckoning, and it will puzzle him to ascertain the source whence we obtained the accurate information that our columns exhibited, though some of the Gentlemen, whom he suspects, and some of whom he has accused, are not the sources. With some trifling mistake, as to the order of proceedings on board the Sisters, our account was literally true, which can be proved by the ship's company of that vessel. If we had charged the *Duke* with cowardice, or imputed bad motives to him, we should not have been surprised; but we gave him, on the contrary, even-handed justice, and no man shall have more, not even a *Duke* of the realm. We are bound to say, therefore, in justice to Mr. Duke, and his ship's company, if the only reason that can be assigned for the suspension of Mr. Tapsell consists in refusing to falsify our statements, the Captain of the Sisters will find himself unpleasantly situate in the long run. We advise him, as his friend, in return for the handsome way in which he gave us his log, to reinstate Mr. Tapsell, unless there be some other offence imputable to him, more criminal than that of refusing to contradict the assertions of the Sydney Gazette. Whilst Mr. Duke is himself protected by the law, those under him also have the benefit of the same law: this should be borne in mind, and, if properly heeded, Mr. Duke will not only replace Mr. Tapsell, in his birth, but give him an equal share, in common with the other officers and crew, of the prize-money. To shew how determined Mr. Duke is to carry his point, we shall subjoin a note *verbatim et literatim*, that he forwarded to his crew on Saturday evening, when the poor fellows entreated a few dollars to enjoy themselves; but, when they found that more was required of them than they could, as English tars, digest consistently with truth, they were content with Mr. Duke's non-indulgence. Why Englishmen should be so treated, because they will not interfere in newspaper squabbles, which the Captain can so easily disprove by his own affidavit, if he thinks proper, is to us most marvellous. And whether any skipper of any whaler is justified in so acting, will be found out in the sequel, though we hope that Captain Duke will feel the policy of treating those under him with justice, for it appears, upon the shewing of this *formidable* epistle, that Mr. Tapsell and the crew acted *under the orders* of their master, though Mr. Duke would not have given such orders but for the English-like remonstrances of his officers and crew. To Mr. Tapsell, and the crew also, this is a valuable document, for it goes to exonerate them, though it by no means falsifies our statements — since they are all able to establish them, in the gross, upon oath. Now for Captain Duke's official despatch:-

"Saturday Night 7 p.m.

"To the residents of the Steereage — has you please to term your selves I have to say unless you are willing to contradict the Statement in the Gazett of Mondey last. I will not advance one. farthineg to any of you has you all must know that great part of it is lies Mr. Tapsell never acted without my orders — with the exception of putting the Spring on the *Caple* — and that afterwards proved of no Servise till the the next morning, when there was nothing done without my Order. "Your Most Obedient Servant,

"ROBT. DUKE."

The Sydney Gazette and New South Wales Advertiser, 27 February 1827[3]

Rumour says, that Messrs. Duke, Tapsell, and the crew of the Sisters, are to have £1800 prize-money. Hurrah for Tapsell!

The Sydney Gazette and New South Wales Advertiser, 1 March 1827[4]

The Sisters. — We perceive that Captain Duke, somehow or other, has found his way into the Monitor [biweekly Sydney newspaper, 1827–1828], or else got into the good graces of His Monitorial Eminence. We are sorry to see that Mr. Hall will be meddling with what he does not understand. Tapsell is the man — recollect that! Captain Duke is a cautious, and we believe a very good commander; but we must ask, whether he would have attacked, conquered, and brought the Wellington into Sydney, but for the degraded and reduced Tapsell? Answer this, ye that are concerned! We have no doubt that Captain Duke, as he richly deserves to be, will be adequately rewarded by the

Government, but every extravagant demand will not be met. We should have allowed the paragraph in question to escape, only that we felt anxious to refute the charge of having abused Captain Duke we say we deny his imputation; and if the Monitor please, let him bring forward chapter and verse to establish the charge. The Wesleyan Missionaries give Captain Duke a very high character as a commander whilst they were onboard his ship — a fact to which we feel pleasure in bearing testimony; but then we must not allow it to be said that, in rendering justice to a poor and gallant tar, like Tapsell, the Sydney Gazette has abused Captain Duke.

The Sydney Gazette and New South Wales Advertiser, 13 March 1827[5]

A PIRATICAL VESSEL, FORTY YEARS AGO.
(From a New Zealand Correspondent.)

Forty years ago the Sydney newspapers contained an account of the heroic rescue of a brig which had been piratically seized by convicts while on her way from Sydney to Norfolk Island, and the restoration of the vessel with its prisoners — eighty-five in number — to the authorities in Sydney, by whom six of the ringleaders were hung, and the remainder transported to Norfolk Island. This was effected in the Bay of Islands, New Zealand, in defiance of his captain, by the mate of a whaling vessel, a brave Dane, who is still alive in New Zealand, and now nearly 90 years of age; His courageous act made him so unpopular with the masters of vessels in these seas that he was unable then, and long afterward, to proceed to England and prefer a request for reward for this signal service, and compelled to remain in New Zealand, where he has spent the subsequent forty years. Once he prepared a petition to the Queen, and once to the Colonial Government of New Zealand, but both fell into negligent hands and never reached their destination.

As he is now beyond the ordinary age of humanity, and cannot in the course of nature expect his life to be much prolonged, he is anxious to make a final effort for the benefit of a numerous family which he will leave behind; and a month or two ago, being informed of the expected visit of Prince Alfred, of whose affable bearing and kind disposition he had heard much, and hoping that the opportunity had come at last to make his case known to, and enlist the sympathies of a member of the royal family, he walked from his home at Whakatane to Maketu, a distance of forty miles, in order to have prepared a petition to his Royal Highness, which he purposed presenting in person.

To this document was appended the following narrative of the occurrence, in the actual words of Mr. Tapsell, the petitioner, which are so simple and graphic that alteration would only have spoiled them.

"On January 26th, 1827, a strange vessel hove in sight at the Bay of Islands. It was customary in those days for the captains of vessels to go out of the harbor and pilot strangers in, which was the case in this instance, for Captain Duke, of the whaling ship Sisters, went out for that purpose, brought this stranger in, and anchored within a cable's length of the Sisters. From that point I observed her with the glass, and had a strong suspicion that there was something not right from seeing a number of people and no apparent discipline amongst them. After Captain Duke came on board I asked him what vessel it was. He said it was a vessel bound from Sydney to Norfolk Island with prisoners, which had put in for wood and water. I told him that I thought there was something wrong, to which he replied, 'No; it is all right.' During the whole day I was viewing them through the glass, and had a strong suspicion that she was a runaway vessel. The next day a man named Walton, who proved to be the pirate captain, was invited on board the Sisters by Captain Duke, to partake of a dinner. After dinner was over, and spirits put on the table, I rose up and challenged Walton in those words:– 'You have run away with that vessel;' to which he answered, 'I have; I could not help it.' I said 'that will do for me', and went away on deck. Duke then came up and asked me what was to be done? I told him to send Walton on board. But in the course of the afternoon his boat came alongside, armed, and inquired for Captain Walton, I told them I know of no Captain Walton, but that there was a man of the name of Walton on board. I then called Walton to go into his boat.

"That night it came on to blow a gale of wind. Mr. Williams, the missionary (late Bishop Williams), came on board, and I had some conversation with him. As he was going over the side he said, 'Tapsell, I hope you will not let her go.' I told him she should not go. Mr. Williams mustered all the Maoris in the bay he could in canoes, all armed, to take the vessel; but they were afraid, and kept behind the rock. That night it came on to blow a gale of wind, being obliged to let go a second anchor. In the morning it moderated, and the wind wore out. Captain Duke and Captain Clarke of the Harriett went on board the Wellington to see her out of the harbour; they hove up the second anchor, and hove short upon the first, the people were up loosing the foretopsail and shooting it home ready to get underway. When I observed that, I called all hands aft, and told them that it was a disgraceful thing to let that vessel go out; knowing that the soldiers with their officers were down below in irons, and would no doubt be murdered. The crew said, 'Speak, whatever you say we will obey.' I then told some of them to get the hawser up and clap a string on the cable, and the rest to mount the guns and get the small arms ready for action, which was done. Walton, observing this, said to Captain Duke, 'You are here to see me out, and now you are preparing to give me a broadside I

223

shall now keep you and Clarke on board.' Duke swore that he know nothing about it, whatever Tapsell did was for his own protection; and he gave his word of honour that the Wellington should go out. On this condition he let them both get into the boat. Captain Duke came on board and asked me what I was doing. I told him I was making preparation to prevent that rogue from going out. He said, 'I gave my word of honor she shall go out.' I replied, 'I gave my word of honor she shall never go out.' He said, 'What can we do, considering there eighty-five desperate characters on board?' I told him those characters proved to be cowards when it came to the trial. He said no one could have anything to do with it but a madman, and Clarke would have nothing to do with it; and Clarke said I will have nothing to do with it. This was on Saturday. On Sunday morning early we hoisted a flag and fired a gun from the quarter dock which took down his foretopmast. The next shot cut his mainmast half through, about two foot from the dock. The mutineers then all bolted down below. I manned a boat and went on board myself, armed with a brace of pistols and a dagger concealed, giving orders to the boat to keep off the side of the ship. Walton came to me saying 'I give up the vessel — I will do anything you wish.' I gave orders for the soldiers to come up to have their irons knocked off, and for the ammunition to be delivered up to me. Walton said he was afraid that he had not treated the soldiers well, to which I answered that was not my look out. Afterwards he asked me down into the cabin, placed liquor on the table, and asked me to help myself. I replied that I had no objection if he would first do the same, for I feared that poison might be in it. After that I went on deck and made preparations to secure the prisoners. The next day I was employed in getting our vessel ready to take the ringleaders on board of us. I gave the proper captain, Harwood, the charge of his own vessel. While taking the prisoners on board of us two of them made their escape to Patua, where Mr. Williams was. Being informed by the Maoris that there were two of them there but they were afraid to take them as they drew their knives when approached, I manned a boat, went to the place indicated, and seized one of them in a hut, the other making his escape by cutting through the raupo. I brought the one I had captured on board. The sentry told me on my return that during my absence he had heard a great deal of noise down below, and that he could see the prisoners' arms going as if they were sawing their irons. I told Mr. Kellett, the second mate, to muster them, and we would overhaul them. I found about twenty of the strongest of them with their irons cut through the thickness of a finger nail. I threatened to punish them, when one man, of the name of Drummond, being afraid of punishment, told me the plan which they had arranged, which was, that when I was in the act of getting the vessel underway, and when my attention would be occupied, they were to leap up and break their irons, get hold of me, out my throat, and throw me over the larboard quarter. Duke was to be saved. After that a strict watch was kept over them, we prepared the vessel for sea, and sailed for Sydney in company with the brig Wellington. We arrived alongside the dockyard in Sydney, and the prisoners were all taken on board the hulk. On coming out of the Court one day after giving evidence Duke came out of a tavern called the Rose and Crown, and asked me if I had seen the papers, at the same time throwing some newspapers to me. I looked at them, and found a full statement from the logbook. I was greatly praised, and Duke was called a coward, for consenting to let the vessel leave the Bay of Islands. He asked me if I could contradict the paper. I told him no, there was nothing but a true statement from the log. The next morning he called all hands aft, and broke me in the presence of them all, told the men not to obey me anymore as a chief officer, and told me there was the shore for me. That I could go ashore or remain in my cabin, which I chose. I told him I should remain, not having any friends in Sydney, and my life being in danger amongst the prisoners. Next day the Rainbow, commanded by the Hon. Captain Rous, came in; I went on board, and made my complaint. Captain Rous told me to come on board the Rainbow and remain, and then wrote to the Governor, and Captain Nicholson, the superintendent of the dockyard, came on board to know whether I was qualified to take charge of a Government vessel, asking me several questions in the presence of Captain Rous and the officers on the quarter-deck. He was satisfied, and said I should have the Alligator, which was then in Hobart Town. When she came in, the captain was to be discharged, and I to take her. Meantime Captain Rous wished me to go round with him to New Zealand as pilot, as he had never been there before, which I did, and on coming back to Sydney found that the Alligator had been there and another captain appointed. The schooner Darling was lying there ready for sea, bound for Tongatabu, for the missionaries, which wanted a captain. I applied, and got her. On my return from Tongatabu, I went to Captain Nicholson and asked if there was a vacancy for me now. He said no, that two lieutenants had come out from England who would step before a sailing-master. I then said I had better leave the country, as my life was in danger, and had been twice attempted. He said it would be the best."

The narrative concludes with Mr. Tapsell's return to the Bay of Islands, subsequent settlement at Maketu, and recounts the ransom of many persons which he effected at his own cost, several of whom were Europeans, as a proof that he has, through his career, endeavoured to serve his fellow-creatures from motives of humanity.

The petition is as follows:–

"To His Royal Highness Prince Alfred Ernest, Duke of Edinburgh,

"The petition of the undersigned, Philip Tapsell, for more than forty years an inhabitant of New Zealand,

"Humbly sheweth, –

"That your petitioner ventures respectfully to make known to your Royal Highness that he is by birth a Dane, born in Copenhagen, who has sailed for sixty years under the English flag.

"That in the year 1827, when chief officer of a whaling vessel in the Bay of Islands, he rendered valuable service to the British Government by rescuing a ship which had been piratically seized by convicts on their way from Sydney to Norfolk Island, and restoring them to the custody of the Government in Sydney notwithstanding the obstruction of the captain of his vessel, who would have permitted the mutineers to leave the harbour, with an English officer and several British soldiers as captives, who, but for your petitioner's resolute and prompt interference, would have been carried to sea and cruelly murdered.

"Your petitioner would respectfully lay stress on the importance of restoring eighty-five hardened criminals to the custody of the British Government at Sydney, by whom six of them were afterwards hanged.

"Your petitioner would also inform your Royal Highness that, on his arrival at Sydney, he received the highest commendation from the public, but incurred the enmity of his captain, who degraded him before his men, and discharged him from his employ, after which your petitioner's life was in constant danger from prisoners and their friends.

"That, under these circumstances, he sought the protection of the Honorable Captain Rous, then commander of her Majesty's ship Rainbow, but now Admiral Lord Rous, who sheltered him on board his ship, recommended him for, and afterwards gave him employment, and who was fully acquainted with the truth of the statements contained in a narrative of the occurrence appended to this petition, to which, though copious, the attention of your Royal Highness is respectfully invited.

"That notwithstanding the unworthy conduct of the captain of your petitioner's ship, that person actually took the vessel to England and obtained a large reward for the service which he had endeavoured to prevent, and which your petitioner had so successfully performed.

"That your petitioner has never been remunerated for this signal service, but on the contrary, exp[e]rienced both danger and privation, in consequence of the conscientious discharge of his duty, in defiance of an unprincipled employer, who reaped the well-earned reward of your petitioner's prompt and vigorous exertions.

"That about sixteen years ago the undersigned entrusted a petition to her Majesty the Queen in private hands, to be forwarded through the Hon. Captain Rous, and during the last year, one to the Colonial Government of New Zealand, neither of which petitions reached their destination, and your petitioner, acquainted by public report, with the kindness of disposition of your Royal Highness, in the belief that your Royal Highness will grant a patient hearing to an Old Sailor, now ventures to obtrude the mention of his services on the notice of your Royal Highness.

"Your petitioner, therefore, humbly and with great respect would pray your Royal Highness to give the subject a favourable consideration, and he pleased to cause this petition to be transmitted with your Royal Highness's recommendation to the throne of her Most Gracious Majesty the Queen; so that her Majesty may be induced to draw the attention of her Ministers of State to devise some means of reparation for this misfortune and injury which your petitioner has for many years suffered in consequence of an opportune and perilous act of service which he performed.

"And your petitioner would humbly add his assurance that, though by birth a Dane, he has spent the greatest part of a very long life under the English flag, and that her Majesty has no more loyal subject, and your Royal Highness no more respectful and sincere well-wisher than your petitioner.

"And your petitioner as in duty bound, &c.

"With sentiments of profound loyalty, your Royal Highness's very obedient and very faithful servant.

"PHILIP TAPSELL.

"Maketu, New Zealand."

Owing to the horrible attempt on the life of the Prince and his consequent departure for England, the opportunity to present this petition did not occur, and with the sanction of Mr. Tapsell the documents were forwarded to Sir George Bowen, Governor of New Zealand, with a request that they might be transmitted to the Prince, to which application the following courteous reply was received from his Excellency's Private Secretary:–

"Government House, Auckland,

"25th April, 1868.

"Sir, — I am directed by Governor Sir George Bowen to acknowledge the receipt of your letter of the 20th instant, and to inform you that the enclosed petition from Mr. Philip Tapsell to his Royal Highness the Duke of Edinburgh will be transmitted to England in due course.

"I have the honor to be, Sir,

"Your obedient servant,

"ALGERNON LEMPRIERE"

"Edward Little, Esq., Tauranga."

The Sydney Herald, 26 August 1868; *Sydney Mail*, 29 August 1868; *The Queenslander*, 5 September 1868; *The Mercury* (Tasmania), 16 September 1868[6]

The sacking of Maketū

March 31 [1836] — We were aroused at midnight by a report, that the fight was close at hand. Among the foremost of the party was Waharoa; and as the great body of the Natives purposed sleeping in the neighbourhood of the Settlement, he came and lay down before the door of Mr. Wilson's house, as a guard for the property. The number of Natives killed by the fight and eaten at Maketu appears to be sixty-five. They have also taken a great many slaves, probably 150; and totally destroyed the Pa. Mr. Tapsell, a flax agent, has had his premises burned to the ground, and all his property either destroyed or carried away. So completely, indeed, was the place ransacked, that the Natives dug up the body of Mr. Tapsell's child, which was deeply buried in his garden, merely for the sake of having the little coffin for a box.

The Missionary Register Containing the Principal Transactions of the Various Institutions for Propagating the Gospel with the Proceedings, at Large, of the Church Missionary Society, Volume 25 (1838)[7]

NEW ZEALAND.

We have been favoured by a gentleman with the perusal of a journal kept at New Zealand, between the 19th of March and the 4th of April last, containing the particulars of a dreadful slaughter and destruction of property committed by the natives of Waikatto, Matamata, and Touranga, at Maketu, where Richard Jones, Esq., M. C, of Sydney, had an establishment, which was totally burnt down, and upwards of one hundred tons of flax destroyed or carried away. The document itself is too lengthy to admit of our publishing it in full; we shall, therefore, bring the reader at once to the scene of murder and devastation, first briefly stating that the alleged ground for the attack was that some natives of the hostile tribe had been killed by those upon whom vengeance was now to to taken. It appears that intelligence of the projected attack was conveyed to Mr. Tapsel, the manager of the establishment at Maketu; but the numbers he was able to muster were almost powerless when opposed to those of the fierce assailants which amounted to about eight hundred well armed men, together with numerous slaves without arms, while the defenders did not amount to more than one hundred and twenty, including women and children. The savage assailants soon cleared every obstacle, killing every man they came across, and making prisoners of the women and children. The scene, says the writer of the journal, 'was now horrid in the extreme.' The unfortunate victims were dragged from their houses; and while held down by the legs and arms, to prevent resistance, savagely butchered with tomahawks. Quarters and heads of men lay scattered about in every direction; while the exulting yells of the conquering party added, if possible, to the surrounding horrors. The party remained at the station several days; and although they had previously disavowed any intention to meddle with the property of Mr. Tapsel, they, emboldened by the success of their main object, soon resorted to further violence and plunder. A friendly Chief strongly advised Mr. T. to remove from the station, to which, after much persuasion, he assented. The natives then commenced removing the stores, despite of every effort to restrain them even by their own Chiefs. At last a 'general rush' was made into the dwelling-house of Mr. Tapsel, and, in about fifteen minutes after, it was in flames. The flax-house close by was emptied of its contents which were carried away in all directions: the river adjoining was crowded with canoes laden with the plunder; and Mr. Tapsel effected his escape with no other clothing than a shirt and trousers. On the following day, Mr. Tapsel was told by one of the few natives who made their escape from the scene of butchery, that the enemy had taken the whole of the flax from two large flax houses — amounting to upwards of one hundred tons — besides a considerable quantity from the dwellings of the natives. After possessing themselves of every article that might prove of use to them, they proceeded to set fire to the houses and the fence, which were wholly consumed. Such was the general terror which these desperate proceedings excited, that the Missionaries at Touranga had sent their wives and most valuable property on board their schooner, which happened to be lying in the harbour, until the natives had passed — those people being generally desperate and prone to the commission of outrage when returning from fighting. This party had also, on their way to Maketu, fallen in with thirteen of another hostile tribe, eleven of whom they murdered, and feasted on their flesh which they baked in ovens. While encamped for this purpose, the Missionaries, who had intelligence of their having set out for Maketu, came to the place and endeavoured to dissuade them from their purpose, but without avail — the Chiefs scarcely attended to what was addressed to them. The establishment of Mr. Scott had also been plundered of a considerable quantity of clothing and cooking utensils, by a party of Touranga natives. At the date of the latest intelligence from New Zealand, tranquillity prevailed in that part of the Country where the occurrences which we have related took place, and the Waikatto tribes had departed for their several settlements.

Sydney Herald, 8 August 1836[8]

NEW ZEALAND. — The Sydney Herald of the 8th August contains a melancholy account of a desperate rencountre between two tribes of natives at a place called Maketoo, where Mr. Tapsel had the management of a flax establishment belonging to Mr. Jones of Sydney. The attacked party amounted to about 125, while the assailants numbered upwards of 800. The conflict is described as truly awful. The superior party killed every man they came across, making prisoners of the women and children. They burned the dwelling house of Mr. Tapsel, and destroyed or carried off about 100 tons of flax from the flax house. How invaluable is the protecting hand of Government which the settler enjoys in this colony, when compared with those sad events at New Zealand and other barbarous countries.

The Hobart Town Courier, 2 September 1836[9]

NEW ZEALAND.

Our readers are already in possession of intelligence from New Zealand, respecting the destruction, by the natives there, of some valuable property belonging to Richard Jones, Esq., M. C., and John Maclaren, Esq., of Sydney. The following extract from a letter to a gentleman here, also a sufferer to a considerable amount, furnishes additional particulars. The letter is dated from Waimate:

'The war at the southward arose from a Rotorua chief killing another chief in cold blood. The murdered man being a brother of Waharoa, the natives of Touranga at first had nothing to do in the matter, as it was said that Waharoa would go direct to Rotorua, and not to Maketa (Town Poert). On a sudden, however, old Toharangi, of Outmoetea, joined Waharoa with two hundred Touranga natives, and to our great surprise, a body of one thousand men, well armed, passed through the settlement on their way to Maketa. This was on a Friday evening. They took Maketa on the Monday afternoon following, and the next day, in the evening, Tapsell's premises, and Mr. Jones's property, were committ[e]d to the flames.

'There were only forty fighting men in the Pa when Waharoa made the attack with seven or eight hundred men. Tapsell had been advised of their approach only three hours before, and urged the people to flee for their lives, but they madly determined to stand their ground, and all were cut off save one, who fled to Rotorua to tell the tale. When I found they would not go, he stood by them and rallied them to the defence, and when Haupapa, a Rotorua chief, received his mortal wound, be was taken into Tapsell's house, who refused to deliver him, while living, to the enemy, and when he died, Tapsell cut off his head that the enemy might not got it.

'Thus Tapsell involved himself in the quarrel, and was obliged at last to cut his way out of the side of the house; he only just escaped with his life, as the hatchets were ready to take off his head, when, through the interference of a native woman, and of old Kiaroa, he was suffered to go. Mr. Wilson and myself were in the neighbourhood of Maketa time enough to see the premises in flames, and Tapsell standing with his face towards them just after he had escaped. He was about to escape in his boat to Wakatane, but the natives would not suffer him to do so that night; he afterwards got to Wakatane, and thence to Rotorua, where he was stimulating the natives to revenge. The last we heard of him was, that the Rotorua natives detained him among them, little better than a prisoner, with scanty food, and scarcely clothes to put on.

'About twenty tons of flax was saved from Maketa by the Tuma natives, and deposited in their Pa in a large house belonging to Tupaia; in every other respect the destruction of Maketa was complete. Mr. Chapman and I visited the place a few days afterwards, when the Rotorua natives had charge of it; scarcely a vestige remained of any of the buildings, and even a grave in which a child of Tapsell's had been buried, was emptied of its contents.

'For some time the movements of the Rotorua natives were very doubtful, and it was thought they had all returned to their place to make ready for a grand attack; when suddenly we heard that the Tuma was taken, and poor old Kiaroa, with Hikareia, Werohia, and Wankaponga, all killed. Before we left Touranga, the Tuma had shared the fate of Maketa, and the twenty tons of flax was, with every thing else in the place, committed to the flames.

'The death of the chiefs and the uncertainty attending the movements of the Rotorua natives, threw the whole of Touranga into greater confusion than before.

'There was every reason to suppose that if the Rotorua people could muster sufficient strength they would soon be in our neighbourhood and we thought it right to remove our wives and children to a place of greater security.'
Sydney Herald, 17 November 1836[10]

The wrecking of the *Falcon*

Kororarika, New Zealand.
December 5th 1842.
My dear Charles,
[...]
We came to anchor off a place called 'Mukatu' on or about the 23rd February to take in Flax (in an open roadstead) but the surf was so heavy the canoes could not come off to us. On the last day of the month February the

weather began to assume a threatening appearance and a heavy swell set in from the N.E. although at the same time there was not a breath of wind out of the Heavens'. During the afternoon we observed the Sea Fowl of different species, even the Stormy Peteril (a bird that delights to sport on the gale) we saw amongst the rest making for the Shore to shun the effects of the approaching gale. These were ill omens and plainly showed there was no time for the watchful eye of the Mariner to sleep — we struck our fore Royal and Top Gallant Masts and sent the yards on deck and struck the Main Topmast. After our preparations were made we sent the seamen below to take rest while it was to be had (for by appearances the time was not many hours distant when they would have to work hard and perhaps struggle for their lives) the Chief Mate and myself remained on deck to keep watch — at length the sun obscured himself at the back of the lofty mountains to the westward of us, still there was not so much wind as would stir a leaf on the loftiest tree — but the heavy swell more increasing and the Vessel rolled very heavy. In the twilight of the evening a light breeze sprang up from the S.W. in which quarter we all sincerely wished it might hold as we were sheltered at that point by the sand, but our hopes were in vain for in less than an hour the wind was at the South — between 8 and 9 in the evening it commenced to thunder and lighten very heavy and was quickly followed by a tremendous squall of wind and rain — called all hands and let go the second anchor — in about half an hour the Thunder and lightning and wind ceased, but rain still continued pouring in torrents and the night was as dark as if we were enclosed in a Tomb. About ten the gale commenced with all its horrors, the much dreaded time had at last arrived — in less than another hour the wind was at East and the elements all in full play and the terrors of the night increasing with the storm (before midnight the wind hauled to the N.E. (which was of all quarters the most dreaded by us, as we were then on a dead lee shore) where it blew with almost tenfold fury, the huge seas burst in quick succession over the Vessel and the last ray of hope seemed to have fled, for each sea that came we expected the Vessel to go down with anchors and ourselves to a watery grave. About one o'clock in the morning our deck stopper, which was stout enough for a Vessel five times her size, broke with a report of Thunder, and in an instant our Starboard cable was gone, the larboard one must have shared the same fate had it not jammed in the weather bit in the windless end. A tremendous sea at that moment struck her in the larboard bow which almost buried her hard round and brought her stern on to the Sea, in a few seconds another sea struck her which drove in her deadlight Cabin Windows and a great portion of her stern frame. The larboard anchor then checked her and as she was casting in a most awful sea burst in her waist which hove her on her beam ends and swept all before it while we were clinging to the shrouds like so many drowning rats, that I made sure was the last for it was the last of my ideas that she could ever recover — neither did I wish that she ever should for death appeared preferable to life in our present situation — but our sufferings were not to end here for she now righted again to the great astonishment of all on board — we could now plainly perceive that the Vessel was drifting but which way we could not tell as there was no light on board and we were deprived of all means of getting one — about 2 o'clock a.m. the Vessel struck violently and we saw but too plainly that she was drifting into the midst of the heaviest of the breakers — we were then obliged to quit the Deck and take refuge aloft in the main rigging to await the event — she continued to strike very heavy until at length the Breakers drove her broadside to the shore, she then fell on her starboard broadside to seaward with her decks perpendicular as a wall, the Chief Mate who was by my side in the Starboard Main rigging were underneath clinging to the shrouds with our arms and legs expecting the next breaker that came would drive her into a thousand pieces, it capsized her right over with her Masts in the shore — a slight ray of hope now seemed to gleam for the first time during the Gale — but it was only for a moment for when the drawback went out it again capsized her into her former position. I now found hope was out of the question for it was utterly impossible the Vessel could hold together long — there were people on board that could not swim — I knew there were few better skilled in that art than myself and as great as the barrier between death and life appeared to be I resolved on making one grand effort to gain the Shore. The distance was but short not being more than 100 yards — but as short as the distance was it appeared utterly impossible to accomplish it I resolved on making one grand effort to gain the Shore. I had hoped if I could gain the Shore to be the means of saving (if not all) some portion of the Crew by watching the Surf and hauling them out as they washed ashore exhausted — accordingly when the next Breakers came and brought her upright before she fell in Shore the Chief Mate and myself let go our hold and dropped on Deck the Captain and the remainder of the Crew remained at the Mast Head as the drawback was coming out, I shook hands with the Chief Mate and overboard I sprang and it was very nearly being the last spring I was ever to make for at that moment it was at its lowest ebb, and consequently my fall much greater than I had anticipated I struck against the bottom and with the violence of the shock severely injured my loins, in an instant I was hurled heels over head to the brow of the Beach where I drove my hands in to the sand and endeavoured to hold on — but the drawback went down with the rapidity of lightning taking me with it nearly under the Vessels bottom thrice I was hauled up the same way and as often taken off again — but the fourth time by a desperate effort I gained the shore — where I crept a few yards on my hands and knees then fell exhausted writhing with the pain in my loins and with anxiety for my Shipmates left in the Vessel, I was on Shore it was true but that assistance which I would have given the world to have rendered to my fellow sufferers that great boon was denied me — for I stood too much in need of that assistance myself — I had not long been in that state before one of my Shipmates fell over me — he enquired who I was and if I were hurt — I answered in the affirmative and begged him for GOD's sake to look out for the others washing ashore and assist them — he immediately obeyed and in a much shorter time than could possibly have been expected by assisting each other every soul was on shore alive, and no time to spare — for scarce were all the people out of her when she broke in midships her topsides parted from her bottom, down came Masts and yards and the illfated 'Falcon' was no more. The rain continued to pour in torrents without the least sign of abating and the large coarse sands flew fit to cut our naked limbs to pieces. Those who were uninjured made holes in the sand and put the Invalids in then made others for themselves, that was the only shelter we could get (if shelter it could be called) at length the day dawned, the rain ceased, and the storm began to abate, and as the day opened out upon us it showed but too plainly our wretched condition — twas then I felt the full force of my situation — for although I can assert with a clear conscience that during the hour of danger fear never once entered my breast — yet when I beheld myself a shipwrecked, houseless, penniless, disabled being, destitute of food and clothing without a friend to consult, and fifteen thousand miles from home, those thoughts I must confess got rather the upper hand of me for a short time for my spirit was such that I would rather die than ask assistance from any one. About 8 o'clock the breeze having considerably abated the Chief Mate and Steward came to assist me to get inshore to a place where there was some grass but we had not proceeded many paces before they were obliged to lay me down the exertion being too great for the wound I had received. About 11 a.m. several of the Natives arrived bringing with them the means of making a fire which they got under weigh close to where I was lying, about an hour afterwards the Crew started for the Trading Station which was about 4 miles distant from where we were wrecked, carrying the Captain with them. The Chief Mate and Steward came to render me some assistance which I positively refused owing to the excruciating pain in my loins. The procession then moved forward and a more wretched spectacle I never beheld — some were half others entirely naked — the only treasure I had left in the world was one shirt minus one sleeve and a pair of trousers minus one leg nearly to the waistband. I regret much losing that watch you made me a present of — but my dear fellow I could not save it, the spyglass was picked up by a Native two days after the gale, the Trading Master purchased it with some tobacco and restored it to me, that is all I recovered. About 4 o'clock p.m. a party of Natives arrived bringing with them a rudely constructed (they were sent by the Trading Master) litter into which they put and conveyed me to the Station where I was confined to my bed for some time.

[...]

Your most affectionate Brother,

W. M. Umbers.

[...]

Letter from William M. Umbers to his brother, Charles Umbers, 5 December 1842[11]

Phillip Tapsell's obituaries and description of funeral

DEATH OF Mr TAPSELL.

We yesterday received intelligence from Maketu of the death (which occurred on the previous day) of Mr Tapsell, sen., one of the oldest settlers in the colony, who visited New Zealand more than two generations ago, when the only white inhabitants consisted of missionaries stationed at the Bay of Islands, and one or two fugitives from whaling ships, who had taken up their abode amongst natives in the interior. Mr Tapsell, whose real name was Hans Homen Falk, by birth a Dane, and son of an official under the Danish Government, was, to the best of his own recollection, born in the year 1777, consequently he must at the period of his death have reached the advanced age of 96, a surprising circumstance when his eventful life of hardships and peril are considered. His maritime experiences commenced with the war in which his own country was engaged against England. When of age sufficient, he obtained command of a privateering cutter, succeeding so well as in a short time to be promoted to a large barque. While at anchor off Elsinore, abreast of the English fleet moored on the opposite side of the Sound, a night attack was made by man of war boats to cut out the privateer. The boats' crews were beaten off with great loss, but Tapsell received a sabre wound which nearly cost him his life, the effects of which he felt to the last. His ship was afterwards taken by the Swedes, and he remained a prisoner for eleven months. After two futile attempts at escape, he recovered his liberty by an exchange of prisoners. By and by he found himself in England, where he took the name of Phillip Tapsell, for the purpose of obtaining employment in British vessels, which were not allowed to carry officials of any other nations. From this period begins his whaling voyages, full of incidents, during one of the earliest of which he had occasion to put into the Bay of Islands, even then, as now, a resort for whaling ships seeking supplies of wood and water. Mr Tapsell's descriptions of those early days of primitive New Zealand, where cannibalism prevailed, were extremely interesting. It is between 40 and 50 years ago that Tapsell's concern in the capture of a runaway convict ship, led by a train of circumstances, to his permanent settlement on the island as a trader on behalf of some Sydney merchant. He chose Maketu as his station, which place he purchased from Hori Tupaea, to whom it had been awarded at a great council of tribes. At his invitation the Ngatiwhakawa and Ngatipikiao (Arawa) came down from Rotorua and settled at Maketu. Here Mr Tapsell became a great chief, and prospered exceedingly, until he was burnt out by an invasion from Waikato and Tauranga. Of his flight, his subsequent settlement at Whakatane, or his shipwreck, it is impossible here to speak. It may suffice to say that a life of almost unprecedented adventure and occasional prosperity, terminated in an old age of dependence, soothed, however, by the affection of dutiful sons, under whose roofs he broke bread in his declining age. Mr Tapsell was remarkable for firmness and intrepidity. Though in his prolonged sojourn he had acquired a large experience, it was not the knowledge to be gained from books, or the graceful amenities of social life, but rather the stern and unconciliating wisdom of an ancient warrior. Nevertheless, he was kindly, affectionate, and, when he had the opportunity, open-handed to a fault. It is pleasing to have to record that in his late years he imbibed a strong devotional feeling, and, in the retirement which his growing infirmities enforced, he read his Bible several hours every day. Never did he sit down to his frugal meal without shading his face with his trembling hand and imploring a Divine blessing. Such as he was he is gone to his rest. Few have passed through similar ordeals, and fewer still have been equally purified by the process.

Bay of Plenty Times, 9 August 1873; *New Zealand Herald*, 13 August 1873, *Nelson Examiner and New Zealand Chronicle*, 22 August 1873[12]

[...] Our 'own correspondent' gives further particulars of his remarkable career:– 'Old Philip Tapsell died at Maketu on the 7th of August, after a fortnight's illness. He might be said to have been dying for some time past, for he had far exceeded the ordinary span of life, being, according to his own reckoning, about ninety-six years of age. For the last six or seven years he has resided at Maketu, where, about forty-five years ago, he first settled as a trader in New Zealand, and where he met ultimately with crushing misfortune. He remained remarkably vigorous till towards the very last, and a very slight stoop detracted from his great height. His faculties were unimpaired, and his memory was good, especially of events long past, on which, in conversation, he loved to dwell. He had always, prior to the visit of the Duke of Edinburgh, had great expectations from a petition which he had got prepared, praying for recompense for former services. When His Royal Highness landed at Maketu, the old man was introduced to him, and was shaken cordially by the hand by His Royal Highness, but poor old Tapsell was so taken by surprise that he had not a word to say. The Prince passed on, and doubtless forgot all about the interview. None of Tapsell's actual contemporaries amongst the natives are now living. The now venerable Hori Tupaea was a young man at the sacking of Maketu, and one or two other comparatively old men among the Arawa were mere striplings at the time, so that of late old Tapsell has been living amongst a new generation, to whom his exploits of olden times are merely traditionary. Not many civilised men have lived entirely for so many years amongst a fierce race of cannibals, and perhaps not many will envy the experience so gained.'

New Zealand Herald, 27 August 1873[13]

FUNERAL OF Mr TAPSELL.

We have been furnished with the following particulars of the funeral obsequies of old Mr Phillip Tapsell. A big gun, mounted by himself alongside of his house, which he had requested to be fired at his death and burial, was exploded immediately intelligence of the death was received, at 10 o'clock on the night of August 6th. On the same night twelve rounds of ammunition were fired off. On Friday, 8th, the big guns continued firing from 10 to 12 a.m., and shortly after which Mrs Simpkins, daughter of Mr Tapsell, arrived from Whakatane, when a *tangi* commenced amongst the natives. On Saturday the big guns were fired from 8 a.m. till noon. The funeral procession started at 3 p.m., the church bell tolling for an hour and a half. Lieutenant Way was in charge of a firing party of twelve, and three rounds were fired over the grave. After the first round one big gun was fired, one after the second, and one after the third. The firing of the big gun was well conducted by Constable McMillan. The burial service was read by Mr Hamlin, R.M., the Rev. Mr Spencer being absent on the coast. There was a large attendance both of Europeans and natives, and several flags in the township were hoisted half mast high. The Vincent also had her ensign at the half-mast. The coffin was handsomely mounted, and the funeral arrangements were under the management of Mr D. Lundon, of Messrs London and Conway, which was a guarantee of their being efficiently performed.

Bay of Plenty Times, 13 August 1873[14]

237

Phillip Tapsell in the letters of Henry Williams

Monday, 24 October 1831.

Fine, west wind. At nine, landed on our way to Maketu; Kiharoa and several other chiefs accompanying us. We were conducted to Paroa, — a beautiful spot, with an extensive view. Sat down to rest, and spoke to the natives there. They were tolerably attentive. At half-past five, arrived at Maketu. Mr Tapsel met us, and invited us into his house.

Assembled all the natives round us in the evening, and spoke to them of the love of God. Pita and Rawiri each said a few words. At ten, lay down to rest much wearied.

Thursday, 3 November 1831.

At half-past six, took leave of Mr Tapsal, after receiving every attention from him, and commenced our journey to Tauranga, leaving several of our party behind, owing to the expressions which had been used respecting Wharetutu, and some of our boys. At two, arrived in view of our little bark, and were soon on board, much rejoiced to be once more on English ground. We soon forgot all our toils, and sent for Kiharoa and Kaiwaiwa, to explain the circumstances of the late report, and also to make arrangements for our departure. They came immediately, and were very civil, wishing us to return to Ngapuhi and say that they had no ill-will towards them, but desired peace.

The cutter arrived from Maketu. A European [Mr Tapsell] came on board, and said he had come to see if Ngapuhi would accept the services of the Rotorua nation against Ngatiawa. He spoke of the cutting up of these poor creatures with apparent relish, as though he would join the natives in their savage feast. A schooner arrived, and anchored at some distance. Sent the boat to the pa to inquire the loss. Answer, four killed and three mortally wounded; could not learn what Ngapuhi had suffered.

The firing did not cease till dusk. A boat came along side from Ngapuhi, and informed us that one was killed, and some wounded. The European who came in the boat expressed his intention of supplying Ngapuhi with arms and ammunition, as much as they required, on trust. His expressions were disgusting, and we were relieved by his departure.

Friday, 15 March 1833.

[...] In the afternoon I heard that Te Amahau, the father of the man shot on Monday, after he had concluded his crying over the corpse, addressed himself generally and said that as he had now lost a child in the war, it was for him to deliver his sentiments and that he should proceed with the Missionaries and make peace. He desired no satisfaction on account of his child, but that these proceedings might be stayed. We went to the Pa to learn the state of feeling, but most were asleep. A few were disposed for conversation, but nothing particularly to the purpose. At length we heard that Te Amahau was enquiring for us. When we met him he spoke of going to the Tumu, for the purpose of consulting upon the propriety of making peace. He had now lost a son and was therefore entitled to speak and proposed to send one of my boys in the morning with a letter to some of the leading men and should they be willing that we should then go round in my boat to Tauranga to meet Titore and the Rarawa. The poor man appeared very earnest in his desires and said he did not want satisfaction on account of his son but peace. He afterwards came to us and gave the needful instruction to the boy who was to go in the morning. I also wrote a letter to some of the leading men in Tauranga of his own dictation, and one to a Mr [David] Scott who resides there as a flax agent requesting that he would render all the aid in his power. Mr Tapsel who resides here for the same purpose begins to feel the necessity of the same thing, and I hope will endeavour to keep the people quiet.

Sunday, 17 March 1833.
Fine morning. The natives in the Pa very busy consulting their sticks as to the probable result of the present conference, whether peace or war — a great noise. Held our service at the usual time; very few persons besides our boys. At the conclusion our old Priest came and desired to say what his Atua had revealed to him, that there would be shedding of blood. I replied that his Atua was the Author of all mischief, by whom the country had been depopulated, that his own arm had been broken by his Atua, and that Te Aramiti [a noted old tohunga of Matauri] a great Priest and his party, the instigators of this war, had been deceived by their Atua, and thus it was continually the case among them, lamentation and mourning and woe. All present assented to what was said that there was no good thing amongst them. I then warned the old man to flee from the wrath to come and seek to obtain peace with God through Jesus Christ.

After dinner went to the Pa; many disposed to cavil, extolling the power and excellency of their Gods; but were soon brought to silence. Others appeared desirous to hear us speak upon these things. The boys returned from the Tumu before sunset, bringing a good report and that they were anxious to see us. Were much encouraged at the conversation of our people, gradually giving way and desiring peace. It is a period of much anxiety and difficulty to do anything with such overgrown self-willed perverse children, where each possesses an opinion independent of the other, and liberty of acting. We should have but little hopes of effecting anything were it not for the promises of the Lord's assistance and blessing. In the evening some of the Chiefs came to converse; tried to prevail with them to allow me to go over to the Tumu, which was opposed, as we must remain until the rear comes up. Mr Tapsel expressed his determination to go over in the morning. The Chiefs were angry with him.

Saturday, 8 June 1833.

Received two letters from Mr Tapsel, a flax agent, residing in Maketu, — the man who opposed us so strenuously last year, when at Tauranga with the natives. At the latter end of his first letter, which is written just at the conclusion of making peace, he says: — 'My people bid me to write to you to send them a Missionary. If you should approve of that, I hope you will send one to Tauranga, Whakatane, and the river Thames, as it would be the means of keeping peace among them.'

This is the testimony of one who has been living several years among this people, and has tried the power of his abilities and strength of his European knowledge in keeping this war in agitation. What he expresses in his letter, I doubt not, is his sincere opinion, — that the influence of Missionaries will alone stay this destructive work. In the course of a few days after peace had been concluded, some of the Rarawa were surprised and killed by some in connection with Tauranga, which immediately involved all in the renewal of hostilities.

Te Wiremu — Henry Williams: Early Years in the North[15]

NOTES

1. John Rawson Elder, *The Letters and Journals of Samuel Marsden, 1764–1838, Senior Chaplain in the Colony of New South Wales and Superintendent of the Mission of the Church Missionary Society in New Zealand* (Dunedin: Coulls, Somerville Wilkie, Ltd. and A.H. Reed for the Otago University Council, 1932), pp. 481, 486–487 (Marsden's Sixth New Zealand Journal, entries for 1830).

2. *The Sydney Gazette and New South Wales Advertiser*, 19 February 1827, p. 2.

3. Ibid, 27 February 1827, p. 2.

4. Ibid, 1 March 1827, p. 2.

5. Ibid, 13 March 1827, p. 2.

6. *The Sydney Herald*, 26 August 1868, p. 3; *Sydney Mail*, 29 August 1868, p. 3; *The Queenslander*, 5 September 1868, p. 7; *The Mercury* (Tasmania), 16 September 1868, p. 3. See also Cecil and Celia Manson, *The Affair of the Wellington Brig: A True and Terrible Tale* (Wellington: Millwood Press, 1978); Henry Williams, *The Early Journals of Henry Williams, Senior Missionary in New Zealand of the Church Missionary Society, 1824–40*, ed. Lawrence M. Rogers (Christchurch: Pegasus Press, 1961), pp. 34–41.

7. *The Missionary Register Containing the Principal Transactions of the Various Institutions for*

Propagating the Gospel with the Proceedings, at Large, of the Church Missionary Society, Volume 25 (1838), p. 293.

8. *Sydney Herald*, 8 August 1836, p. 2.
9. *The Hobart Town Courier*, 2 September 1836, p. 4.
10. *Sydney Herald*, 17 November 1836, p. 3. See also Ron D. Crosby, *The Musket Wars: A History of Inter-Iwi Conflict 1806–1845* (Auckland: Libro International, 2012 [1999]), pp. 303–307; Enid Tapsell, *Historic Maketu. Hui Hui Mai!* (Rotorua: Rotorua Morning Post, 1940), pp. 56–60.
11. Letter from William M. Umbers to his brother, Charles Umbers, 5 December 1842, typescript copy in Tauranga Public Library Archives, New Zealand (excerpt).
12. *Bay of Plenty Times*, 9 August 1873, p. 3; *New Zealand Herald*, 13 August 1873, p. 3; *Nelson Examiner and New Zealand Chronicle*, 22 August 1873, p. 3 (abbreviated version).
13. *New Zealand Herald*, 27 August 1873, p. 3.
14. *Bay of Plenty Times*, 13 August 1873, p. 3.
15. Caroline Fitzgerald, *Te Wiremu — Henry Williams: Early Years in the North* (Wellington: Huia, 2011), p. 157, 160, 177–78, 198–99, 199–200, 207–208.

Bibliography

Barnes, Robert Harrison. *Sea Hunters of Indonesia: Fishers and Weavers of Lamalera*. Oxford: Clarendon Press, 1996.

Belich, James. *Making Peoples: A History of the New Zealanders from Polynesian Settlement to the End of the Nineteenth Century*. Rosedale, NZ: Penguin, 1996.

Bell, F. Dillon. *Maori Deeds of Old Private Land Purchases in New Zealand, From the Year 1815 to 1840, with Pre-Emptive and Other Claims*. Wellington: George Didsbury, 1882.

Bentley, Trevor. *Pakeha Maori: The Extraordinary Story of the Europeans who Lived as Māori in Early New Zealand*. Auckland: Penguin, 1999.

——. 'Images of Pakeha-Maori: A Study of the Representation of Pakeha-Maori by Historians of New Zealand from Arthur Thomson (1859) to James Belich (1996)'. Unpublished PhD thesis. Hamilton: University of Waikato, 2007.

——. *Cannibal Jack: The Life and Times of Jacky Marmon, a Pākehā-Māori*. Auckland: Penguin, 2010.

Bevan-Smith, John. '[Review] Paul Moon, This Horrid Practice: The Myth and Reality of Traditional Maori Cannibalism'. *New Zealand Journal of History*, 44.2 (2010), pp. 203–205.

Binney, Judith. *The Legacy of Guilt: A Life of Thomas Kendall*, rev. edn. Wellington: Bridget Williams Books, 2005.

Blom, K. Arne, and Jan Moen. *Försvunna städer i Skåneland*. Lund: LiberFörlag, 1983.

Bluitgen, Kåre. *Hans Falk: i menneskeædernes land*, illustrated by Lars Gabel. Copenhagen: ABC, 2010.

Bush, Ernest E. 'The Three Wives of Philip Tapsell'. *Te Ao Hou. The Maori Magazine*, 74 (1973), pp. 11–13.

Caldwell, Russell. *Tapihana: Brothers in Arms*. Christchurch: Iwi-Link Management, 2004.

Cowan, James. *The Adventures of Kimble Bent*. London: Whitcombe and Tombs, 1911.

——. *A Trader in Cannibal Land. The Life and Adventures of Captain Tapsell*. Dunedin: A.H. & A.W. Reed, 1935.

——. *Hero Stories of New Zealand*. Wellington: Harry H. Tombs, 1935.

Cronin, Bernard, and Arthur Russell, '"Gentleman Brady": Bushranger of Breeding'. *The Queensland Times*, 26 February 1932, p. 5.

Crosby, Ron D. *The Musket Wars: A History of Inter-Iwi Conflict 1806–1845*. Auckland: Libro International, 2012 [1999].

Davis, Robert C. *Christian Slaves, Muslim Masters: White Slavery in the Mediterranean, the Barbary Coast, and Italy, 1500–1800*. New York: Palgrave Macmillan, 2003.

Dich, Preben. *Blandt hvaler og kannibaler. Hans Falk — en dansk eventyrer i New Zealand*. [Lyngby]: Holkenfeldt 3, 2006. [e-book: Copenhagen: Lindhard og Ringhof, 2019].

Doak, Wade. *The Burning of the Boyd: A Saga of Culture Clash*. Auckland: Hodder & Stoughton, 1984.

Earle, Augustus. *A Narrative of a Nine Months' Residence in New Zealand in 1827; together with a*

Journal of Residence in Tristan d'Acunha, an Island Situated between South America and the Cape of Good Hope. London: Longman, 1832.

Elder, John Rawson (ed.). *The Letters and Journals of Samuel Marsden, 1765–1838: Senior Chaplain in the Colony of New South Wales and Superintendent of the Mission of the Church Missionary Society in New Zealand*. Otago: Coulls Somerville Wilkie, 1932.

——. *Marsden's Lieutenants*. Dunedin: A.H. Reed, 1934.

Falk-Rønne, Arne. *Sydhavets syv bølger*. Copenhagen: Lindhardt og Ringhof, 1969.

Halliday, Stephen. *Newgate: London's Prototype of Hell*. Stroud: The History Press, 2007.

Hilliard, Chris. 'James Cowan and the Frontiers of New Zealand History'. *The New Zealand Journal of History*, 31.2 (1997), pp. 219–233.

Holcomb, Janette M. 'Captain Robert Duke, (1796–1845): A Biographical Case Study of Investment in the Colonial Whaling Industry'. *The Great Circle*, 32.2 (2010), pp. 9–30.

——. *Early Merchant Families of Sydney: Speculation and Risk Management on the Fringe of Empire*. London: Anthem Press, 2014.

Jennings, William. 'The Debate over *kai tangata* (Māori Cannibalism): New Perspectives from the Correspondence of the Marists'. *Journal of Polynesian Society*, 120.2 (2011), pp. 129–48.

Laugesen, Ruth. 'Close to the Bones'. *New Zealand Listener (Online)*, 227 no. 3694 (26 February 2011).

Manson, Cecil, and Celia Manson. *The Affair of the Wellington Brig: A True and Terrible Tale*. Wellington: Millwood Press, 1978.

Matheson, Alister. 'Tapsell's Big Guns'. *Historical Review: Bay of Plenty Journal*, 37.1 (1989), pp. 1–12.

——. 'Law and Order in Maketu'. *Bay of Plenty Journal of History*, 43.2 (1995), pp. 106–122.

——. 'The Storm that Wrecked the Falcon, 1 March 1840'. *Historical Review: Bay of Plenty Journal*, 48.1 (2000), pp. 8–24.

McKay, Joseph Angus. *Historic Poverty Bay and the East Coast, North Island, New Zealand*. Gisborne: McKay · Poverty Bay-East Coast Centennial Council, 1949.

McNab, Robert. *Murihiku: A History of the South Island of New Zealand and the Islands Adjacent and Lying to the South, from 1642 to 1835*. Wellington: Whitcombe and Tombs, 1909.

——. *The Old Whaling Days: A History of Southern New Zealand from 1830 to 1840*. Christchurch: Whitcombe and Tombs, 1913.

Meredith, [Louisa]. *Notes and Sketches of New South Wales during a Residence in that Colony from 1839 to 1844*. London: John Murray, 1844.

Moon, Paul. 'Correspondence'. *New Zealand Journal of History*, 45.1 (2011), pp. 146–47.

——. *This Horrid Practice: The Myth and Reality of Traditional Māori Cannibalism*. Rosedale, NZ: Penguin, 2008.

Munch-Petersen, Thomas. *Defying Napoleon: How Britain Bombarded Copenhagen and Seized the Danish Fleet in 1807*. Stroud: Sutton, 2007.

Nielsen, Aage Krarup. *Hans Falk fra Maketu. En dansk Sydhavsfarers Liv og Eventyr*. Copenhagen: Gyldendal, 1940.

Ocampo, Emilio. 'The Attempt to Rescue Napoleon with a Submarine: Fact or Fiction?' *Napoleonica. La Revue*, 11 (2011–2012), pp. 11–31.

Pike, Douglas, et al. (eds.). *Australian Dictionary of Biography*. Vol. 2: 1788–1850, I–Z. Melbourne: Melbourne University Press, 1967.

Ramsden, Eric. *Marsden and the Missions: Prelude to Waitangi*. Sydney: Angus & Robertson, 1936.

Reed, A.W. *An Illustrated Encyclopedia of Traditional Māori Life · Taonga Tuku Iho*, edited by Buddy Mikaere. Auckland: New Holland, 2002 [1963].

Reunion Committee (ed.). *1778–1978: The Descendants of the Union of a Viking of the North to That of a Viking of the South*. Maketū: Reunion Committee, 1978.

Rogers, Lawrence M. (ed.). *The Early Journals of Henry Williams, Senior Missionary in New Zealand of the Church Missionary Society, 1824–40*. Christchurch: Pegasus Press, 1961.

Salesa, Damon Ieremia. *Racial Crossings: Race, Intermarriage, and the Victorian British Empire*. Oxford: Oxford University Press, 2011.

Salmond, Anne. *Between Worlds: Early Exchanges between Maori and Europeans, 1773–1815*. Honolulu: University of Hawai'i, 1997.

Schaniel, William Carl. 'The Maori and the Economic Frontier: An Economic History of the

Maori of New Zealand, 1769–1840'. Unpublished PhD thesis. Knoxville: The University of Tennessee, 1985.

Smith, Stephenson Percy. *Maori Wars of the Nineteenth Century*. Christchurch: Whitcombe and Tombs, 1910.

Stafford, Donald Murray. *Te Arawa: A History of the Arawa People*. Auckland: Reed, 1991 (1st edition 1967).

Tapsell, Enid. *Historic Maketu. Hui Hui Mai!* Rotorua: *Rotorua Morning Post*, 1940.

Tapsell, Paora [Paul]. 'Te Haupapa', in *The Lives of Colonial Objects*, edited by Annabel Cooper, Lachy Paterson and Angela Wanhalla. Dunedin: Otago University Press, 2015, pp. 24–31.

Tapsell, Paul. *Pukaki: A Comet Returns*. Libro International, 2000.

—— and Quentin Tapsell. *Whanau-a-Tapihana Reunion 1830–2004*. Maketū: Reunion Committee.

Thornley, Andrew. *A Shaking of the Land: William Cross and the Origins of Christianity in Fiji · Na Yavalati Ni Vanua: Ko Wiliame Korosi kei na i Tekitekivu ni Lotu Vakarisito e Viti*. Suva: Institute of Pacific Studies, University of the South Pacific, 2005.

Turner, J.G. *The Pioneer Missionary: Life of Rev. Nathaniel Turner, Missionary in New Zealand, Tonga, and Australia*. London: Wesleyan Conference Office, 1872.

Vennell, C.W. *The Brown Frontier; New Zealand Historical Stories and Studies, 1806–1877*. Wellington: A.H. & A.W. Reed, 1967.

Wakefield, Edward Jerningham. *Adventure in New Zealand, from 1839 to 1844*. London: John Murray, 1845.

White, John. *The Ancient History of the Maori, his Mythology and Traditions: Tai Nui*. Vol. 6. London: Sampson Low and Co., 1890.

Yarwood, Alexander T. *Samuel Marsden: The Great Survivor*. Melbourne: Melbourne University Press, 1977.

Acknowledgements

I WOULD LIKE TO THANK the staff of the following libraries and repositories in New Zealand: the Alexander Turnbull Library, Wellington, especially Jocelyn Chalmers, Paul Diamond and Linda McGregor; the Whakatāne & District Historical Society, especially Morley West); and Archives New Zealand · Te Rua Mahara o te Kāwanatanga, The Department of Internal Affairs · Te Tari Taiwhenua, Wellington.

I am grateful to the following correspondents in New Zealand, Denmark and Iceland who kindly answered queries and sent references: Anna Pétursdóttir, Reykjavík; Caroline Fitzgerald, Dunedin; Chanel Clarke and Zoe Richardson, Auckland War Museum · Tamaki Paenga Hira; Henriette Gavnholdt Jakobsen, Museet for Søfart, Helsingør; Paula Karkkainen, the Whakatāne Museum and Research Centre; Preben Dich, Frederiksberg; Rhonda Paku, formerly Mātautanga Māori, Museum of New Zealand Te Papa Tongarewa; Tony Pecotic, Reporoa, and Tonya Dunn, Tauranga City Libraries.

I would also like to thank Peter Dowling and the wonderful staff at Oratia Media, especially the reader, Susan Brierley, who provided many helpful comments and suggestions on the book manuscript, and the editorial director, Carolyn Lagahetau, who carefully managed publication. Without their support and hard work this book would never have appeared. I owe a particular debt of gratitude to Paora Tapsell, who kindly read a draft of this book manuscript making invaluable suggestions and corrections and encouraged its publication. Thanks to his efforts, this book was greatly improved. Ngā mihi nui ki a koe mo tō tautoko!

The publication of this book has been generously supported by Alfred Good's Personhistoriske Fond, Den Hielmstierne-Rosencroneske Stiftelse, Konsul George Jorck og Hustru Emma Jorck's Fond and Lillian og Finks Fond.

The Knut and Alice Wallenberg Foundation, The Royal Swedish Academy of Letters, History and Antiquities and the Hilda Kumlin Foundation provided funding to pay for research trips to New Zealand and I am deeply grateful for their financial support. On parts of these trips I was accompanied and assisted by the tireless Christian Brix and Niels Krause Brix-Thomsen — tusind tak til jer begge for jeres kærlighed og tålmodighed!

This book is dedicated to my dear dad, John W. Adams, for taking me on my first flight overseas, showing me that there is a world beyond the Ridgeway and supporting me ever since — no matter what I have chosen to do and where I have ended up.

Index